THE BEST OF
Thymes
by Marge Clark

Herbs and Recipes

My Favorite Things Recipes

A Collection of New and Old Favorites

Illustrated by Lynda Haupert

Book Design by Angela Haupert Hoogensen

Copy Editing by Sheila Mauck

Herb Editing by Charles Voigt and Michael Bettler

PUBLISHER

Thyme Cookbooks

Marge Clark

Oak Hill Farm

6242 W. State Road 28

West Lebanon, IN 47991

Other books by Marge Clark:
It's About Thyme!
Christmas Thyme at Oak Hill Farm

Published by Thyme Cookbooks, Marge Clark,
Oak Hill Farm, 6242 W. State Road 28, West Lebanon, IN 47991

Library of Congress Catalog Card Number
97-60074

Clark, Marge
The Best of Thymes
Index Included
1. Herbs and Recipes 2. My Favorite Things Recipes
3. A Collection of New and Old Favorites

ISBN 0-9640514-1-9

First Printing

Printed by
RR Donnelley & Sons Company

TABLE OF

Contents

Acknowledgments

Anyone who writes a book and self-publishes it must depend on a countless number of people to help in some way with the production of that book. Obviously, it has taken many people to create *The Best of Thymes*. My first thanks will always go to my husband (and best friend), Dick. He never sees an obstacle. He says, "Just do it!" So with his help, in many ways, this book has become a reality.

I am fortunate to have Angie Hoogensen for my book designer. She is certainly the only person I can think of I would trust with such a task. From the beginning, she instinctively knew how I wanted the book to look and feel. Through deadlines, childrens' illnesses, and running a household full time, Angie always came through on time. This became Angie's book, too, and I think that's obvious as you page through it.

The beautiful illustrations were done by Lynda Haupert. We thought Lynda captured the beauty of each herb she illustrated as well as all the illustrations throughout the book. The fabulous one-of-a-kind borders Lynda created add originality and charm. She would be quick to tell you the borders took as much time to design and paint as the herbs themselves!

Thanks also to Sheila Mauck for all the hours of proofreading, correcting, and re-arranging she performed as my copy editor. Special thanks, also, to two knowledgeable "herb" friends, Charles Voigt and Michael Bettler, for helping me with the Latin names, varieties, species, and other confusing things about plants that I wanted to be accurate.

I asked several friends to contribute recipes to this book, especially the herb chapters. I was overwhelmed with their generosity and enthusiasm. Thanks so much Carla Nelson, Kate Jayne, Kim Snyder, Wilma Clark, Bertha Reppert, Beulah Hargrove, Susan Wittig Albert, Carolee Snyder, and Joyce Wagner. And I can't leave out all the friends who have sent me their special recipes over the years. Some of these people I know, but most of them I don't. Where possible, I have given credit.

There are three other people who contributed much time and effort in the production of this book. Chuck Harpel and Deanie Silcox from the RR Donnelley Company patiently and professionally worked with me until the book was just as I wanted it. And Megan Hammond, from Unisource, who must have sent me fifteen paper samples before we all found the one we thought was just right! Thanks, Megan.

Introduction

This book came as a complete surprise to me! When I finished *Christmas Thyme at Oak Hill Farm,* I said to family and friends, "This is it!" But then I realized I had learned so much in the last few years that I felt compelled to share all those good things with you. So I surprised myself one day when I realized I was mentally outlining another book. That mental outline has become this book, *The Best of Thymes.*

Twelve herbs have evolved as my favorites so I have devoted an entire chapter to each of those twelve — sweet basil, chives, dill, French tarragon, lemon verbena, mint, oregano and marjoram, parsley, rosemary, sage, scented geraniums, and thyme. I certainly cook with more than those twelve herbs, so there also is a section on fifteen more culinary herbs I think we should be acquainted with.

I give somewhere between 30 and 70 speeches per year (that year was a killer!), and the audience loves to see what I do with herbs from my garden. They also love to see how an ordinary kitchen staple (such as vinegar) can become something very special when herbs or other seasonings are added. Many of the vinegars, seasonings, herbed butters, oils, jams, and jellies that I talk about in my speeches are included in "My Favorite Things" chapter. The book ends with new and old favorite recipes — some herb, some not.

When I started this book, I was afraid I wouldn't have enough material to fill it up. The laugh is on me as I look at the whopper it has become. I hope you'll find many wonderful things here to add to your collection of recipes.

Was it all worth it? All the time, expense, overnight letters, telephone calls, faxes, proofreading, late nights, and long days. Well, in retrospect, honestly it was!

Unlike Charles Dickens, there is no "worst of times" here, just "the best of thymes!"

Marge Clark
Oak Hill Farm
Winter 1997

Sweet
Basil

OCIMUM BASILICUM

Sweet Basil

OCIMUM BASILICUM

I love all the herbs I talk about, but sweet basil (and its many varieties) is my favorite. Much has been written about basil through the ages. We know that it is native to India and Africa and has been a part of those civilizations for 4,000 or more years. Sweet basil is an annual plant. In India, it has been revered for centuries and still is held in high esteem today. **Indian basil** (*O. sanctum*) is dedicated to Krishna and sprigs of the plant are placed on the chest of a dead person to ensure protection. **Common** or **sweet basil** (*O. basilicum*) became a popular culinary herb in France and southern European countries centuries ago. The discussion on these pages applies to **sweet basil** (*O. basilicum*) only. There has always been some confusion about the meaning of basil. In some ancient writings, the author says basil has terrible and evil power while other writers say it is an object of worship. Still others, namely the French, say it is an herb for royalty only. In Italy, a man offers a lady a sprig of basil to express his love. Generally speaking, leaves of the basil plant are oval — some round oval, some long oval. They are pale green to dark green to purple, and some are mottled green and purple. Green basils have white flowers and purple basils have pink to purple flowers. All these variables depend on which basil we're talking about. More on all this later. The stems are somewhat tender, but get tough and woody close to the ground. The leaf, not the stem, is the plant part to cook with. Seeds are miniscule in size. Most basils have a wonderful clovelike and spicy aroma. 🍃 The basils are very sensitive to cold weather and cold winds. Below 40° F is harmful to the plant and the first hint of frost will turn the leaves black and unusable. 🍃 Basil is easy to grow once the plants are established. I much prefer to set out basil plants in late spring when the days are warm and the ground temperature is above 55° F. You certainly can sow basil seeds, but must realize that they are slow to germinate. I also have found it's very difficult to keep the planted area weed-free while waiting for the basil to come up. 🍃 More and more seed houses are offering basil seeds that are free of fusarium wilt and I heartily suggest you look for plants from these seeds. This wilt has been a problem for me the last 3 or 4 years. 🍃 Plant basil in a rich, well-drained soil that has been enriched with well-rotted manure or compost. Basils like plenty of sun, but they don't mind a little midday shade, either. This is one herb that likes plenty of moisture, but on the other hand, new seedlings (particularly the purple varieties) are prone to "damping off," so you need to learn what the happy medium is — moist soil but not too wet where the stem meets the soil. 🍃 I find basil is rather difficult to dry to retain flavor. I've tried several ways and all have a degree of success, but the best method for me is to hang branches upside down in a cool, dry, dark room or closet. If you can spare it, a closet is the best drying chamber I have found. Let them dry for a couple of weeks, strip off the leaves and store them in glass or plastic containers out of heat and light. I store the leaves whole and crumble them when I'm ready to use them. 🍃 In the field of medicine, basil is said to be good to relieve headaches and nausea. It's such a terrific herb to cook with (as you'll see by the splendid array of recipes that follow) that most of my attention goes to the culinary aspects of this herb. 🌿 There are a couple of other things that need to be said about basil. 1. It is very important to keep the blooms cut off, particularly on the green varieties. In the peak growing season, you may need to scout the basil patch every day or two to keep this done. Keeping the blooms removed allows the plant to branch and keeps it from getting leggy and woody-stemmed. 2. There is nothing to match the aroma of basil in the garden after a soft, warm summer rain. Take a chair, go sit in the midst of it, and inhale. Ahh, basil! 🌿 Following is a list of some popular basil varieties. There are many more, of course, but these are my favorites. All varieties listed are in the **sweet basil** (*Ocimum basilicum*) family. 1. *O. b.* **crispum** or lettuce leaf basil — large light green curled leaves that resemble a small lettuce leaf, hence the name. Grows 18 inches to 2 feet tall. A very good basil to cook with. 2. *O. b.* **purpurascens** or 'Dark Opal' basil — beautiful smooth purple leaves often mottled with green splotches. Leaves have soft jagged edges. Pink flowers appear in midsummer. Grows about 18 inches tall and is very aromatic. Makes a gorgeous red vinegar. 3. *O. b.* **citriodorum** or lemon-scented basil — grows 1½ to 2 feet tall. Has lovely lemon-scented small green leaves. Its flowers are white. Of all the basils, this variety is the most difficult to keep the flowers picked off — a very prolific bloomer if you let it! 4. *O. b.* **minimum** or 'Greek Mini' basil — a lovely round mound of tiny fragrant green leaves. Grows 8 to 10 inches tall. The leaves are small, nearly round with a very good sweet and spicy flavor. 5. *O. b.* **'Purple Ruffles'** or purple ruffles basil — this was a 1987 All America plant winner. The plant has dark purple ruffly leaves with saw-tooth edges and grows about 18 inches tall. There are pink flowers in midsummer. The best vinegar I make is with purple ruffles basil — it is a beautiful ruby red color.   6. *O. b.* 'Genovese' or perfume basil — very fragrant with smooth, dark green, long, pointed leaves. A terrific basil to cook with. Grows about 2 feet tall.   7. *O. b.* **'Napoletano'** — another great basil to cook with. Also very fragrant with large, round, deeply wrinkled medium-green leaves. Grows about 2 feet tall. A truly wonderful basil flavor. Either 'Napoletano' or 'Genovese' makes excellent pesto.   8. *O. b.* 'Anise-Scented' or 'Licorice' basil — grows about 18 inches tall and has a distinct licorice and clove flavor and aroma. This plant has green leaves with serrated edges, purple stems, and pink flowers.   9. *O. b.* **'Cinnamon'** — has a good cinnamon taste and aroma. Grows about 18 inches tall, has green, smooth leaves and the stems are purplish green. The flowers are pink. The taste is basil-like, but also intensely spicy.   10. *O. b.* **'Green Ruffles'** — looks like purple ruffles only it has deeply ruffled green leaves, white flowers, and grows a little shorter than purple ruffles. Not a good culinary herb, but a beautiful border plant. Doesn't bloom as profusely as some of the other green varieties. Doesn't "damp off" as readily as purple ruffles. But it also doesn't taste very good!   11. *O. b.* **minimum 'Fino Verde'** — also called Piccolo basil. The leaves are about 1 inch across and grow in clusters. It grows 12 to 15 inches tall. Makes a lovely mounding border plant. The Italians love to cook with this basil. 12. *O. b.* 'Red Rubin' — a new breed of the dark opal basil. It holds its color much better than dark opal and doesn't tend to revert to the green mottling of dark opal leaves. Makes an outstanding vinegar or jelly.   13. *O. b.* **'Mrs. Burns Lemon'** — this variety is often difficult to find, but well worth the search! The leaves are larger and have a better lemon flavor than the older lemon varieties. I love this one with fish and seafood. ❦

How do I use sweet basil?

- with chicken
- with beef, veal, lamb
- with fish
- with pasta dishes
- in egg dishes
- with vegetables, especially with eggplant, onions, tomatoes, potatoes, summer squash
- with sun-dried tomatoes
- with fruit dishes
- with melons
- with apples
- with oranges
- with lemons
- in soups, especially beef soup, chicken soup, tomato soup
- in salads
- in salad dressings
- in cheese dishes
- with cream cheese, cottage cheese, sour cream
- in breads, muffins
- in cakes
- in marinades
- in sauces
- in drinks, such as lemonade
- in pesto
- in butters
- in vinegar
- in oil
- in jellies
- with olives
- with garlic

INDEX

Sweet Basil Recipes

Sweet Basil Recipe Index continued on the facing page

INDEX

Sweet Basil Recipes, continued

MENU

Viva la Basil!

Molded Italian Cheese Spread with Crudites (p. 14) *

Fresh Spinach Salad with Lemon Yogurt Vinaigrette (p. 320)

Chicken Cacciatore (p. 22) *

French Bread with Herbed Olive Oil Dip (p. 26) *

Basil-Lime Pound Cake (p. 25) *

* Recipe contains basil

Basil-Nectarine Lemonade

3½ cups water
1   cup fresh basil leaves
2   ripe nectarines
¾   to 1 cup sugar
1   cup fresh lemon juice

In a small saucepan, combine 2 cups water, the basil, 1 chopped nectarine and the sugar. Bring mixture to a boil, stirring until sugar is dissolved. Reduce heat and simmer for 5 minutes. Let cool, then strain mixture into a pitcher. Stir in remaining 1½ cups water, the other nectarine, thinly sliced, and the lemon juice. Serve over ice. Makes about 5 cups. Recipe can be doubled. Makes a delicious summer drink.

Appetizer Shrimps on French Bread Rounds

2   cloves garlic, finely minced
¼   cup dry white wine
¼   cup olive oil
1   tablespoon fresh lemon juice
1   tablespoon fresh basil, minced
¼   teaspoon salt, or more to taste
¼   teaspoon crushed red pepper flakes
12   large cooked, deveined shrimps
½   cup grated Parmesan cheese*
12   slices French bread

Combine garlic, wine, oil, lemon juice, basil, salt and red pepper flakes in a large zip-top plastic bag. Add shrimps, close bag and make sure shrimps are coated well with the marinade. Refrigerate for 2 hours or longer. Split each shrimp in half lengthwise. Sprinkle about 1½ teaspoons Parmesan cheese over each bread slice. Place 2 shrimp halves on each slice, cut side down. Spoon a little marinade over each appetizer. Sprinkle more cheese over each. Place bread rounds on a broiler rack and broil 6 inches from the heat source just until bubbly, about 4 to 6 minutes. Watch closely. Serve warm. Makes 12 appetizers.

* PARMESAN CHEESE —
THERE IS ONLY ONE TRUE
PARMESAN CHEESE AND THAT IS
PARMIGIANO REGGIANO FROM
PARMA, ITALY. ALL OTHER
PARMESAN CHEESE TYPES PALE
IN COMPARISON TO THIS GREAT
CHEESE. ANY GOOD CHEESE
SHOP SHOULD HAVE IT. IF THIS
IS NOT AVAILABLE, BUY THE
NEXT BEST BRAND. PARMA IS A
TOWN NEAR MILAN — THE
FOOD FROM NORTHERN ITALY
IS SUPERB.

Pesto Cheesecake

Crust

1 tablespoon butter, softened

¼ cup Italian seasoned bread crumbs

Filling

2 8-ounce packages cream cheese, softened

1 cup ricotta cheese

½ cup grated Parmesan cheese

3 large eggs

½ cup pesto (recipe follows, at right)

Chopped fresh basil for garnish

Roasted peppers

Sliced rounds of French or Italian bread, toasted

Roast the peppers: Clean 2 or 3 red and/or yellow bell peppers. Cut them in half lengthwise, remove seeds and place on a baking sheet. Broil close to the heat element until pepper halves are blackened all over. Place blackened peppers in a brown paper bag. Close the top and let them stand for 10 minutes to loosen the skins. Hold each pepper under cold running water and peel off the skins. Drain peppers on paper towels. Cut peppers into strips. Place in a covered container and refrigerate.

And now for the cheesecake!

Make the crust: Rub the 1 tablespoon butter over bottom and halfway up sides of a 9-inch springform pan. Sprinkle the bread crumbs evenly over the bottom. Set pan aside.

Make the filling: Combine cream cheese, ricotta cheese and Parmesan cheese in a food processor. Process until very smooth. Add eggs and mix thoroughly. Pour half of cheese mixture into a small bowl. To the half remaining in the food processor, add the ½ cup pesto and mix well. Pour pesto-cheese mixture into prepared pan. Carefully pour plain mixture over pesto mixture and smooth to cover the entire surface. Bake at 350° for 35 to 40 minutes, or until cake is set in the middle. Cool. Cover and refrigerate overnight. To serve, loosen from sides of pan with a knife. Remove pan sides. Chop some fresh basil and sprinkle over top of cheesecake. Dice several strips of roasted pepper and scatter over the basil. Cover and refrigerate any leftover peppers. Let guests slice cheesecake to spread on toasted bread rounds. Serves 15 to 20. Wonderful, wonderful!

THIS TAKES SOME TIME TO ASSEMBLE, BUT FORTUNATELY IT NEEDS TO BE MADE THE DAY BEFORE SERVING. A PERFECT APPETIZER FOR A SPECIAL PARTY. PREPARE THE PESTO AND ROAST THE PEPPERS FIRST, THEN ASSEMBLE.

The Best Pesto

4 cups fresh green basil leaves, coarsely chopped
1 cup pine nuts
1/2 cup extra virgin olive oil
1 cup grated Parmesan cheese
1/4 cup butter, softened
2 cloves garlic, crushed
Salt

In food processor, purée the basil with pine nuts, oil, Parmesan cheese, butter, garlic and a little salt. Place in a glass jar. Pour a thin layer of olive oil over top. Screw on lid and refrigerate until ready to use. When ready to use, stir the thin layer of olive oil into the pesto.

THE BEST RECIPE I KNOW OF! THIS RECIPE WILL MAKE MORE PESTO THAN YOU NEED FOR THIS CHEESECAKE. PLACE LEFTOVER PESTO IN A JAR, COVER WITH A THIN LAYER OF OLIVE OIL AND FREEZE FOR OTHER USES.

some thoughts on
PESTO

Pesto is a marvelous Italian recipe that showcases basil at its best. As I stated earlier, I particularly like 'Genovese' and 'Napoletano' varieties for pesto. I also like 'Piccolo' and 'Lettuce Leaf' varieties. Basil pesto can only be made with the fresh leaves.

The traditional method of making pesto (and the one still adhered to in Italian kitchens) is with a mortar and pestle. The shortcut (and it really is a shortcut!) method of making it in a food processor is almost as good and a whole lot easier and faster. Regardless of the method chosen, do make this splendid concoction when basil is plentiful.

If you wish to make some for winter use, pesto freezes beautifully. Just remember to add a thin layer of olive oil on top of the pesto so it won't turn black or dark. When you want to use some, thaw, stir the layer of oil into the pesto and it's ready to serve.

If you like, you can substitute a cup of fresh Italian (flat leaf) parsley for 1 cup of the basil in "The Best Pesto" recipe.

Pesto is splendid in pasta dishes, in cheese-based dishes, with vegetables, and of course in tomato-based dishes. Nothing helps a spaghetti or pasta sauce as much as 1/2 cup or so of pesto added to the sauce at the last minute. It will give the sauce a wonderfully fresh taste.

Thank you, Italy!

My Pesto Torte

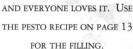

I OFTEN MAKE THIS AND TAKE TO LECTURES FOR TASTING. IT'S VERY EASY TO PUT TOGETHER AND EVERYONE LOVES IT. USE THE PESTO RECIPE ON PAGE 13 FOR THE FILLING.

For a 4½" x 6½" pâté dish:

1   8-ounce package cream cheese, softened and divided
²/₃   cup prepared pesto (see recipe on p. 13)
2   tablespoons diced sun-dried tomatoes

Take ½ of the cream cheese and spread on the bottom of the pâté dish. Spread pesto over the cheese. Scatter sun-dried tomato bits over pesto. On a piece of waxed paper, pat out the other half of the cream cheese so it will fit the pâté dish. Carefully peel cheese off the waxed paper and lay it on top of pesto and tomato layer. If necessary, use your fingers to push cheese all the way to dish edges. The pesto layer must be sealed completely so pesto doesn't turn black. Serves 10 to 12 as an appetizer. Serve with crackers or French bread pieces.

Molded Italian Cheese Spread

I HAVE HAD THIS RECIPE FOR YEARS. IT'S VERY GOOD AND A PARTY FAVORITE. SERVE IT COLD WITH CRISP RAW VEGETABLES OR CRACKERS.

2   cups sour cream
½   cup green pepper, finely chopped
½   cup celery, finely chopped
¼   cup pimiento-stuffed green olives, coarsely chopped
¼   cup onion, finely chopped
2   teaspoons fresh lemon juice
1   teaspoon Worcestershire sauce
    Dash of paprika
3   or 4 drops bottled hot pepper sauce
1½   cups cheese cracker crumbs

In a large bowl, thoroughly combine all ingredients, except cracker crumbs. Line a 1 quart bowl with clear plastic wrap. Spread about ½ cup sour cream mixture in bottom of bowl. Sprinkle with about ¼ cup cheese cracker crumbs. Repeat layers using crumbs and sour cream mixture until sour cream is used up. Top with any remaining crumbs. Cover with plastic wrap and chill thoroughly. To serve, unmold on a large platter. Peel off plastic wrap. Surround cheesecake with assorted vegetables for dipping, or crackers for spreading. Serves 15 to 20.

Court Café Fruit Soup

1	cup water
3	tablespoons instant tapioca
3	tablespoons sugar
$^1/_8$	teaspoon salt
1	6-ounce can frozen orange juice concentrate
$1^1/_2$	cups ice water
1	tablespoon fresh lemon juice
1	banana, diced
1	ripe peach, peeled and diced
1	navel orange, all peel and pith removed, diced
$^1/_2$	cup fresh blueberries, washed
$^1/_2$	cup white seedless grapes, washed and cut in half
$^1/_2$	cup fresh strawberries, washed and sliced
1	tablespoon fresh basil, chopped

Combine water, tapioca, sugar and salt. Cook and stir until thickened. Remove from heat. Add orange juice concentrate, ice water and lemon juice. Stir well and refrigerate. This step may be done the day before serving. At serving time, prepare all fruits and add to the tapioca base. Stir in the fresh basil. Serve immediately, or chill up to 2 hours, then serve. Serves 8.

THERE IS A SMALL OPERA COMPANY IN RICHMOND, INDIANA, CALLED THE WHITEWATER OPERA COMPANY. FOR A FUND-RAISER, THE CHAIRMAN, PAT JARVIS, OWNER OF THE COURT CAFÉ (AND A GREAT COOK), ASKED ME TO SPEAK TO A LADIES' LUNCHEON GROUP. IT WAS A HOT SUMMER DAY AND THIS COLD SOUP WAS THE HIT OF THE ENTIRE MEAL. SHE GRACIOUSLY GAVE ME THE RECIPE. I HAVE SERVED IT MANY TIMES SINCE TO APPRECIATIVE GUESTS.

Tomato, Onion, Mozzarella and Basil Salad

THIS IS STILL MY FAVORITE SALAD. IT EXUDES SUMMER. USE ONLY THE BEST AVAILABLE INGREDIENTS. IT IS A BEAUTIFUL SALAD TO SERVE.

Peel ripe **tomatoes** and cut into rather thick slices. Slice **sweet onions** and separate into rings. Slice **mozzarella cheese** about $^1/_4$ inch thick. Wash and dry large tender **green basil leaves**. On a large tray or platter, place a tomato slice, overlap 2 or 3 onion rings on top of the tomato, a slice of cheese, then a basil leaf. Continue this order to cover the platter with rows. Cover with plastic wrap and refrigerate. Make a dressing of $^2/_3$ cup **extra virgin olive oil** and $^1/_3$ cup **herbal vinegar** (I particularly like **My Mixed Herb Vinegar**, page 291), or **Basil Vinegar** (page 26). Shake dressing well. When ready to serve, remove platter from refrigerator. Remove plastic wrap. Drizzle the dressing over all. Add a grating of **fresh ground pepper** and a sprinkling of **salt**. Sprinkle 2 tablespoons **chopped fresh parsley** over the top. Serve immediately. Serves 8 or more.

Tomato, Bacon and Basil Salad

1 tablespoon olive oil

1 clove garlic, peeled and smashed

1 slice firm white bread, cut into $1/2$-inch cubes

6 strips bacon

2 medium to large tomatoes

Lettuce leaves

$1/2$ cup fresh basil, finely chopped

$1/2$ cup mozzarella cheese, diced

Salt and pepper

2 tablespoons basil-infused olive oil (recipe follows)

1 tablespoon sherry vinegar or red wine vinegar

FRESH TOMATOES AND BASIL TEAM UP TO MAKE ONE WONDERFUL SALAD. ACTUALLY, THIS RECIPE SERVES 2, BUT YOU COULD DOUBLE IT TO SERVE 4! MAKE THE INFUSED OIL SEVERAL HOURS BEFORE USING.

Heat olive oil in a large skillet. Add garlic and bread cubes. Toss over medium heat, until bread is browned, about 5 minutes. Remove cubes with a slotted spoon and set aside. Remove and discard garlic. In same skillet, fry bacon until crisp. Drain, then crumble bacon. Set aside. Peel, core and dice tomatoes. Line 2 plates with lettuce leaves. Pile diced tomatoes in middle of each plate. Top with basil and cheese. Sprinkle with bacon and season with salt and pepper to taste. Combine 2 tablespoons basil oil and the vinegar in a small bowl. Drizzle dressing over salad and sprinkle with bread cubes. Serves 2.

Basil-Infused Olive Oil

1 cup olive oil

1 cup fresh basil leaves, coarsely chopped

Combine oil and basil in a medium saucepan. Heat just to a boil. Immediately remove oil from heat. Cover and let set until oil is cool. Discard basil. Cover and refrigerate leftover oil. Use to dress green salads or use for sautéing. Use any leftover oil within 10 days to 2 weeks.

some thoughts on
CUTTING BASIL

Basil is one of the best herbs to cut to add to your flower and herb summer bouquets. Cut stems and place in slightly warm water to condition them (2 or 3 hours, or more, is ideal). Then arrange with other herbs or flowers for fragrant and beautiful bouquets. Imagine pink zinnias and purple ruffles basil together in an iron-stone bowl or an antique basket!

Chicken Waldorf Salad with Fresh Basil

The Salad

2	pounds cooked white chicken meat, cubed
1	cup celery, diced
1	cup cantaloupe, cubed
1	cup green apple, cubed
$^1/_2$	cup toasted walnuts, chopped
1	tablespoon fresh basil, chopped

The Dressing

$^3/_4$	cup Japanese rice vinegar
3	cups mayonnaise
1	tablespoon Dijon mustard
$^1/_2$	cup honey
$^1/_2$	cup soy sauce
1	cup vegetable oil, not olive oil

Prepare the dressing first. Combine vinegar, mayonnaise and mustard. Mix until smooth. Add honey and soy sauce. Slowly add the oil and blend thoroughly. Place chicken, celery and cantaloupe in a large salad bowl. Gradually add the dressing until the mixture is well coated. Scatter apples, walnuts and basil on top. Serve salad on lettuce-lined salad plates. Serves 8 to 10.

Note: You will not need all the dressing. Cover and refrigerate any leftover dressing for green salads.

THIS RECIPE WAS SENT TO ME BY AN UNKNOWN FRIEND. I SURE WISH I KNEW WHO IT WAS SO I COULD PROPERLY THANK HER — IT IS A FABULOUS SALAD WITH AN EQUALLY FABULOUS DRESSING. HERE IS WHAT SHE SAYS ABOUT THIS RECIPE: "THIS IS FROM THE OLD LORD AND TAYLOR RESTAURANT. I KNEW ONE OF THE MANAGERS AND SHE GAVE THIS RECIPE TO ME — THE DRESSING IS GOOD ON LOTS OF THINGS." INDEED IT IS. THE BASIL IS MY ADDITION.

Orange and Basil Salad

4   navel oranges, with all traces of rind and pith cut away
2   medium red onions, thinly sliced
$^{1}/_{2}$ cup extra virgin olive oil
3   tablespoons balsamic vinegar
     Freshly ground black pepper
3   tablespoons coarsely chopped walnuts or pine nuts
2   cups fresh basil leaves

Cut peeled oranges into thin slices. Save any juice that collects from slicing. Place orange slices and juice in a glass or crystal bowl. Add onion slices to the orange bowl. Combine $^{1}/_{2}$ cup olive oil, the vinegar and pepper in a small bowl. Pour over orange and onions and toss. Cover and let set at room temperature for at least an hour. In a small skillet, toast nuts over medium heat for 3 to 5 minutes. Shake pan often to toast evenly. Set aside to cool. Rinse and dry fresh basil leaves. Coarsely chop the leaves. To serve, add toasted nuts and basil to the salad bowl. Toss gently and serve. Serves 4 to 6.

Basil Vinaigrette

3   tablespoons white wine vinegar
2   teaspoons Dijon mustard
1   clove garlic, chopped
     Freshly ground black pepper
$^{2}/_{3}$ cup olive oil
2   tablespoons fresh basil leaves, minced

Combine vinegar, mustard, garlic and pepper in a blender. Blend until smooth. With motor running, add the olive oil in a steady stream to blend thoroughly. Stir in the basil and blend 2 or 3 seconds only. Place dressing in a jar. Cover tightly and refrigerate. To serve, bring to room temperature and shake well. Dress salad greens. Makes 1 cup.

Pasta with Gorgonzola and Tomatoes

3 tablespoons extra virgin olive oil
1 medium onion, chopped
4 cloves garlic, chopped
1 14½-ounce can Italian plum tomatoes, drained and chopped
½ cup chopped fresh basil
6 ounces Gorgonzola cheese, at room temperature
½ cup butter, softened
1 pound penne pasta
  Salt and pepper
1 cup best available Parmesan cheese

Heat oil in a large heavy skillet over medium heat. Add onion and garlic and sauté until tender, 6 or 8 minutes. Do not brown onion and garlic. Stir in tomatoes. Cook until mixture thickens, stirring occasionally, for 15 minutes. Add the fresh basil and simmer for 5 more minutes. In a small bowl, combine Gorgonzola and butter. Cook pasta in boiling salted water until just tender, or al dente. Drain, then return pasta to the pot. Using a whisk, combine the Gorgonzola mixture into the tomato sauce. Add sauce to pasta and toss to coat well. Season with salt and pepper. Sprinkle with Parmesan cheese and serve immediately. Serves 4.

ALL GOOD THINGS ITALIAN COME TOGETHER IN THIS DELICIOUS PASTA DISH. GORGONZOLA, THE BEST BLUE CHEESE OF ITALY, AND PARMESAN ARE TWO SUPERB CHEESES THAT MAKE THIS RECIPE SPECIAL.

Pasta in Bacon and Basil Sauce

8 strips bacon, fried, drained and crumbled
4 cups cooked pasta (linguine or fettuccine)
½ cup whipping cream
½ cup chicken broth
3 tablespoons fresh basil, chopped
  Freshly ground pepper
  Freshly grated Parmesan cheese

Prepare bacon in a large skillet and set aside. Discard all but 2 tablespoons bacon grease. Add pasta, cream, broth and basil to skillet. Cook and stir over high heat until the cream has thickened slightly, 6 or 8 minutes. Remove from heat and add bacon, pepper and Parmesan cheese. Toss and serve to 4.

SOME TIME AGO, I DID A COOKING CLASS FOR THE ILLINOIS PORK PRODUCERS WOMEN'S GROUP IN SPRINGFIELD, ILLINOIS. NATURALLY, ALL THE DISHES I PREPARED USED PORK PRODUCTS. THIS PASTA DISH WAS A BIG HIT.

My wish is that everyone could at some time in their lifetime visit the south of France, or the Provence. If you like to cook, or even if you don't, this is an area to be savored for its sights, aromas and foods. A mental picture of the Provence includes sun — lots of sun; fields of lavender; ancient aqueducts; medieval walled cities (Carcasonne, for one); olive oil; basil, basil and more basil; cheeses so good they are indescribable; red ripe tomatoes; watching a farmer force-feed a goose so the liver will grow fat which then becomes pâté de foie gras; precious truffles in any form; sun-ripened fruits; small-town marketplaces filled with fruits and vegetables; big brown mushrooms harvested from nearby woods and fields; and bunches of herbs, the varieties too numerous to mention. There is no gastronomic area of the world that can compare with the Provence. After saying all that, this recipe brings all the above to mind.

Fettuccine Provençal

¹/₂	cup softened, chopped sun-dried tomatoes
2	tablespoons extra virgin olive oil
1	teaspoon garlic, finely chopped
¹/₂	cup pine nuts
1	teaspoon salt
¹/₂	teaspoon pepper
2	tablespoons fresh basil, finely chopped
1	pound fettuccine
¹/₂	cup grated Parmesan cheese

Place sun-dried tomatoes in a bowl. Cover with boiling water and let stand for 5 minutes. Drain. Chop tomatoes into small pieces. Set aside. In a medium frying pan, heat olive oil over medium heat. Sauté sun-dried tomatoes, garlic, pine nuts, salt and pepper. Remove pan from heat and stir in the chopped fresh basil. Set aside. Cook fettuccine, according to package directions, in salted boiling water to al dente stage. Drain. Add tomato mixture to the fettuccine and toss to mix well. Sprinkle Parmesan cheese over fettuccine and serve immediately. Serves 4.

Pesto-Dressed Pasta

1   pound pasta of your choice
     Olive oil
1/2 to 1 cup prepared pesto, to your taste
     Parmesan cheese, grated

Prepare the pesto on page 13. Cook pasta according to package directions. Drain. Sprinkle a little olive oil over hot pasta to add flavor and to keep noodles separated. Immediately toss with the pesto. Serve at once. Pass Parmesan cheese. Serves 6 or 8 as a side dish, or 4 as an entrée.

A WELCOME CHANGE OF PACE FROM POTATOES AND RICE. A SIDE DISH OF THIS PASTA IS PERFECT WITH BROILED SALMON, OR WITH ALMOST ANYTHING.

Fresh Tomato Strata

3   large fresh tomatoes
16 slices firm white bread, crusts removed
2   tablespoons butter, melted
1/2 pound bacon, fried, drained on paper towels, and left in strips
2   cups shredded sharp cheddar cheese
8   eggs
3   cups half-and-half cream
1   tablespoon fresh basil, finely chopped
1   tablespoon fresh parsley, finely chopped
1   teaspoon salt
1/4 teaspoon black pepper

Core tomatoes. Cut a thin slice from top and bottom of each tomato (use for another dish). Cut each tomato into 4 equal slices. Set aside. Lightly grease a 15x10x2-inch baking dish. Place bread in a single layer in the baking dish, covering the entire bottom. With a pastry brush, lightly brush bread slices with the melted butter. Turn buttered slices over so buttered side is on bottom of dish. Arrange bacon over bread. Sprinkle 1 1/2 cups cheddar cheese over bacon. Set aside. In a large bowl, lightly beat eggs with half-and-half. Add the basil, parsley, salt and pepper and blend well. Slowly pour egg mixture over the bread, bacon and cheese. Bake at 350° for about 15 minutes. Remove from oven. Arrange tomato slices over the top. Bake another 8 to 10 minutes. Sprinkle with the remaining 1/2 cup cheese. Cover with foil and let set for 5 minutes to melt cheese. Remove foil, cut into squares and serve. Serves 6 or 8.

BAKE AND SERVE THIS STRATA AS YOU MAKE IT. UNLIKE MOST STRATAS, THIS ONE DOESN'T GO INTO THE REFRIGERATOR OVERNIGHT.

Chicken Cacciatore

3	pounds boneless white chicken meat
1	cup olive oil
1	stick margarine
2	cups onion, chopped
1	green pepper, chopped
1	tablespoon fresh basil, or 1 teaspoon dried
1	teaspoon salt
	Pepper
2	cups whole tomatoes, cut up
1	cup fresh mushroom slices
$1/2$	cup red wine
$1^1/_2$	pounds spaghetti, fettuccine or linguine
	Parmesan cheese (optional)

Sauté chicken in hot olive oil and margarine until light brown. Add remaining ingredients, except the wine. Simmer for $1^1/_2$ hours with lid tilted to allow steam to escape. Add wine and simmer another 5 minutes. Cook pasta according to package directions. Drain and place pasta on a very large serving platter. Lift chicken pieces from the sauce and lay them around edge of platter. Ladle sauce over pasta and serve immediately. Sprinkle with Parmesan cheese, if desired. Serves 8 to 10.

Turkey-Basil Roll-Ups

For each 8-inch tortilla:

2	teaspoons mayonnaise
2	leaves romaine lettuce, center ribs removed
6	very thin slices ripe tomato
3	or 4 thin slices cooked turkey breast, or chicken breast
6	fresh green basil leaves
	Salt and pepper to taste

Spread tortilla with mayonnaise. Cover with romaine leaves. Arrange tomato slices over lettuce, followed by turkey slices. Arrange basil leaves over turkey. Season with salt and pepper. Beginning at top edge, roll tortilla toward you to form a roll. When rolled, trim ends to square off. Cut into large pieces for an individual serving, or cut into $1/2$-inch slices for appetizers.

Layered Scalloped Tomatoes with Basil

2½	pounds fresh tomatoes, peeled
2	cups fresh bread crumbs*
3	tablespoons grated onion
1	tablespoon sugar
1	teaspoon salt
½	teaspoon pepper
1	tablespoon fresh basil, chopped, or 1 teaspoon dried, crumbled
3	tablespoons butter

Cut tomatoes into thick slices. Butter an 8-inch baking dish. Sprinkle ½ cup bread crumbs over bottom of the dish. Arrange tomato slices in dish in 3 layers, sprinkling each layer with some of the onion, sugar, salt, pepper, basil and about ½ cup bread crumbs. Dot each layer with butter. Bake at 375° for 30 minutes. Serves 4 to 6.

Process 3 or 4 slices bread in food processor to make soft bread crumbs.

TOWARD THE END OF SUMMER AND WHEN THE DAYS ARE COOLER, THIS HOT TOMATO DISH IS WELCOME. I LOVE IT WITH FRIED CHICKEN AND FRESH GREEN BEANS.

Pesto Bread

1½ packages active dry yeast
1 tablespoon sugar
1²/₃ cups warm water, 105° to 115°
6 to 7 cups bread flour
1½ teaspoons salt
²/₃ cup pesto (see page 13)

Proof yeast in a small bowl with the sugar and warm water. Let stand until foamy, about 5 minutes. Combine 6 cups flour and the salt in a large bowl. Make a well in the center of the flour and add the yeast mixture. Stir to form a soft dough. Add prepared pesto and add more flour as necessary. Turn dough onto a floured board and knead until smooth and elastic, 8 to 10 minutes. Grease a large bowl. Turn dough into bowl and cover with a slightly damp towel. Let rise in a warm place until dough has doubled in bulk, about 1 hour. Punch down and divide into 2 equal portions. Form into 2 round loaves and place on a large greased baking sheet. Cover again with the towel and let rise until doubled, about 45 minutes. Bake loaves at 400° for 35 to 40 minutes or until well browned and loaves sound hollow when tapped. Cool loaves and slice.

IF YOU LOVE PESTO, OR THE TASTE OF FRESH BASIL, THIS MAY BE THE BEST BREAD YOU'LL EVER EAT. SERVE WITH SOFTENED UNSALTED BUTTER.

Quick Basil Bread

1 cup mayonnaise
1 cup grated Parmesan cheese, best quality available
1½ teaspoons garlic, finely minced
1 1-pound round sourdough bread, cut in half horizontally
   Softened butter to spread on bread
2 tablespoons fresh basil, finely chopped, or 2 teaspoons dried, crumbled

Preheat broiler. Mix mayonnaise, Parmesan cheese and garlic in a bowl. Blend well. Place bread, cut side up, on a large cookie sheet. Butter the bread halves. Broil until crisp and golden brown. Spread Parmesan cheese mixture over the browned bread. Broil until top is puffed and golden brown. Sprinkle with the chopped basil. Cut bread into wedges and serve to 6 or 8.

WHAT A GREAT WAY TO SEASON AN ALREADY BAKED SOURDOUGH ROUND! PUT THIS TOGETHER WHEN UNEXPECTED GUESTS ARRIVE.

Basil-Lime Pound Cake

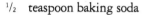

¹/₂   teaspoon baking soda
1   cup sour cream
1   cup sweet basil
1   cup granulated sugar, plus a little to prepare the pan
1   cup confectioner's sugar
3   large eggs
¹/₂   cup butter
¹/₂   cup margarine
1   tablespoon grated lime rind, green only
1¹/₂ tablespoons fresh lime juice
¹/₂   teaspoon salt
1   teaspoon vanilla
2¹/₄ cups flour
     Cream Cheese-Lime Frosting (recipe follows)

In a small bowl, mix baking soda with sour cream. Set aside. With metal blade in place and motor running, drop basil down feed tube. Add sugars and process a few seconds longer. Add eggs, butter, margarine, sour cream and baking soda mixture, lime rind, juice, salt and vanilla. Process until mixture is smooth. Add flour and pulse on/off only until the flour has been mixed in well — do not over-process. Grease an angel food or bundt cake pan. Sprinkle a little granulated sugar in the pan and tap out any extra sugar. Place batter in the prepared pan and bake in a 350° oven for 1 hour or until a tester comes out clean. Cool 10 minutes, then invert cake onto a large platter. Spread with Cream Cheese-Lime Frosting. Serves 10 to 12.

Cream Cheese-Lime Frosting
4   ounces cream cheese, softened
¹/₂   stick butter, softened
1   cup confectioner's sugar
1   teaspoon grated lime rind, green only
1   teaspoon fresh lime juice
¹/₂   teaspoon cream of tartar

Blend all ingredients together until smooth. Spread on top of warm (not hot) cake.

SHARON MASSAGLIA FROM SOUTH HOLLAND, ILLINOIS, SENT THIS TERRIFIC RECIPE TO ME. MAKE THIS IN THE SUMMER WHEN BASIL IS PLENTIFUL. A PERFECT CAKE FOR A SUMMER PARTY. IN SHARON'S WORDS, "THIS CAKE IS WONDERFUL!" USE YOUR FOOD PROCESSOR FOR THIS RECIPE.

Herbed Olive Oil Dip
for Bread

1 cup tightly packed fresh green basil leaves
²/₃ cup walnuts or pine nuts
¹/₂ cup fresh parsley leaves
¹/₄ cup grated Parmesan cheese
2 cloves garlic, coarsely chopped
1 tablespoon fresh lemon juice
¹/₄ teaspoon salt
³/₄ to 1 cup olive oil

In food processor, process basil, walnuts or pine nuts, parsley, cheese, garlic, lemon juice and salt until finely chopped. With motor running, slowly pour olive oil through feed tube until mixture is well combined. Add more olive oil if mixture seems too thick. Transfer mixture to a jar, cover and refrigerate. Keep refrigerated at all times, except to serve. To serve, spoon a little oil into small serving dishes, one for each guest. Guests dip chunks of French or Italian bread — they'll rave!

Basil Vinegar

To make 1 gallon:

1 sterilized glass or plastic jar
  Fresh basil leaves and tender sprigs (any variety you choose) (pack leaves in to fill the jar)
1 gallon white distilled vinegar, or white wine vinegar, or rice vinegar,
  or red wine vinegar

Clean the basil sprigs in tepid water, shake off excess water and allow basil to dry so that no moisture clings to leaves. Place leaves and sprigs in the jar. Pour vinegar, either hot or cold, over the basil. Place a nonmetallic lid* on the jar and set in a cool, dark place for 3 or 4 weeks to develop flavor. Remove basil and discard. Fit a coffee filter into a small funnel and filter the vinegar from the jar into sterilized bottles. Cork and seal.

* If your jars have metal lids, as most of mine do, tear off a piece of plastic wrap about 16" long. Fold that in half and then into quarters to make a 4-inch, or so, square. Place on the jar opening and screw the lid on over the wrap.

LEAVE THE BUTTER IN THE REFRIGERATOR ONCE IN A WHILE AND SERVE THIS HIGHLY FLAVORED HERBED OIL WITH CRUSTY FRENCH OR ITALIAN BREAD.

BASIL VINEGAR IS TRULY ONE OF THE BEST VINEGARS WE CAN MAKE IN OUR KITCHENS. I USE IT THROUGHOUT THE YEAR FOR SALAD DRESSINGS, MARINADES, IN MAYONNAISE DISHES AND TO DEGLAZE THE FRYING PAN, TO NAME A FEW. MAKE PLENTY FOR YOURSELF AND FOR YOUR UNFORTUNATE FRIENDS WITH NO HERB GARDEN.

Basil-Orange Jelly

1½ cups packed fresh basil leaves (I love the purple ruffles or opal basil here)
3   cups frozen reconstituted orange juice or 1½ cups orange juice plus 1½ cups water
1   1¾-ounce package powdered pectin (Sure Jell)
4   cups sugar
    Green food coloring, if desired, for green basil
    Red food coloring, if desired, for red basil

Crush basil leaves. Combine them with juice or juice and water. Bring to a boil. Remove from heat. Cover and let stand 10 minutes. Strain and measure 3 cups of infusion, adding water if necessary. Add food coloring — drop by drop — if desired. In a large kettle, combine the liquid and the pectin. Place over high heat and stir until it comes to a full boil. Stir in sugar and return to a rolling boil. Boil 1 minute, stirring constantly. Remove from heat. Skim off foam and pour into sterilized jelly glasses. Seal immediately. Makes about six 6-ounce glasses. Perfectly wonderful with meats.

Green Basil Jelly

1½ cups packed fresh basil leaves
2¼ cups cold water
3   tablespoons fresh lemon juice
3½ cups sugar
2   drops green food coloring
1   3-ounce pouch plus 2 tablespoons liquid pectin

Rinse, dry and finely chop the basil. Place in a heavy saucepan with 2¼ cups water. Cover and bring to a full boil over medium heat. Remove from heat and let mixture steep, covered, for 15 minutes. Pour the mixture into a cloth jelly bag. Hang bag over a large bowl and let the liquid drip through for 1 hour. Do not squeeze the bag, but you can scrape the juices from the outside of the bag into the bowl. If there is less than 1¾ cups of basil liquid, add a small amount of hot water to make 1¾ cups. In a heavy large kettle, combine the liquid, lemon juice, sugar and food coloring. Over high heat, bring mixture to a full rolling boil, stirring constantly, that cannot be stirred down. Stir in the pectin. Return to a full rolling boil, stirring constantly, for 1 minute. Remove kettle from heat. Skim off any foam. Ladle into hot sterilized jelly jars, leaving ¼ inch headspace. Adjust caps accordingly to jar manufacturer's directions. Process in a boiling water bath for 5 minutes.

THIS IS A TASTY JELLY TO SERVE
WITH MEATS AND POULTRY. IT'S
ALSO GOOD TO ADD A LITTLE TO
A FRUIT SALAD DRESSING.

Chives

ALLIUM SCHOENOPRASUM

Chives

C hives are a member of a large family of plants called alliums, or onions. The Latin word for allium is *unio*, meaning "one large pearl." In Chinese, the name means "jewel among vegetables." We're familiar with several members of this family, especially those we use in the kitchen. Well-known members are onions, garlic, shallots, leeks, and of course chives. I think if you visited most any part of the world, one or more members of the allium family would be a staple in that country's cuisine. Chives were recorded more than four thousand years ago in China. Marco Polo, that traveler of all travelers, spread the word about chives wherever he went.   Chives are a true harbinger of spring. In late March when everything else in the garden is either dormant or very drab-looking, chives can be found poking through the soil. The most common chive in the garden is *Allium schoenoprasum*. These are hardy perennial bulbs that grow in most temperate climates. They grow wild in Greece and Italy. *A. schoenoprasum* has hollow, long, cylindrical leaves that grow about 1 foot tall. This is the smallest member of the onion family. This chive plant has a soft, delicate flavor.   Chives need to be planted (either seeds or small clumps of bulblets) in light but rich, well-drained soil and in a mostly sunny location. Be sure the clumps have adequate moisture. After harvesting 2 or 3 times in a season, dress the soil with compost or a balanced fertilizer to boost further production. You may cut throughout the growing season, but do not cut lower than 2 inches. I find that the stems that had flowers on them are hard and tough, so I do not cut them to cook with.

In mid-June, chives will send up beautiful purple round blossoms that have a very pronounced onion flavor. My grandchildren call these blooms clover blossoms. I gather these blossoms, add some white wine vinegar or white distilled vinegar to them and make the most beautiful mauve-colored vinegar that has a very oniony flavor and aroma. 🌿 Chives are rich in vitamin C and some minerals. Medicinally, they can be used as an antiseptic and as a stimulant. The oil in chives is used in medicines to help reduce blood pressure. 🌿 This is one herb that grows well in the house. Divide a clump and place a few bulblets (still in a clump) in a 4- or 5-inch pot. Place the pot in a kitchen window and snip fresh chives all winter long. Again, don't cut lower than 2 inches. 🌿 Drying chives is not very successful. They will lose their flavor very quickly. I have found a very good way to preserve chives. I chop them, spread them on a cookie sheet, and freeze them for about 30 minutes. Quickly scrape the frozen pieces into sealable bags and immediately place in the freezer. The flavor lasts a long time and the pieces will stay separated from each other. Dry flower heads (not used in flavored vinegars) for dried arrangements or to add to potpourris. Following are three varieties to grow for fun, and also to cook with. 1. **Chinese chives** (*A. tuberosum*) or commonly called garlic chives — the leaves are flat, not hollow, and the blooms are white. The flavor is distinctly garlic. Be careful with this plant in the garden — it is a prolific spreader. 2. **Egyptian onion** (*A. cepa proliferum*) — has hollow 3-foot stems and grows small bulblets on top. These bulblets can be harvested and used as a chive/garlic flavoring. The bulblets drop and root and new plants grow. 3. **Curly chives** (*A. senescens*) — is a fun plant to grow because of the gray-green twisting and curling leaves. The flowers are pinkish-purple. The stems are hollow. 🌿 Any of the chives make wonderful border plants in either the herb garden or the flower garden. 🌿 Chives are truly one of the indispensable herbs we cook with. Much of the allium family falls into that category. 🌿

How do I use chives?

- in egg dishes
- with cheeses, especially cottage cheese and in cheese spreads
- in other dairy products, such as sour cream and yogurt
- in salads
- with many vegetables, especially new little potatoes
- in soups
- with mayonnaise
- in butters
- with tomatoes

- in sausages
- in marinades
- in vinegars (the blossoms)
- in cream sauces
- with seafood, especially salmon, shrimp, and delicate-flavored fish
- in breads and muffins
- in salad dressings
- with mushrooms
- with chicken
- in rice dishes

MENU

Delicate Chives

Stuffed Mushrooms with Chives (p. 38) *

Old Fashioned Coleslaw (p. 315)

Perfect Pan-Fried Fish with Tartar Sauce (p. 350)

Herbed New Potatoes (p. 42) *

Cheese and Chive Muffins (p. 43) *

Florida Lime Pie (p. 378)

* Recipe contains chives

Smoked Salmon Cheesecake

The Crust

- $1/2$ cup dried bread crumbs
- $1^1/4$ cups Parmesan cheese, best quality, grated and divided
- 3 tablespoons butter, melted

The Filling

- 5 or 6 ounces smoked salmon (remove any skin or bones)
- 2 pounds cream cheese, at room temperature
- 4 large eggs
- $3/4$ cup fresh chives, chopped and divided
- 2 teaspoons grated lemon zest (yellow only)
- $1/2$ teaspoon salt
  Pepper
- 1 cup sour cream
  Chive Toast (see recipe, page 37)

Lightly grease a 9-inch springform pan, or spray with nonstick vegetable cooking spray. Combine bread crumbs and $1/4$ cup Parmesan cheese and toss to mix. Stir in melted butter. Press this crumb mixture onto the bottom of the pan. Set pan aside.

For the filling, finely chop smoked salmon in a food processor. Set aside. With electric mixer, beat cream cheese at medium speed until smooth, about 2 minutes. Beat in remaining cup of Parmesan cheese. Blend well. Add eggs, one at a time, and mix well after each addition. Add $1/2$ cup chives, lemon zest, salt and pepper and mix well. Gently fold in sour cream, then the chopped salmon. Spoon mixture evenly over the crumb crust and level with a spatula.

Bake in a 350° oven for 45 minutes. Turn oven off and set door ajar. Leave cheesecake in oven for 30 minutes. Remove from oven and cool at room temperature. Cover well and refrigerate for up to 2 days before serving. To serve, bring cheesecake to room temperature. Place cheesecake on a large serving tray. Sprinkle with the remaining $1/4$ cup chives. Serve with Chive Toasts.

Chive Toasts

20 or more slices very thin white bread (I like Pepperidge Farm)
5 tablespoons unsalted butter, melted
5 tablespoons olive oil
1¹/₂ tablespoons fresh chives, finely chopped

Remove crusts from bread. Cut bread squares into triangles. Will have 40 pieces of bread. Combine butter, oil and chives in a small bowl. With a brush, paint butter mixture on both sides of the triangles and place triangles on a baking sheet. Bake at 350° until golden brown, about 10 minutes. Turn triangles and bake another few minutes until that side is golden brown. Watch and do not burn. Let toasts cool completely, then cover with foil and let stand at room temperature until ready to serve.

Easy Cheese Spread

6 tablespoons butter, at room temperature
8 ounces cream cheese, at room temperature
1 clove garlic, finely minced
2 tablespoons fresh chives, chopped
1 tablespoon fresh lemon juice
1 tablespoon fresh parsley, chopped
¹/₄ teaspoon salt
¹/₈ teaspoon pepper

In food processor, blend butter and cream cheese. Add garlic, chives, lemon juice, parsley, salt and pepper. Process until smooth. Taste and add more salt and pepper if necessary. The chives add a nice delicate flavor to this spread.

NEED A QUICK APPETIZER FOR UNEXPECTED COMPANY? MIX THIS IN YOUR FOOD PROCESSOR IN A HURRY. SERVE WITH CRACKERS OR PIECES OF FRENCH BREAD.

Stuffed Mushrooms with Chives

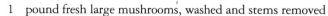

STUFFED MUSHROOMS MAKE
WONDERFUL APPETIZERS, BUT
THEY ALSO CAN BE USED AS A
FIRST COURSE. THIS RECIPE
SERVES 6 AS APPETIZERS, BUT IT
CAN EASILY BE DOUBLED.

1 pound fresh large mushrooms, washed and stems removed
2 tablespoons fresh chives, chopped
5 tablespoons butter
1 egg, beaten
1/2 cup dry bread crumbs
2 teaspoons brandy or sherry
1 teaspoon fresh French tarragon, chopped, or 1/3 teaspoon dried
Salt and pepper to taste
Butter for broiling

Chop mushroom stems. Sauté stems and chives in butter. With a slotted spoon, remove mushroom pieces to a medium bowl. Add beaten egg, bread crumbs, brandy, tarragon, salt and pepper to stem mixture. Combine and set aside.

In same skillet, sauté mushroom caps. Place caps on baking sheet. Stuff each cap with some of the stem mixture. Dot each cap with a little butter, then broil until golden brown. Serve. These may be prepared a few hours in advance, refrigerated, then broiled when guests arrive. Serve hot.

Creamy Bleu Cheese Salad Dressing with Chives

I HAVE MADE LOTS OF
BLEU CHEESE DRESSINGS, BUT
THIS ONE TAKES THE
BLUE RIBBON!

3/4 cup sour cream
3 tablespoons mayonnaise
1 tablespoon fresh lemon juice
1 teaspoon Worcestershire sauce
1/4 cup fresh chives, chopped
6 ounces bleu cheese, crumbled*

Combine all ingredients in a small bowl. Mix well. Use blender or food processor, but don't over-process. Cover and chill well. Makes about 1 2/3 cups.

I particularly love Saga Bleu cheese for the recipe. It is not as harsh or salty as the Roquefort or Stilton or even Gorgonzola. The delicate flavor of Saga is a perfect match for the delicate flavor of chives.

Strawberry–Spinach Salad

The Salad

1   pound fresh spinach, washed, dried, ribs cut out of middle, and leaves torn into bite-size pieces
1   large or 2 small heads bibb lettuce, washed, dried and torn into bite-size pieces
1   pint best quality fresh strawberries, washed, dried and sliced
½   to 1 cup pecan halves, toasted
1   to 2 tablespoons fresh chives, chopped

The Raspberry Vinaigrette Dressing

⅓   cup raspberry vinegar (see Summer Berries Vinegar, p. 292)
¼   teaspoon salt
½   cup sugar
1   tablespoon poppy seeds
1   tablespoon minced sweet onion
1   cup canola oil

Place spinach, lettuce, strawberries, chives and pecans in a large bowl. Combine dressing ingredients in a small bowl and whisk until the sugar is dissolved. Pour over salad ingredients and toss. Serve immediately.

Another time, dress the salad with a strawberry vinaigrette (a wonderful way to use some of your strawberry vinegar).

FRESH SPINACH AND STRAWBERRIES TEAM WITH A DELICIOUS RASPBERRY VINAIGRETTE FOR A MEMORABLE SPRING SALAD. SERVE 6 TO 8 FOR LUNCH ENTRÉES, OR 8 TO 10 FOR DINNER SALADS. IT'S DELICIOUS.

Strawberry–Chives Vinaigrette

1   cup strawberry vinegar (see Summer Berries Vinegar, p. 292)
¼   cup honey
2   teaspoons fresh chives, finely chopped
¼   teaspoon salt
¼   teaspoon pepper
6   tablespoons olive oil

Combine vinegar, honey, chives, salt and pepper. Gradually whisk in the oil. Add to salad ingredients, toss and serve.

Baked Salmon with Chive Cream Sauce

THIS MAY BE THE BEST SALMON
ENTRÉE YOU'LL EVER PREPARE.
THE SAUCE IS ACTUALLY VERY
SIMPLE BUT COMPOSED OF
TERRIFIC SEASONINGS, PLUS
WINE, CREAM AND BRANDY.
SERVE WITH FRESH ASPARAGUS,
A NICELY FLAVORED PILAF AND
HERB BREAD. SERVES 4.

4	6-ounce pieces salmon (I like the flat fillets)
2	teaspoons seasoned salt (your own if you have it)
¹⁄₂	cup vegetable oil (not olive oil)
1	cup white wine
1	tablespoon fresh lemon juice
4	tablespoons margarine
1	tablespoon onion, finely chopped
1	tablespoon fresh chives, chopped
1	tablespoon fresh parsley, chopped
1	teaspoon garlic, finely chopped
¹⁄₄	cup unflavored brandy
1	cup heavy cream
	Chopped chives for garnish

Season the fillets with seasoned salt. Place them in a baking dish with the oil. Marinate about 20 minutes, turn fillets and marinate another 20 minutes. Pour wine and lemon juice over fillets. Bake in a 350° oven for 15 minutes. Remove fillets and set aside, but keep warm.

In a heavy saucepan, melt margarine. Sauté onions, chives and parsley, but do not brown. Add remaining juices from baking dish, the garlic and the brandy. Heat to a simmer. Add the cream and simmer until sauce is reduced by about half. Divide sauce between 4 plates. Place a salmon fillet on sauce. Sprinkle a few chopped chives over salmon and serve immediately.

The Perfect Roast Chicken

1   4- to 5-pound whole chicken (I like to use a roaster rather than a fryer, if possible)
1   lemon, thinly sliced
1   large onion, chopped
3   tablespoons fresh parsley, finely chopped and divided
2   tablespoons fresh chives, finely chopped and divided
1   tablespoon olive oil
    Salt and pepper
1   lemon, cut in half
2   cups chicken broth
    Gravy (see below)

YOU'LL FIND SEVERAL ROASTED CHICKEN RECIPES IN THIS BOOK. THIS ONE IS ESPECIALLY GOOD. IN MY OPINION, YOU HAVE REACHED THE RANK OF A GREAT COOK WHEN YOU HAVE LEARNED HOW TO ROAST THE PERFECT CHICKEN!

Wash and pat dry the chicken. Combine sliced lemon and half the chopped onion, 1 tablespoon parsley and 1 tablespoon chives. Stuff this mixture into the cavity of the chicken. Use kitchen string and loosely tie legs of bird together to help hold in stuffing. Rub bird with oil, then season with salt and pepper. Lightly grease a heavy roasting pan and scatter remaining onion pieces on bottom of pan. Place chicken, breast side up, on top of onion. Squeeze both halves of lemon over the chicken.

Roast chicken in a 350° oven for 1½ to 2 hours, basting occasionally with the chicken broth. Roasting time will depend on the size of the bird. Use a meat thermometer, or look for a chicken at the market that has a pop-up timer inserted — no guesswork then on when it's done. Be sure to not overcook or the meat will be dry. When done, remove chicken from oven, cover loosely with foil and let stand for 10 or 15 minutes before carving.

For delicious gravy, combine the pan juices, the remainder of the broth and the remainder of the herbs in a heavy saucepan. Bring to a boil. Make a paste of ¼ cup flour and 1 cup water. Whisk into the boiling mixture and stir until gravy is smooth and thickened. Salt and pepper if necessary. Serves 4 to 6, depending on size of chicken.

Herbed New Potatoes

THIS IS ONE OF OUR FAVORITE SPRING DISHES. SERVE THIS DISH WITH SPRING LAMB, HAM OR REALLY WITH ANYTHING!

2   pounds little new red potatoes
4   tablespoons butter, melted
1   tablespoon fresh lemon juice
$^1/_2$ teaspoon salt
1   tablespoon fresh chives, chopped
1   tablespoon fresh parsley, chopped

Wash potatoes. Pare a thin strip around middle of each potato. Cook in boiling salted water just until tender, 20 minutes or so. Drain and return potatoes to pan. Combine butter, lemon juice, salt (if needed), chives and parsley. Toss with the potatoes. Place lid on pan and let stand for 3 or 4 minutes to release the flavor from the herbs. Serves 6 or 8.

Herbed Rice

I LOVE THIS PERFECTLY SEASONED RICE WITH BEEF ENTRÉES.

1   cup long grain white rice
2   cups canned beef bouillon
1   cup fresh mushrooms, sliced
2   tablespoons butter
2   tablespoons fresh chives, chopped
$^1/_2$ teaspoon dried basil, crumbled
$^1/_2$ teaspoon dried sweet marjoram, crumbled
     Salt and pepper to taste

Combine rice and bouillon in a medium saucepan. Set aside. In a small skillet, sauté sliced mushrooms in butter until mushrooms are lightly browned. Add the chives, basil, sweet marjoram and salt and pepper to taste. Add skillet contents to rice and bouillon. Stir well. Cover and simmer for 20 minutes, or until rice is tender. Serves 6 to 8.

Cheese and Chive Muffins

¹/₂ cup cornmeal
1 cup flour
1 tablespoon baking powder
1 tablespoon sugar
¹/₂ teaspoon salt
³/₄ cup milk
1 egg, beaten
1 tablespoon butter, melted
1 tablespoon chives, fresh or freeze dried, chopped
¹/₂ cup shredded cheddar cheese

Combine cornmeal, flour, baking powder, sugar and salt in a medium bowl. Add milk gradually, stirring only until just mixed. Stir in egg, butter, chives and cheese. Spoon into greased muffin cups. Bake at 375° for 25 minutes, or until tester comes out clean. Makes 8 or 9 muffins.

REMEMBER THIS RECIPE WHEN YOU WANT A MUFFIN THAT ISN'T SWEET OR FRUITY. THESE ARE GOOD WITH BEAN SOUP OR POTATO SOUP OR WITH CHICKEN DISHES.

Chive Blossom Vinegar

2 cups chive blossoms
1 quart white distilled vinegar, or white wine vinegar

Have a sterilized half gallon jar available. Place chive blossoms in bottom of jar and pour the vinegar (I like room temperature best) over the blossoms. Seal with a nonmetallic lid and let jar stand for about 2 weeks to extract all color and flavor from the blossoms. Discard blossoms. Strain vinegar through a coffee filter into a pretty, sterilized bottle. Cork and seal. This vinegar has a very pronounced onion flavor and aroma. It is nice to splash on vegetables or to make salad dressings and marinades. Go easy — it's potent!

MAKE THIS GORGEOUS VINEGAR WHEN THE CHIVES ARE IN FULL BLOOM, IN MID- TO LATE JUNE IN THE MIDWEST. A BOTTLE OF THIS MAUVE-COLORED VINEGAR ADDS REAL BEAUTY TO YOUR VINEGAR DISPLAY.

Dill

ANETHUM GRAVEOLENS

Dill

....

ANETHUM GRAVEOLENS

Dill is an indispensable flavoring agent in our kitchens. As you can see by my "How I use dill" page, it can be used in many, many foods. When I first started gardening, I thought dill was a perennial plant — after all, it kept coming up in the same spot each spring. I finally discovered it is a hardy annual that self-seeds prolifically. I have learned to leave at least 2 or 3 heads in the garden for the soil and the birds to share. Dill resembles fennel in looks (of course not in taste), though dill usually produces only 1 main stem, whereas fennel can produce several. It is best to sow dill seeds. Dill has a long taproot that doesn't allow it to be easily transplanted. The feathery leaves of the plant are called dillweed. Beautiful umbels of yellow flowers, 4 to 6 inches across, appear at the top of the stem. Eventually, seeds appear here. Dill is native to western Asia but is cultivated throughout the world. No one loves dill more than the Scandinavians. You'll find a patch of dill in every Scandinavian garden. Many items on the smorgasbord are flavored with dillweed or dill seed. The old Norse name for dill was "dilla," which means "to lull." In the Middle Ages, dill was said to protect against witchcraft. Dill grows best in full sun and in well-drained soil. It is important to find the right spot for dill. The stems are hollow and fairly rigid, but the plant definitely needs protection from the wind. Dill grows from 1½ to 5 feet tall, depending on the variety. Three varieties I particularly like are dukat, fernleaf, and bouquet. ❧ 1. *A. g.* '**Dukat**' is a European variety and the one most often found in Sweden, Denmark, Norway or Finland. This is a good choice if you're interested in more weed than seed. It is very leafy and slower to bolt. The leaves have a very "dill" taste. 2. *A. g.* '**Fernleaf**' dill was a 1992 All America winner (developed by Burpee) for use in small gardens and in containers. It grows 18 inches tall, has dark green foliage, and grows rather compact. Fernleaf branches from the base and produces foliage over a longer season than other varieties. It is an excellent plant for the home garden. I love it in one corner of my herb garden. Some of my herb friends don't think it has the excellent dill flavor of other varieties, but I disagree — I'm sure the flavor depends a lot on soil and other conditions. 3. The *A. g.* '**Bouquet**' variety is widely grown and popular because of its large seed heads (this would be the one to grow for seeds rather than the weed). Especially prized for pickling, the stems of bouquet dill will reach 4 to 5 feet tall. Dillweed dries quickly, in just 2 or 3 days. The taste is very fragile and when cooking with dillweed, add it only at the end of cooking to avoid destroying the flavor. Dill seeds, on the other hand, are much more potent in flavor — this flavor is similar to caraway flavor. The seeds can be used fresh or dried with about the same results. Seeds shatter badly if allowed to dry fully in the garden. Cut umbels with seeds, and hang upside down to dry. Place a bag, a container larger than the umbel, or a cloth underneath the umbel to catch the seeds as they dry and fall. ❧ There are numerous medicinal uses for dill. It is said to aid digestion and the old-timers will tell you that chewing dill seeds will stop the hiccups! ❧

How do I use dill?

- with fish and shellfish, especially salmon and shrimps
- in salad dressings
- in mustards
- in vinegars
- with lamb
- with pork
- in salads
- in soups, especially bean soup and tomato soup
- in sauces
- with vegetables, such as carrots, potatoes, peas, cabbage
- in sour cream
- in cream cheese
- in cottage cheese
- with other cheeses, such as Havarti

- in breads, especially rye bread
- with egg dishes
- in pickling
- in cole slaw
- in yogurt
- in tuna salad
- in horseradish sauce
- in tartar sauce
- in seafood salads
- with mushrooms
- in rice dishes
- in butters
- in potato salad
- in meatballs
- with garlic
- in sauerkraut
- in dips and appetizer spreads

INDEX

Dill Recipes

MENU

*It's a Dilly
of a Spring Menu!*

Carla Nelson's Adger's Wharf Crab Dip (p. 53) *

Crackers

Strawberry-Dill Spinach Salad (p. 58) *

Roast Leg of Spring Lamb (p. 340)

Scalloped Asparagus (p. 358)

Biscuits with Dill Butter (p. 61) *

Wonderful Rhubarb Cake (p. 369)

* Recipe contains dill

THESE ARE SPECIAL ON AN APPETIZER TRAY OR SERVE 2 OR 3 ON A LUNCHEON PLATE FOR A WONDERFUL "SANDWICH." MAKE YOUR OWN LEMON-FLAVORED MAYONNAISE BY ADDING FRESH LEMON JUICE AND LEMON ZEST TO STORE-BOUGHT MAYONNAISE — ABOUT 1 TABLESPOON JUICE AND $1/2$ TEASPOON ZEST PER 1 CUP MAYONNAISE.

Smoked Salmon and Dill Roll-Ups

Flour tortillas (10 to 12 per package)
Lemon-flavored mayonnaise
Sweet onions, thinly sliced
Dillweed, freshly chopped
Smoked salmon, thinly sliced

Work with 1 tortilla at a time. Spread tortilla with a thin layer of lemon mayonnaise. Add a layer of onions. Sprinkle with the dillweed, then arrange smoked salmon slices over all. Beginning at the top, roll tortilla toward you to form a log. Trim off ends, then cut tortilla into 5 or 6 equal pieces for sandwiches, or into thinner slices for appetizers. Place on a serving dish, cover with plastic wrap and refrigerate for at least an hour or two to develop flavors. Wonderful!

Cheese Swirls with Dill

I HAVE MADE THESE LITTLE CHEESE BISCUITS FOR YEARS. I SERVE THEM AS AN APPETIZER WITH THIN SLICES OF HAM OR ROAST BEEF OR ROAST PORK. THEY WILL MELT IN YOUR MOUTH.

2	cups flour
$1/2$	teaspoon salt
3	teaspoons baking powder
$1/2$	teaspoon dried dillweed
3	tablespoons margarine, softened, or Crisco
$2/3$	cup milk
$1/2$	cup grated cheddar cheese

Sift flour, salt and baking powder together. Stir in the dillweed to distribute evenly. Cut in shortening. Add milk and mix to a soft dough. Do not over-handle the dough. Divide dough into 2 balls. Roll each ball $1/4$-inch-thick into a rectangle. Sprinkle half the cheese on the dough. Roll up tightly and cut into $1/4$-inch-thick slices. Bake slices on a lightly greased baking sheet at 425° for about 8 minutes. Check — may need to bake 2 or 3 minutes longer. Makes about 2 dozen little biscuits.

Carla Nelson is the editor/publisher of a very informative herb newsletter called "Herb Gatherings, The Newsletter For The Thymes." Six issues a year for $15, address is 10949 E. 200 S., Lafayette, IN 47905-9453. Carla tells me, and I quote, "The four of us (Carla, husband, sister and brother-in-law) spent quite a number of very enjoyable hours on Folly Beach, James Island, South Carolina, talking our heads off over a bowl of Adger's Wharf Crab Dip and vodka tonics."

Here is what Carla says about this superb recipe:

"My sister, Judy, and her husband, Joe, discovered Adger's Wharf on James Island in South Carolina some years ago. It was a quaint little restaurant noted for its wonderful crab dip. It's gone now — a victim of rampant progress — but luckily Judy was able to get the recipe before they closed. The original recipe called for "mayo." Initially we were disappointed that we couldn't seem to duplicate the flavor and then we discovered the secret. In the South, JFG Mayonnaise is widely used. As soon as we made this dip with JFG, we had a perfect match. But it's great with any brand."

Carla Nelson's Adger's Wharf Crab Dip

1	cup crab meat, coarsely shredded
1	cup mayonnaise
$^1/_2$	cup cheddar cheese, grated
1	teaspoon French dressing
1	teaspoon Worcestershire sauce
1	teaspoon horseradish
1	teaspoon fresh dillweed, finely chopped

Mix all ingredients together. Serve on crackers.

MARGE ADDS: "I DON'T LIVE IN THE SOUTH, SO I DIDN'T HAVE JFG MAYONNAISE TO MAKE THIS WITH, BUT I CAN'T IMAGINE IT COULD BE ANY BETTER!"

Tomato-Dill Soup

2   10 ½-ounce cans cream of tomato soup
1   15-ounce can crushed or diced tomatoes
1   teaspoon dried dillweed, or less to suit your taste
½   teaspoon garlic powder
1   10 ½-ounce soup can heavy whipping cream
     Salt and pepper
     Sour cream for garnish

Mix together the soup and tomatoes. Add dill and garlic powder. Heat thoroughly.
Lower heat and add heavy whipping cream. Heat slowly or cream may curdle. Don't
allow it to boil. Season with salt and pepper. Top each serving with a dollop of sour
cream. Serves 4 or 5. No one will know this isn't homemade.

Dilled Cucumber and Tomato Salad

1   large firm cucumber, thinly sliced
⅓   cup oil
3   tablespoons vinegar or herbal vinegar
½   teaspoon dillweed
1   teaspoon sugar
⅛   teaspoon pepper
3   large tomatoes, firm and ripe

Place cucumber slices in a 9x13x2-inch baking dish. Combine remainder of ingredients,
except the tomatoes, and mix well. Pour marinade over cucumber slices, cover with
plastic wrap and refrigerate several hours or even overnight. When ready to serve, slice
tomatoes. Remove cucumbers from marinade. Arrange tomato and cucumber slices on a
lettuce-lined platter. Drizzle marinade over all. Serves 4 to 6.

My Potato Salad

5   pounds red potatoes, medium size
6   hard-boiled eggs
3   tablespoons green onion, finely diced
1   cup sweet gherkins, drained and diced
1   small jar pimiento, or ½ cup of your own roasted and marinated red peppers
1   cup celery, diced
    Salt to taste
2   cups mayonnaise
½   cup sour cream
1   tablespoon yellow mustard*
1   teaspoon fresh dillweed, or ½ teaspoon dried
1   tablespoon fresh parsley, finely chopped

Cook potatoes in their jackets. Cool, then peel. Boil eggs, cool and peel. Slice potatoes and eggs into a large bowl. Add the onion, sweet gherkins, pimiento, celery and salt. Toss to mix. Combine mayonnaise, sour cream, mustard, dillweed and parsley. Combine with salad ingredients and mix gently but thoroughly. Refrigerate several hours to blend flavors. Serves 10 or more.

*Another time, omit the mustard and add 1 or 2 tablespoons of an herbal vinegar. My choice would be dill vinegar.

Dill or Dill-Garlic Vinegar

To make 1 quart:

1   quart white distilled, white wine or cider vinegar
2   or 3 heads dill
2   cloves garlic, chopped, if making dill garlic vinegar

Stuff dill heads into a sterilized half-gallon jar. Pour vinegar over dill. Add garlic if using. Tightly cover jar and set in a cool, dark place for about 3 weeks. Remove dill heads, strain vinegar through a coffee filter and place in a sterilized bottle. Seal bottle. Remember, use no metal when making your vinegars.

I DISLIKE "FLAT-TASTING" POTATO SALAD. THE ADDITION OF DILL AND PARSLEY SURELY HELPS TO BRIGHTEN THIS OR ANY POTATO SALAD.

THIS IS THE EASIEST VINEGAR YOU'LL MAKE. TASTES LIKE DILL PICKLES WITHOUT THE PICKLES!

Joyce Wagner
AND HER ORIENTAL DILL SALAD

There is a wonderful herb shop and gardens (numerous gardens) just outside New Carlisle, Ohio, called Hampton Herbs. Bob and Betty Leonard are the owners. I think their middle initial must be "P," which stands for "Perfection," which stands for the way they run this business. If you live in Ohio or eastern Indiana, you owe yourself a trip to Hampton Herbs. They are blessed with a talented staff who seemingly can do anything — from cooking, to weeding, to creating some of the loveliest herbal wreaths and swags I've seen anywhere. One such staff member is Joyce Wagner, who made this delicious salad for about 100 people for an herbal luncheon on a day I was there for an herb presentation. The salad is a rather strange combination of ingredients, but I found it absolutely delicious. I think you will too.

Joyce Wagner's Oriental Dill Salad

A NOTE FROM JOYCE —
YOU MAY SUBSTITUTE ONE-FOURTH LETTUCE FOR THE CABBAGE AND YOU MAY ADD OTHER DICED VEGETABLES OF YOUR CHOICE. SHE HAS, AT TIMES, ADDED CHOPPED, COOKED CHICKEN BREAST TO THE SALAD.

2 packages Ramen noodles (beef, Oriental or chicken) DO NOT COOK NOODLES!
1 pound cabbage, finely chopped
$^1/_3$ cup red onion, finely chopped
1 sweet red pepper, finely chopped
$^1/_2$ to 1 cup sunflower meats
$^1/_4$ cup toasted slivered almonds
2 tablespoons dried dillweed
2 tablespoons fresh parsley, chopped

Break up the uncooked noodles and place in a large resealable plastic bag. Add remainder of ingredients. Close bag and refrigerate. Just before serving, add the following dressing:

$^3/_4$ to 1 cup oil
$^1/_3$ cup white distilled vinegar, or an herbal vinegar
$^1/_2$ cup sugar
Seasoning packets from the noodles packages

Toss salad and dressing together in the bag. Serves 8.

Luncheon Salmon Mousse with Cucumber-Dill Sauce

2   1-pound cans red salmon
¹/₃   cup fresh lemon juice
1   cup sour cream
1   cup shredded cheddar cheese
2   tablespoons onion, grated
1   teaspoon salt
1   teaspoon dillweed
2   envelopes plain gelatin
¹/₂   cup water
1   tablespoon vinegar
1   cup heavy cream, whipped
    Cucumber Dill Sauce (recipe follows)

Drain salmon. Discard skin and bones. Flake salmon into a large bowl. Add the lemon juice, sour cream, cheddar cheese, onion, salt and dillweed. Heat gelatin, water and vinegar together until gelatin dissolves. Carefully stir gelatin mixture into salmon mixture. Fold in whipping cream, just to combine. Turn into a 6-cup mold. Cover and refrigerate for several hours or until thoroughly chilled and jelled. To serve, turn mousse out of mold onto a lettuce-lined serving platter. Drizzle a little cucumber dill sauce over the mousse. Pass the extra sauce. Serves 8 to 10.

Cucumber Dill Sauce

1   cucumber, peeled, cut in half lengthwise and seeds removed with the bowl of a spoon
    Salt
1   cup sour cream, or ¹/₂ cup sour cream and ¹/₂ cup mayonnaise
1   tablespoon fresh lemon juice
1   teaspoon dillweed
1   teaspoon chopped chives

Shred cucumber with a grater. Sprinkle with salt. Let stand at room temperature for 1 hour. Drain thoroughly. Combine with remainder of ingredients. Refrigerate. Makes about 1¹/₂ cups.

A SPLENDID COLD SALMON SALAD. SERVE WITH A HOT GREEN VEGETABLE, A CRUSTY BREAD, FRESH FRUIT AND RASPBERRY CHEESECAKE (P. 373)

Strawberry-Dill Spinach Salad

6	cups fresh spinach leaves, cleaned and torn (remove stem ends)
1	teaspoon toasted sesame seeds
2	cups fresh strawberries, cleaned and cut in half
$1/4$	cup salad oil (not olive oil)
2	tablespoons red wine vinegar*
$1^1/2$	tablespoons sugar
$1^1/2$	teaspoons fresh dillweed or about $1/2$ teaspoon dried
$1/8$	teaspoon salt
$1/8$	teaspoon onion powder
$1/8$	teaspoon garlic powder
$1/8$	teaspoon dry mustard
$1/8$	teaspoon pepper

Place spinach in a large salad bowl. Toast sesame seeds in a small skillet — shake skillet over heat for 2 or 3 minutes. Add sesame seeds and strawberries to bowl. Toss to distribute evenly. In a screw-top jar, combine remainder of ingredients. Cover and shake well. Pour dressing over mixture. Toss gently. Serves 6.

* If you have some Garlic and Parsley Red Wine Vinegar (p. 163) made, use that here.

Dill Salad Dressing

$3/4$	cup salad oil
$1/4$	cup fresh lemon juice
$1/2$	teaspoon salt
$1/2$	teaspoon black pepper
$1/4$	teaspoon dillweed
1	clove garlic, minced
$1/3$	cup mayonnaise

Combine oil, juice, salt, pepper and dillweed. Mix well. Stir in garlic. Add mayonnaise and blend thoroughly. Especially good to serve with cooked artichoke hearts and hearts of palm. Makes $1^1/3$ cups.

Danish Meatballs in Sour Cream–Dill Sauce

Meatballs

1 small onion, minced
1 tablespoon butter or margarine
$1/2$ pound ground beef, preferably chuck
$1/2$ pound ground veal shoulder
$1/2$ cup fine dry bread crumbs
1 egg, slightly beaten
1 tablespoon cold water
1 teaspoon salt
$1/2$ teaspoon dillweed
$1/8$ teaspoon ground nutmeg
$1/8$ teaspoon pepper
1 tablespoon vegetable oil
    Sour Cream-Dill Sauce (recipe follows)

Sauté onions and butter in a large skillet until onions are tender, but do not brown. Mix in meats, bread crumbs, egg, water, salt, dillweed, nutmeg and pepper. Shape into $1^1/2$-inch balls. Place oil in a large skillet and heat. Sauté meatballs in hot oil until brown on all sides and cooked through. Roll them around in pan to cook evenly. Transfer to a heated platter. Cover with foil to keep warm. Pour Sour Cream-Dill Sauce over meatballs, toss lightly and serve to 4 as a main course.

Sour Cream-Dill Sauce

    Meatball drippings plus enough melted butter to make $1/2$ cup
$1/4$ cup flour
2 cups hot beef broth
1 cup sour cream, at room temperature
2 tablespoons freshly snipped dill, or 2 teaspoons dried
$1/8$ teaspoon nutmeg
$1/8$ teaspoon salt
$1/8$ teaspoon pepper

Heat meatball drippings in a skillet. Blend in flour and cook and stir until flour is light brown. Whisk in broth and cook and whisk until sauce thickens and boils. Mix in sour cream, dill, nutmeg and pepper. Heat thoroughly, but do not boil or sour cream will curdle.

NO SECTION ON DILL WOULD BE COMPLETE WITHOUT AT LEAST ONE AUTHENTIC SCANDINAVIAN RECIPE. THIS IS ABOUT AS AUTHENTIC AS IT GETS. SOMETIMES I SERVE THESE MEATBALLS AS AN APPETIZER, BUT I OFTEN SERVE THEM AS A MAIN COURSE OVER HOT BUTTERED NOODLES.

GRILL THE STEAK OUTSIDE FOR
EXTRA ADDED FLAVOR. I LIKE
TO CUT THIS GRILLED STEAK
INTO THIN SLICES. COMBINE
WITH SOME OF THE
HORSERADISH-DILL SAUCE AND
STUFF INTO POCKET OR PITA
BREAD. THESE ARE GREAT
PICNIC SANDWICHES.

Flank Steak with Horseradish-Dill Sauce

1	tablespoon olive oil
$^1/_2$	teaspoon salt
$^1/_2$	teaspoon ground cumin
$^1/_4$	teaspoon cayenne pepper
$1^1/_2$	pounds flank steak
	Horseradish Dill Sauce (recipe follows)
4	to 6 pita breads, toasted if desired

Combine oil, salt, cumin and pepper. Rub evenly over both sides of steak. Let steak stand at room temperature 15 minutes before grilling. Grill steak over low coals for 5 to 6 minutes per side for medium. May need to grill another 2 or 3 minutes, but don't overcook. Remove from heat and let stand 5 minutes. Slice into thin slices and serve with pita bread and Horseradish-Dill Sauce. Serves 4.

Horseradish-Dill Sauce

1	cup plain yogurt
1	to 2 tablespoons prepared horseradish
2	tablespoons minced fresh dill, or 2 teaspoons dried
3	green onions, finely diced

In a small bowl, combine yogurt, 1 tablespoon horseradish, dill and green onions. Taste and add more horseradish if desired. Makes 1 cup sauce.

Baked Stuffed Halibut with Dill

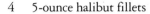

4	5-ounce halibut fillets
3	ounces crab meat
3	ounces bay shrimp
3	ounces Brie cheese, cut into small cubes
1	tablespoon fresh dill, chopped
$^1/_8$	teaspoon salt
$^1/_8$	teaspoon pepper
3	tablespoons mayonnaise

Split fillets lengthwise to form a pocket — do not split all the way through. Set aside. In mixing bowl, combine remainder of ingredients. Divide stuffing among the four pocketed fillets. Hold pockets closed with toothpicks. Place fillets in a lightly buttered baking dish. Bake at 400° for 12 to 15 minutes or until fish is firm and cooked through. Serves 4. (Lucky 4!)

I CLIPPED THIS RECIPE FROM A NEWSPAPER BECAUSE IT SOUNDED PERFECTLY DELICIOUS. IT IS. THE RECIPE CAME FROM McCORMICK'S FISH HOUSE AND BAR IN BEAVERTON, OREGON. THANK YOU FOR SHARING IT WITH ALL OF US.

Dill Butter

2	sticks butter, softened
$^1/_3$	cup snipped fresh dill, or 3 teaspoons dried
$^1/_3$	cup minced fresh parsley
2	green onions, minced
2	tablespoons chopped fresh French tarragon, or 2 teaspoons dried
1	tablespoon chopped fresh celery leaves
2	tablespoons fresh lemon juice

Combine all ingredients in a medium bowl and mix with a wooden spoon to make a smooth butter. Makes 1 cup.

DAB THIS BUTTER ON FISH AS IT BROILS OR BAKES. IT'S A WONDERFUL SPREAD FOR HOT BISCUITS.

Salmon Loaf with Dill Sauce

THIS IS ONE OF THE BEST
LUNCHEON OR SUPPER DISHES I
KNOW OF. USE ONLY THE BEST
QUALITY CANNED SALMON —
RED SOCKEYE IS MY FAVORITE.
THE WONDERFUL DILL SAUCE
CAN BE USED WITH OTHER
FISH DISHES.

1 cup celery, finely chopped
$^3/_4$ cup onion, finely chopped
2 tablespoons salad oil
2 $7^3/_4$-ounce cans salmon, skin and bones discarded
2 eggs
2 $5^1/_3$-ounce cans evaporated milk
2 cups fresh bread crumbs
$^1/_2$ to 1 teaspoon salt
   Dash of pepper
   Dill Sauce (recipe follows)

In a 2-quart saucepan over medium-high heat, cook celery and onion in hot oil until tender, about 10 minutes. Remove pan from heat. Add salmon and its liquid and remaining ingredients, except Dill Sauce. Combine the mixture until well mixed and smooth. Grease a 9x4-inch loaf pan. Spoon salmon mixture evenly into the pan. Bake in a 350° oven for 55 to 60 minutes. Remove salmon from pan. Serve hot or cold with Dill Sauce. Serves 4.

Dill Sauce

$^1/_2$ cup mayonnaise
$^1/_4$ cup sour cream
1 tablespoon fresh lemon juice
1 tablespoon milk
2 teaspoons chopped fresh dillweed, or $^1/_2$ teaspoon dried
$^1/_2$ teaspoon salt
$^1/_2$ teaspoon sugar
$^1/_8$ teaspoon pepper

Combine all ingredients in a small bowl and whisk until smooth. Refrigerate until ready to use. Makes $^3/_4$ cup sauce.

Overnight Cheese Soufflé

4	tablespoons butter
1	cup sliced fresh mushrooms
1	large onion, diced
16	slices firm white bread, crusts removed
1	pound lean bacon, fried crisp and crumbled
2	Anaheim or other hot chilis, seeded, peeled and diced
$^3/_4$	cup celery, diced
1	pound sharp cheddar cheese, grated
	Salt and pepper
2	tablespoons snipped fresh dill, or 2 teaspoons dried
1	large tomato, peeled and sliced
6	eggs, slightly beaten
3	cups half-and-half cream
1	tablespoon Dijon mustard

Melt butter in a sauté pan over medium heat. Cook mushrooms and onions for 2 or 3 minutes or until tender. Remove with a slotted spoon and set aside. Dip 8 of the bread slices in sauté pan to butter one side. Place bread, butter side down, in a 13x9x2-inch baking dish. Layer half the mushrooms, onions, bacon, chilis and celery on top of the bread and finish with half the cheese. Season with salt, pepper and $^1/_2$ of the dill. Repeat bread layer and the remaining half of ingredients as above, but add tomato slices before the cheese. Thoroughly mix eggs, cream and mustard. Pour over contents in baking dish. Cover top with waxed paper. Wrap with plastic wrap. Refrigerate overnight. Before baking, allow casserole to stand 30 minutes at room temperature. Bake casserole, uncovered, at 350° for 45 minutes. Remove from oven and cool 5 minutes before serving. Cut into squares to serve. Serves 10 to 12.

LOOKING FOR A WONDERFUL BRUNCH OR LUNCHEON DISH THAT IS PREPARED THE DAY BEFORE? HERE IT IS. JUST REMOVE FROM THE REFRIGERATOR, BAKE IT AND SERVE IT FROM THE SAME DISH. WHAT COULD BE EASIER?

French Tarragon

ARTEMISIA DRACUNCULUS SATIVA

French Tarragon

ARTEMISIA DRACUNCULUS SATIVA

French tarragon is a member of the vast family of artemisias. Some of its relations would be wormwood (*Artemisia absinthium*), southernwood (*Artemisia abrotanum*), and mugwort (*Artemisia vulgaris*), to name a few. ❦ How many of you have bought a packet of tarragon seeds in the spring, planted the seeds, then were disappointed when the plant grew and you couldn't detect the licorice (anise) flavor when you cooked with it? Go out and pull all those plants, because true French tarragon can be propagated only by cuttings or root divisions. You probably have planted Russian tarragon (*A. dracunculus*) seeds and in my opinion, the plant is nearly worthless for culinary uses. This is another plant (along with Greek oregano) that must be tasted at the nursery or greenhouse before bringing it home. It must have a sharp licorice flavor. ❦ The word tarragon derives from the French word *esdragon* and the Latin word *dracunculus*, meaning little dragon. Unlike basil, for example, the leaves have no aroma unless they are bruised. Tarragon is a perennial plant that needs winter protection in cold climates. French tarragon is a native of southern Europe, whereas Russian tarragon is a native of Siberia. ❦ The leaves of French tarragon are smooth, dark green, long, and narrow. The plant grows from 2 to 3 feet tall on stems that are woody, but are greenish-brown and tender at the top. Tarragon likes to be planted in a sunny location in well-drained, but not too rich, soil. I have never seen blooms on my tarragon (therefore no seeds so it must be French!), but I understand the Russian tarragon blooms, which then produces tiny seeds. 	The French trace tarragon back to the 12th century. Throughout the centuries, the French are given credit as the big users of this plant. However, all Mediterranean countries love and use French tarragon extensively. It is one of four herbs (parsley, chervil, chives, and French tarragon) the French have made into their classic seasoning called Fines Herbes. Equal parts of these four herbs make this seasoning. In any restaurant or café in France, you will no doubt see the word *esdragon* on menus. You know then they are serving a dish that contains tarragon. When fresh, tarragon should be used rather sparingly in cooking, as its flavor is quite potent. Unfortunately, much of that flavor is lost in the drying process. 	French tarragon needs to be harvested in late June or early July (at least in Indiana). That's when I see a few yellow or dried leaves near the stem base. I have found it is best to cut the plant almost to the ground in late fall, then mulch the area well for winter. Whether you mulch or not is your choice. Drainage is the most critical thing to consider — French Tarragon will not live in standing water. Divide tarragon, or at least cut through it with a spade, every 3 or 4 years to keep the flavor at its peak. 	In my research, I found that tarragon has not been widely used medicinally. But I did find that it has been used as an appetite stimulant, and like many other herbs, used as a digestive aid. 	As I mentioned earlier, tarragon is difficult to dry successfully. Drying temperature should not exceed 80° to 90° F.

Hotter than that and the flavor, or much of it, will be destroyed. I dry small batches of tarragon two ways. One, I gather 4 or 5 leafy stems, wash them, and let them dry until the leaves are moisture-free. Then I hang them upside down in a warm shaded area. They should dry in 10 days to 2 weeks if the conditions are right. Strip the leaves off the stems and store in an airtight container. Another method of drying is to strip the leaves off the stem, lay them on a clean screen in a warm and humid-free area. The leaves will dry quickly — 4 or 5 days. Regardless of which method you use, the minute they are dry, store the leaves in airtight containers out of heat and light. Tarragon easily and readily re-absorbs moisture if opened to the air. The main way I preserve French tarragon is to make a vinegar with the leaves. Tarragon vinegar is a necessary item in the French kitchen and in many other kitchens throughout the world. ❦ There are many plants in the herb world with a licorice flavor, but French tarragon is probably the winner of the group in the culinary world. ❦

How do I use French tarragon?

- in appetizer dips
- with vegetables, such as zucchini, green beans, carrots, broccoli, tomatoes, peas, and asparagus
- with chicken and turkey
- with lamb
- with veal
- in vinegar
- in salads
- in salad dressings
- in cream sauces
- in mustards
- in breads
- in butters
- with egg dishes
- in oil
- with many fish and seafood dishes
- in Fines Herbes blend
- with mayonnaise
- in tartar sauce
- with sour cream, yogurt, cream cheese
- in Béarnaise sauce
- in liqueurs
- in soups, especially chicken soup

French Tarragon Recipes

MENU

Oui, Oui, Tarragon!

Tarragon Party Dip (p. 73) *

Pear and Bleu Cheese Salad (p. 313)

Chicken and Mushrooms in Tarragon Sauce (p. 79) *

Buttered Noodles

Carrots with Orange and Ginger (p. 356)

Wonderful Sour Cream Rolls (p. 326)
with Tarragon Butter (p. 81) *

Velvet Angel Cake (p. 367)
with Sliced Peaches and Raspberry Sauce (p. 401)

* Recipe contains French tarragon

Tarragon Party Dip

1 cup mayonnaise
3 hard-cooked eggs, finely chopped
2 tablespoons green onions, finely chopped
2 tablespoons fresh parsley, finely chopped
2 tablespoons capers (optional, but a good addition)
2 teaspoons Dijon mustard
1 tablespoon French tarragon vinegar
1 tablespoon fresh lemon juice
1 clove garlic, finely chopped
1 teaspoon prepared horseradish
2 teaspoons fresh French tarragon, chopped, or 1 teaspoon dried, crumbled

Combine all ingredients thoroughly. Cover and refrigerate for several hours or overnight. Serve with crackers, shrimps or raw vegetables.

THIS IS A WONDERFUL SHRIMP OR VEGETABLE DIP. IT IS BEST TO MAKE IT THE DAY BEFORE THE PARTY SO ALL THE FLAVORS CAN BLEND. MY TWIN SISTER, MARTHA, GAVE THIS RECIPE TO ME MANY YEARS AGO.

Tarragon-Green Bean Salad

$^1/_2$ cup vegetable oil, not olive oil
$^1/_2$ cup red wine vinegar
2 teaspoons salt
2 teaspoons fresh French tarragon, finely chopped, or 1 teaspoon dried tarragon, crumbled
1 clove garlic, minced
$^1/_4$ teaspoon seasoned pepper
6 1-pound cans whole green beans, drained, or equal amount of cooked fresh green beans
4 tomatoes, cut into eighths
1 14-ounce can hearts of palm, drained and cut into fourths

Make a vinaigrette of the first 6 ingredients. Add to the combined vegetables in a large bowl. Cover bowl and refrigerate 3 or 4 hours before serving. Good for 2 or 3 days in the refrigerator. Serves 10 to 12.

YOU'LL LOVE HAVING THIS SALAD IN THE REFRIGERATOR TO SERVE ON HOT SUMMER DAYS. WHEN THE SALAD IS GONE, USE ANY LEFTOVER VINAIGRETTE TO DRESS A GREEN SALAD.

Cold Marinated Vegetables

THE MARINADE FOR THIS SALAD IS ESPECIALLY GOOD. SERVE THE SALAD IN A GLASS BOWL BECAUSE IT'S SO BEAUTIFUL!

8 medium carrots, scraped and sliced
2 medium cucumbers, sliced
2 ribs celery, sliced
1 green pepper, seeded and cut into strips
1 red pepper, seeded and cut into strips
1 small head cauliflower, divided into flowerets
1/2 pound fresh green beans, cooked slightly
12 small white onions, peeled and cooked slightly
1/2 teaspoon salt
1/2 pound fresh mushrooms (to be added later)

Combine the above vegetables except mushrooms and sprinkle with 1/2 teaspoon salt. Cover and refrigerate for 2 hours. Rinse vegetables, spread them out on a clean towel to dry.

Meanwhile, make this marinade:

3 cups cider vinegar, or half cider vinegar and half French Tarragon Vinegar (see recipe, p. 81)
3 cups water
1 1/2 cups sugar
1/4 cup mustard seeds
2 teaspoons fresh French tarragon, chopped, or 1 teaspoon dried, crumbled
3/4 teaspoon celery seed
3/4 teaspoon mace

Combine all ingredients in a large saucepan and bring to a boil. Reduce heat and simmer 2 or 3 minutes. Add rinsed and dried vegetables, plus 1/2 pound cleaned and sliced fresh mushrooms. Bring to a boil. Immediately remove pan from heat.
Let cool, then refrigerate for several hours. Will keep for 1 week in the refrigerator.
Serves 8 to 10.

Cobb Salad

Vinaigrette

2	shallots, finely minced
3	tablespoons fresh French tarragon, finely chopped
1	teaspoon salt
1/4	teaspoon pepper
2/3	cup olive oil
6	tablespoons white wine vinegar
2	tablespoons smooth (not grainy) Dijon mustard

Combine vinaigrette ingredients and blend thoroughly.

IF I EVER SEE THIS SALAD ON A MENU, I ORDER IT. THE VINAIGRETTE WITH FRESH TARRAGON IS THE SECRET HERE — WITHOUT IT, IT WOULD BE ANOTHER CHEF'S SALAD.

Salad Ingredients

12	cups cleaned assorted salad greens, torn into bite-size pieces
3	cups cooked chicken breast, cut into thin strips
4	small tomatoes, peeled, seeded and diced
2	hard-cooked eggs, chopped
1	ripe avocado, peeled and cut into small pieces
6	slices bacon, cooked until crisp, then crumbled
1/2	cup bleu cheese, crumbled
1	tablespoon fresh chives, chopped

Place the salad greens on a large deep platter. Drizzle about half the vinaigrette over the greens. Arrange other ingredients on the greens. Drizzle a little more vinaigrette over the salad. Pass any remaining vinaigrette. Serves 6.

Tarragon Salad Dressing

3	tablespoons French tarragon vinegar (see recipe, p. 81)
	Dash of salt and pepper
1/2	cup olive oil
2	tablespoons fresh French tarragon, chopped, or 1 tablespoon dried, crumbled

Combine all ingredients in a screw-top jar. Shake well before using. Makes 1/2 cup.

USE THIS VERY TARRAGON DRESSING TO DRESS SALAD GREENS.

Crab au Gratin

$^1/_2$ cup butter
$^1/_4$ cup flour
1 cup milk
1 cup half-and-half cream
$^1/_2$ cup dry white wine
$^1/_2$ teaspoon salt
$^1/_4$ teaspoon paprika
2 teaspoons fresh French tarragon, chopped, or 1 teaspoon dried, crumbled
2 tablespoons onion, grated
$^1/_4$ pound fresh mushrooms, cleaned and sliced
1 cup sharp cheddar cheese, grated
1 pound crabmeat, fresh, canned or frozen, picked over carefully
$^1/_3$ cup bread crumbs
1 tablespoon butter, melted

Melt the $^1/_2$ cup of butter in a medium saucepan. Stir in flour and cook 2 minutes. Add milk, cream and wine. Cook and stir until thick and smooth. Add salt, paprika, tarragon, onion, mushrooms and cheese. Stir over low heat until cheese melts. Fold in crabmeat. Spoon into a 2-quart buttered casserole. Sprinkle with bread crumbs. Drizzle the 1 tablespoon melted butter over the crumbs. Bake at 350° for 15 to 20 minutes until hot and bubbly. Serve on toast triangles or in toast cups. Serves 6.

Tarragon Roasted Turkey

- 1¼ cups butter, softened
- 2 tablespoons dried French tarragon
- 3 tablespoons orange juice concentrate
- 1 15-pound turkey

Combine butter, tarragon and orange juice concentrate. A food processor makes quick work of it. Set aside. With your fingers, carefully loosen the skin of turkey all around the breast area. Be careful not to tear skin. With your hands, push the butter mixture under the skin, covering all the breast area. Save a little to rub on the outside of the bird. Place turkey on a rack, breast side up, in a large roasting pan. Tie legs and wing tips close to the carcass. Roast, uncovered, at 375° for 15 to 20 minutes per pound. Do not baste. Cover loosely with foil the last hour of baking if skin appears to be browning too much. Do not bake past 185° on a meat thermometer. Remove turkey from oven and let stand, loosely covered, for 20 to 30 minutes before carving. Make gravy with pan juices. Serves 12.

Wild Rice and Turkey or Chicken Casserole

- 1½ cups wild rice
- 1 pound bulk unseasoned pork sausage
- 1 cup fresh mushrooms, cleaned and sliced
- 1 tablespoon butter
- 1 teaspoon fresh lemon juice
- 2 10½-ounce cans condensed cream of mushroom soup
- 1 teaspoon dried French tarragon, crumbled
- 1 teaspoon Worcestershire sauce
- 12 slices roasted turkey or chicken (or cook 2 fryers and use all the meat)
- 1½ cups Ritz cracker crumbs
- ¼ cup butter, melted

Cook wild rice according to package directions. Cook sausage in a skillet until browned, stirring often. Drain off and discard fat. In a small skillet, sauté mushrooms in butter and lemon juice until liquid is reduced. Stir the mushrooms, soup, tarragon and Worcestershire sauce into the sausage skillet. Gently stir in the cooked rice. Spoon half of mixture into a greased 12x8x2-inch baking dish. Place turkey or chicken slices on top. Spoon remaining rice over turkey or chicken. Sprinkle with the cracker crumbs. Drizzle melted butter over the crumbs. Cover and refrigerate. To serve, heat oven to 375° and bake for 45 minutes. If made and placed in oven without refrigerating, bake only 30 to 35 minutes. Serves 8 to 10.

IF YOU'RE TIRED OF PREPARING THE TURKEY THE SAME WAY EACH TIME, TRY THIS METHOD. I CAN GUARANTEE A JUICY, WELL-SEASONED BIRD — JUST FOLLOW THE DIRECTIONS. I LIKE THIS TURKEY MUCH BETTER UNSTUFFED.

HERE IS A DELICIOUS, MAKE-AHEAD PARTY CASSEROLE. THE SAUSAGE AND FRENCH TARRAGON ARE SPECIAL "SEASONING" FOR THIS DISH.

Homestyle Chicken Pot Pie

Pastry

1½	cups flour
1	teaspoon salt
⅓	cup cold butter, cut into pieces
1	large egg
2	to 3 tablespoons ice water

In a medium bowl, mix flour and salt. Use a pastry blender and cut butter into flour until coarse crumbs form. In a small bowl, beat egg and water. Add to flour mixture and mix until a soft dough forms. Do not overwork dough. Gather into a ball and wrap in plastic wrap while preparing the chicken filling. Refrigerate the dough.

Chicken Filling

4	cups cooked chicken, cubed
1	tablespoon butter
1	pound fresh mushrooms, cleaned and sliced
1	cup frozen peas, uncooked
½	cup pimiento, chopped
¼	cup dry white wine or water
1½	cups whipping cream
2	tablespoons flour
1½	teaspoons paprika
½	teaspoon salt
½	teaspoon pepper
1	teaspoon dried French tarragon, crumbled
¾	cup low-sodium chicken broth

Place chicken cubes in a buttered deep dish 2-quart casserole. In a large skillet, melt butter over low heat. Add mushrooms, increase heat and sauté until browned and liquid has evaporated, about 5 minutes. Add peas and pimiento. Add the wine or water and cook until almost evaporated, about 2 minutes. Add to chicken in the casserole. Stir gently. In a medium saucepan, combine cream, flour, paprika, salt, pepper and tarragon over low heat. Cook until thickened, about 5 minutes. Stir in broth and cook until bubbly. Pour sauce over chicken mixture. Remove dough from the refrigerator. On a lightly floured surface, roll pastry to fit top of the casserole. Place pastry on top of pie. Trim and seal edges. Decorate with leftover pastry trimmings, if desired. Cut a few vent holes. Beat 1 egg slightly and brush over the top of the pastry to glaze the dough. Bake at 400° for about 30 minutes. Cool slightly, then serve. Serves 6.

Chicken and Mushrooms in Tarragon Sauce

¹⁄₄	cup butter
1	tablespoon vegetable oil
6	chicken breast halves, boneless and skinless
8	ounces fresh mushrooms, cleaned and sliced
1	tablespoon flour
1	10 ¹⁄₂-ounce can condensed cream of chicken soup
1	cup dry white wine
1	cup chicken broth or water
¹⁄₂	cup whipping cream
1	teaspoon salt
¹⁄₄	teaspoon pepper
1	tablespoon fresh French tarragon, chopped, or 1 teaspoon dried, crumbled
	Chopped green onions for garnish
	Chopped fresh parsley, for garnish

Heat butter and oil in a large skillet. Add chicken and brown on both sides, about 5 minutes. Place in a large buttered baking dish. Add mushrooms to the chicken skillet. Cook and stir 5 minutes. Stir in flour, soup, wine and broth or water. Simmer about 10 minutes, stirring occasionally. Stir in cream, salt, pepper and tarragon. Heat thoroughly but do not boil. Pour over the chicken pieces. At this point, you may cover and refrigerate chicken until guests arrive. Bring to room temperature 1 hour before baking. If baking immediately following preparation, bake, uncovered, at 350° for about 45 minutes, or until hot and bubbly. Sprinkle with chopped green onions and parsley. Bake another 5 minutes, then serve. Serves 6.

THIS IS A TERRIFIC PARTY DISH BECAUSE IT CAN BE ASSEMBLED AHEAD OF TIME AND BAKED AFTER GUESTS ARRIVE. THIS RECIPE SERVES 6, BUT IT CAN EASILY BE DOUBLED FOR A LARGER CROWD. SERVE WITH BUTTERED NOODLES AND A GREEN VEGETABLE. IT'S SUPERB.

Tarragon Chicken

1/4 cup flour

Salt and pepper

4 boneless, skinless chicken breast halves

1 tablespoon olive oil

1 small onion, peeled and sliced

1 medium carrot, scraped and sliced

1 cup dry vermouth

1 cup chicken broth

1 tablespoon fresh French tarragon, chopped, or 1 teaspoon dried, crumbled

2 tablespoons whipping cream

Season flour with salt and pepper. Flour both sides of each chicken breast. Heat oil in a medium skillet. Brown chicken on both sides, 3 or 4 minutes per side. Remove breasts and place on a plate. Cover with foil to keep warm. Add onion and carrot to skillet and cook about 5 minutes. Add vermouth and increase heat. Boil gently and reduce liquid by half. Add chicken broth and reduce by half again. Add salt and pepper to taste. Strain mixture into a clean skillet. Discard onion and carrot pieces. Return chicken to the skillet and finish cooking, another 3 or 4 minutes. Sprinkle tarragon into the sauce and cook a minute or two to warm. Add the cream and heat, but do not boil. Serve chicken with rice. Serves 4.

HIGHLY FLAVORED. SERVE THIS NEXT TIME YOU HAVE COMPANY. IT'S QUICK AND DELICIOUS.

Zucchini and Cheese with Tarragon

3 cups zucchini, washed (but not peeled), then finely grated

1 cup soda cracker crumbs

1 cup grated cheddar cheese

2 eggs, beaten

2 tablespoons onions, finely chopped

1 teaspoon fresh French tarragon, finely chopped, or 1/2 teaspoon, dried and crumbled

Combine all ingredients and place in a buttered 2-quart baking dish. Bake in a 350° oven for 45 minutes to 1 hour. Watch after 45 minutes. Serves 6.

IF YOU HAVE THE SAME PROBLEM THINKING OF WAYS TO USE AN ABUNDANT SUPPLY OF THIS SUMMER SQUASH, AS I DO, THEN HERE IS AN EASY SOLUTION. THIS IS GOOD WITH ANY MEAT AND TAKES THE PLACE OF POTATOES, RICE OR PASTA AS A SIDE DISH.

Tarragon Butter

¹/₂	cup butter, softened
2	tablespoons onion, finely chopped
2	tablespoons fresh French tarragon, finely chopped
1	teaspoon grated lemon rind
2	teaspoons fresh lemon juice
1	tablespoon fresh parsley, finely chopped
	Dash of salt and pepper

Mix all together. Cover and refrigerate until ready to use. Can be wrapped well and frozen.

DAB THIS WONDERFUL BUTTER ON CHICKEN, STEAKS OR CHOPS AS YOU GRILL OR BROIL THEM. ALSO GOOD ON THICK SLICES OF FRENCH BREAD, THEN PLACE UNDER THE BROILER FOR A MINUTE OR SO.

French Tarragon Vinegar

Fill a sterilized gallon glass or plastic jar two-thirds full with clean, moisture-free **tarragon sprigs**. Pour **white distilled or white wine vinegar** over the leaves to cover. Seal with a nonmetallic lid*. Set in a cool dark place for 3 weeks or so. Discard the tarragon and strain the vinegar though a coffee filter into a sterilized bottle. Seal or cork.

* If a nonmetallic lid is not available, cover jar with 3 or 4 layers of plastic wrap and secure with a rubber band.

THIS IS ONE OF THE SIMPLEST VINEGARS I MAKE. BUT ONE I REACH FOR OFTEN.

Tarragon Mustard

¹/₂	cup fresh French tarragon leaves
4	tablespoons minced shallots
2	cups mild Dijon-style mustard
2	teaspoons white wine

Clean tarragon leaves and dry them until no moisture remains on leaves. Finely chop. Place all ingredients in a food processor and blend until smooth. Seal and refrigerate up to one month, or freeze. Makes 2¹/₂ cups.

MAKE THIS IN EARLY JULY WHEN FRENCH TARRAGON IS AT ITS BEST. IF YOU WOULD LIKE TO MAKE SOME FOR CHRISTMAS GIFT-GIVING, MAKE AS USUAL, SEAL AND FREEZE. ADD A JAR OF THIS MUSTARD TO A BASKET OF OTHER HERBAL GOODIES FOR A WELCOME GIFT.

Lemon
Verbena

ALOYSIA TRIPHYLLA

Lemon Verbena

ALOYSIA TRIPHYLLA

I love lemon — anything lemon. And so it is not surprising that I love lemon verbena. It is such a great and versatile herb. It is native to South and Central America. Lemon verbena is a symbol for unity. ❧ Lemon verbena is woody-stemmed and has an extraordinary lemon aroma when the leaves are bruised. It grows 2 to 4 feet tall. Tiny blooms appear at the top of the stems. The leaves are long, narrow, pale green, and feel rather rough to the touch. ❧ I love the way lemon verbena adds tremendous lemon flavor to foods, such as shellfish, fish, chicken, jelly, oils, vinegars, and drinks, just to name a few. The dried leaves of this plant add wonderful aroma and soft green color to potpourris. Medicinally, the leaves can be infused into a soothing and delicious tea. This tea is said to relieve cold congestion in the nose and lungs. It is also soothing for an upset stomach. ❧ Lemon verbena likes a sunny location. It is perennial in temperate climates. Where I live — the Midwest — I treat it as an annual. The plant can be taken inside during the winter months (a heated garage is a good spot), but will lose all or most of the leaves because it is a deciduous shrub. Water sparingly during dormancy. When spring arrives, take plants outside, trim off about half the old growth, and let the rain and sun work their magic. Eventually there should be new leaves — give it plenty of time for this to happen. Don't despair if leaves don't appear. I take in 2, preferably 3, plants and hope that one will make it to spring. So far, one always has. By the way, lemon verbena grows just fine in the herb garden, but I particularly like growing it in containers — large containers with good drainage and filled with soilless mix or a mixture of soilless mix and potting soil. Lemon verbena requires plenty of sunshine, rain, air circulation, and an occasional shot of fertilizer. I use a balanced fertilizer of 20-20-20, but a nutrient-rich homemade compost is still the best. ❦ This plant is very easy to dry. I bring in large stems covered with leaves. Tie a string around the stem end and hang from a nail or hook (out of sun or direct light) for a week or two until the leaves are curled and crispy dry. They are now ready to strip from the stems and store for potpourri making and for some culinary uses, such as tea. I treat dried lemon verbena leaves like bay leaves. Since the leaves are rather coarse and dry, I try to use them whole-leaf so they can be removed at the end of cooking. If leaves are not or cannot be used whole, then chop them fine or, better yet, whirl in food processor or blender to make a powder. I find that fresh leaves are best for cooking. ❦

How do I use lemon verbena?

- in or on chicken, turkey
- with beef, veal
- in stuffings, especially for poultry and fish
- to flavor certain vegetables, such as peas, carrots, mushrooms, cabbage, cauliflower, brussels sprouts
- in salads
- to flavor fruit dishes
- in custard sauces

- in dessert sauces
- in cakes
- in cookies
- in breads
- in jellies
- in vinegar
- in oil
- in potpourris
- in teas and tisanes

INDEX

Lemon Verbena Recipes

MENU

A Lovely Lemon Luncheon

Asparagus Salad with Raspberry Vinaigrette (p. 316)

Lemon-Garlic Chicken (p. 90) *

Individual rice timbales, or other rice dish

Lemon Verbena Blueberry Muffins (p. 93) *

Lemon Verbena Jelly (p. 97) *

Iced Tea

Cranberry Ice (p. 395)

* Recipe contains lemon verbena

Kate Jayne
AND THE SANDY MUSH HERB NURSERY

*M*y husband pointed out the following Lemon Garlic Chicken recipe to me that he found in an issue of Farm Journal magazine. It is light, lemony and delicious. I really became interested when I saw it was from Kate Jayne and her daughter, Nicketie, who own and operate Sandy Mush Herb Nursery in North Carolina. On our way to the International Herb Conference in Raleigh, NC, we decided we would love to stop at this nursery and take in the sights. We had been told about their outstanding gardens and plots and about the thousands of plants they have for sale. Try as hard as we could, we could not find the place (and we are country folks used to country roads!), and had to give up so as to be in Raleigh in time for the conference. When I saw Kate and Nicketie's recipe, I called to ask if I might use it. Kate graciously said yes and also sent me a copy of their handbook. I chuckled when I read on the first page how some people have a difficult time finding them! We'll try harder the next time. To order this outstanding catalog and handbook, send a check or money order for $6.00 to The Sandy Mush Herb Nursery, 316 Surrett Cove Road, Leicester, NC 28748-9622.

Lemon–Garlic Chicken

And now for the recipe — altered only slightly.

4   to 6 cloves garlic (depending on how much garlic you like)
$^1/_2$ cup fresh lemon juice
$^1/_4$ cup olive oil
2   teaspoons chopped fresh lemon verbena leaves
6   boneless, skinless chicken breasts
    Salt and pepper
1   teaspoon chopped fresh lemon thyme leaves

In a small bowl, crush garlic and stir in lemon juice, olive oil and lemon verbena. Place chicken in a glass, plastic or stainless steel bowl or plastic bag. Pour marinade over chicken. Place bowl or bag in refrigerator for about 30 minutes. Place chicken pieces in single layer in a roasting pan. Pour marinade evenly over the chicken. Salt and pepper to taste. Bake in a 350° oven for 30 to 45 minutes or until juices run clear when pricked with a fork. Do not overbake. Sprinkle chicken with chopped fresh lemon thyme leaves. Serves 6.

My Lemon Verbena Chicken

THIS RECIPE IS FOR
WHEN YOU'RE RUNNING LATE
AND NEED TO GET THE CHICKEN
IN THE OVEN RIGHT NOW!

1   2½ to 3 pound whole frying chicken
½   to 1 cup lemon verbena leaves, washed and dried
½   cup butter or margarine
4   or 5 lemon verbena leaves, coarsely chopped
    Juice of 1 fresh lemon
    Salt and pepper

Wash and dry chicken inside and out. Stuff cavity with the ½ to 1 cup lemon verbena leaves.
Melt butter; add chopped lemon verbena leaves and lemon juice. Mix well. Pour over the
entire chicken. Salt and pepper chicken. Bake at 350° for about 1 hour or until it tests
done on a meat thermometer. Baste chicken occasionally with pan juices. Serves 4 to 6.

Lemony Carrots

A SPECIAL CARROT RECIPE
FOR FAMILY OR FRIENDS AND
BEAUTIFULLY SEASONED WITH
LEMON VERBENA.

12   medium carrots, washed and scraped
 4   tablespoons butter
 2   tablespoons honey
¼   teaspoon grated lemon peel
 1   tablespoon fresh lemon juice
 1   tablespoon sugar
 1   teaspoon finely chopped lemon verbena leaves

Boil carrots until barely tender. Melt butter in a small skillet. Add honey, peel, lemon juice,
sugar and chopped lemon verbena leaves. Blend well. Add drained, cooked carrots and
sauté gently over low heat to glaze well. Shake pan to sauté and glaze evenly. Serves 4 to 6.

Lemon Verbena Tisane

Pour 6 to 8 ounces boiling water over 6 to 8 fresh, clean, bruised **lemon verbena leaves**,
or 1 to 2 teaspoons dried, crumbled leaves. Let steep for 5 minutes. Strain and enjoy.
Makes 1 cup. If desired, sweeten with a little **honey**.

Ann Greenfield's Lemon Verbena Bread

1	cup sugar
6	tablespoons margarine
1	tablespoon lemon rind, grated
1	tablespoon lemon verbena leaves, finely chopped
2	eggs
1¹/₂	cups flour
1	teaspoon baking powder
¹/₂	teaspoon salt
¹/₂	cup milk
¹/₂	cup chopped pecans, almonds or walnuts

Glaze

¹/₄ cup sugar
Juice of 1 lemon

In mixer bowl, cream sugar and margarine. Add lemon rind and lemon verbena leaves. Beat in eggs, one at a time. Sift together flour, baking powder and salt. Add flour alternately to batter with milk. Stir in chopped nuts. Pour into a greased and floured 9x5x3-inch loaf pan. Bake at 325° for 35 to 45 minutes, or until a tester comes out clean. For the glaze, in a small pan combine ¹/₄ cup sugar and the lemon juice, stirring until thoroughly dissolved. Pour over cake, a little at a time. Allow cake to cool in pan. Then remove from pan. Slice and serve with softened butter.

Note: Ann says it is best to bake, cool, then freeze this bread for a few days before thawing to serve. Freezing improves the flavor.

Lemon Verbena Blueberry Muffins

8	fresh lemon verbena leaves
1	cup super-fine sugar
3	tablespoons fresh lemon verbena leaves, finely chopped
1½	cups fresh blueberries
1	cup walnuts or black walnuts, finely chopped
2	cups flour
1	tablespoon baking powder
¾	cup sugar
½	cup milk
⅓	cup safflower oil
1	egg

One day before making muffins, bury the 8 lemon verbena leaves in the 1 cup sugar. Place in a closed container.

Grease a 12-cup muffin pan, with cups about 2½ inches across. In a medium bowl, combine the chopped lemon verbena leaves, blueberries and nuts. In a large bowl, mix the flour, baking powder and sugar. In another bowl, beat together the milk, safflower oil and egg. Pour milk mixture into flour mixture and stir just until blended. Add the blueberry mixture and fold in gently. Divide the batter between the prepared muffin cups. Sprinkle each muffin with 1 teaspoon of the lemon verbena sugar. Bake at 400° for 25 minutes, or until a tester comes out clean. Cool a few minutes, then remove muffins. Makes 12 muffins.

Use remaining lemon verbena sugar to flavor other desserts or to sweeten your tea. Delicious.

BY NOW, YOU SEE JUST WHAT LEMON VERBENA CAN DO TO IMPROVE THE ALREADY GREAT TASTE OF FRESH LEMON. MAKE THESE MUFFINS WHEN BLUEBERRIES AND LEMON VERBENA ARE IN SEASON.

Lemon Verbena Cake

1½ cups flour
1 teaspoon baking powder
½ teaspoon salt
6 tablespoons fresh lemon juice
2 teaspoons vanilla extract
Peel from 2 medium lemons, yellow only
1 cup sugar
1 tablespoon lemon verbena leaves, finely chopped
1 cup unsalted butter or margarine, at room temperature
3 large eggs
Creamy Lemon Frosting (recipe follows)

Lightly grease an 8-inch springform pan or two 8-inch cake pans. Line bottoms with waxed paper. Lightly grease the paper. Dust pans with flour and tap out excess. Mix flour, baking powder and salt. Mix lemon juice and vanilla. In a food processor, process lemon peel, sugar and lemon verbena leaves until peel and leaves are finely ground. Put into a large mixer bowl with butter and beat until pale and fluffy. Beat in eggs, one at a time. Add flour mixture and juice mixture alternately, mixing well after each addition. Pour in prepared pan or pans. Bake at 350° about 40 minutes for the springform pan or about 20 minutes for the 8-inch pans. A pick inserted near the center must come out clean. Cool in pan or pans, then turn out. Peel off waxed paper. Horizontally slice a large cake into 3 equal layers or the 2 cakes into 2 layers each. Frost with Creamy Lemon Frosting (recipe follows). Refrigerate until ready to serve. Serves 8 or 10.

Creamy Lemon Frosting

Peel from 1 medium lemon, yellow only
⅓ cup sugar
2 8-ounce packages cream cheese, at room temperature
2 tablespoons fresh lemon juice

Combine peel and sugar in bowl of a food processor. Process until finely ground. Add the softened cream cheese and lemon juice and process until smooth and creamy. Chill, then spread on cake layers.

Lemon Verbena Pound Cake

1   cup cake flour
$1/2$ teaspoon baking powder
$1/4$ teaspoon salt
3   tablespoons lemon verbena leaves, finely chopped
1   tablespoon grated lemon zest
$1/2$ cup unsalted butter, softened
1   cup sugar
3   large eggs
1   teaspoon vanilla
2   tablespoons milk
2   tablespoons fresh lemon juice

Glaze

$1/2$ cup confectioner's sugar
1   tablespoon fresh lemon juice

Butter and flour a 8x5x3-inch loaf pan. Tap out excess flour. In a medium bowl, combine flour, baking powder, salt, lemon verbena leaves and zest. In a large mixer bowl, beat butter and sugar until light and fluffy. Beat in eggs, one at a time, beating well after each addition. Beat in vanilla. Blend in half the flour mixture. Beat in milk and lemon juice. Add remainder of flour and mix until just combined. Pour batter into pan. Push batter into corners and smooth top. Bake at 325° for 45 to 50 minutes, or until a tester comes out clean. Cool cake in pan for 15 minutes, then turn out onto serving tray to cool completely. Combine glaze ingredients and drizzle over cake. Decorate edge of cake with fresh lemon verbena leaves, if desired.

THIS IS A LOVELY POUND CAKE WITH A BEAUTIFUL, FINE-GRAINED TEXTURE. UNBEATABLE WITH FRESH SLICED STRAWBERRIES OR FRESH WHOLE RASPBERRIES ON THE SIDE. A DOLLOP OF WHIPPED CREAM WOULDN'T BE AMISS.

Lemon Herbs Vinegar

1   quart white wine vinegar
1   cup cleaned and bruised lemon verbena leaves
$^1/_2$ cup cleaned and bruised lemon thyme leaves
     Peel of 1 fresh lemon (yellow only — no white)

Heat vinegar, but don't let boil. Pour vinegar over herbs and lemon peel in a 2-quart glass or plastic container. Let cool. Cover container tightly (use no metal). Let stand in a cool, dark place 2 to 3 weeks. Discard herbs and peel. Strain vinegar through a coffee filter into a sterilized bottle. Seal or cork. I refrigerate any of this leftover vinegar.

RECENTLY, I MADE CHICKEN SALAD FOR A BRIDAL LUNCHEON. THE DAY WAS HOT AND HUMID AND I WANTED A SALAD THAT WAS REALLY GOOD AND REALLY COLD. I ALSO WANTED IT TO BE CLEAN AND CRISP, AND NOTHING DOES THAT JOB BETTER THAN FRESH LEMON. SINCE THE BRIDE AND HER ATTENDANTS WERE "THIS" BIG, I KNEW THEY WOULD APPRECIATE A LOW-CALORIE LUNCHEON TO KEEP THEM THAT WAY! SO I MADE THE FOLLOWING VINEGAR ABOUT 2 WEEKS BEFORE I WAS TO USE IT TO HELP SEASON THE SALAD. THE VINEGAR RECIPE IS FIRST, THE CHICKEN SALAD IS NEXT.

The Chicken Salad

For 8 servings:

8   skinless, boneless chicken breast halves, cooked and cut into small pieces
1   cup finely chopped celery
1   cup green seedless grapes, halved
$^1/_2$ to $^3/_4$ cup chopped pecans, walnuts or almonds
$^1/_2$ teaspoon salt, or to taste
     Dash of pepper
1   cup low-calorie mayonnaise
2   or 3 tablespoons Lemon Herbs Vinegar
     Lettuce leaves
     Fresh lemon verbena leaves for garnish
     Lemon rind curls for garnish
     Viola or nasturtium flowers for garnish

Combine chicken, celery, grapes and nuts. Season with salt and pepper, if desired. Combine mayonnaise and vinegar. Add mayonnaise to chicken mixture to moisten. It may not require all the mayonnaise. If any is leftover, use as a sandwich spread. Serve salad in lettuce cups and decorate with fresh lemon verbena leaves and lemon rind curls. Top each serving with a fresh viola or nasturtium flower.

Lemon Herbs Oil

- 2 cups canola oil
- $^1/_2$ cup cleaned and bruised lemon verbena leaves
- $^1/_4$ cup cleaned and bruised lemon thyme leaves
- 1 tablespoon crushed coriander seeds (optional, but I do like this flavor)
  Peel of 1 fresh lemon (yellow only)
- 2 or 3 drops of Boyajian* pure lemon oil (secret ingredient)

Heat oil until hot but do not allow to boil. Pour oil over herbs, seeds and lemon peel. Let cool, then put oil in a wide-mouth jar or container. Add the Boyajian lemon oil and seal container. Keep refrigerated for 2 weeks to develop flavors. Discard herbs and peel. Strain and pour oil into a clean jar or bottle. Seal and refrigerate. Fabulous stuff!

Boyajian oils I am familiar with are lemon, lime and orange. They are pure food grade oils that add tremendous flavor to citrus dishes or drinks. The oils are available through gourmet food shops and many cooking catalogs. They aren't inexpensive, but they last a long, long time if stored tightly sealed in the refrigerator between uses.

I USE THE SAME HERBS HERE AS FOR THE LEMON HERBS VINEGAR RECIPE. THIS OIL IS A BEAUTIFUL GOLDEN YELLOW AND IS REDOLENT OF LEMON FLAVOR. IT IS WONDERFUL TO ADD TO A SHRIMP OR FISH MARINADE, TO DRESS A BIBB LETTUCE SALAD, OR FOR SAUTÉING CHICKEN BREASTS OR SEAFOOD. IT IS SIMPLY A SUPERB OIL. DON'T MAKE TOO MUCH AT A TIME AND KEEP ANY LEFTOVER OIL REFRIGERATED.

Lemon Verbena Jelly

- 2 heaping cups fresh lemon verbena leaves, cut up
- $2^1/_2$ cups boiling water
- $^1/_4$ cup fresh lemon juice
- $4^1/_2$ cups sugar
- 2 to 4 drops yellow food coloring
- 1 3-ounce package liquid pectin (I like Certo)

Place cut up leaves in a large bowl. Pour boiling water over leaves. Cover and let stand for 15 minutes. Strain and measure 2 cups of the herb liquid into a heavy saucepan. Add lemon juice and sugar. Stir well. Bring to a full rolling boil over high heat, stirring often. Add food coloring. Stir in pectin and return to a full rolling boil. Boil hard for 1 minute, stirring constantly. Pour into hot, sterilized jelly jars, leaving $^1/_4$ inch head space. Adjust lids and process in a boiling water bath for 5 minutes. Makes about 2 pints of jelly.

THIS RECIPE IS FROM "CHRISTMAS THYME AT OAK HILL FARM," BUT IT'S SIMPLY TOO GOOD NOT TO REPEAT IN THIS LEMON VERBENA CHAPTER. THIS IS A WONDERFUL JELLY TO SERVE WITH MEATS, BUT IT'S ALSO A GREAT SPREAD FOR TOAST, BISCUITS OR BAGELS. MAKE THIS IN THE LATE SUMMER FOR A REALLY SPECIAL CHRISTMAS GIFT, BUT MAKE PLENTY FOR YOURSELF ALSO.

Mint

MENTHA, VARIOUS SPECIES

Mint

MENTHA, VARIOUS SPECIES

int, mint, and more mint. What was originally native to the near East, is now grown worldwide. Literally dozens of species and varieties exist. The plant is referred to in pre-Christian times. It is mentioned several times in the Bible and played major roles in some Greek mythology. Mint is considered a symbol of hospitality and virtue. ❧ All mints are perennial (although some are tender perennials), have square stems, and have paired leaves — opposite each other on the stem. Most stems are green, but some are colored, such as the black-stemmed peppermint which actually has purple stems! The stems are tender, but sturdy. Mints grow from 1 inch tall (the Corsican mint) to as tall as 5 feet (the Bowles mint). Leaves range in size from tiny, to large and round, to long and narrow. They are generally green or gray-green, but many varieties have gold or purple color in their leaves. Mints flower in late summer with rather insignificant white, pink, or purplish blooms. Mints like a rich, moist, but well-drained, soil. They need sun, but most varieties tolerate and actually need some shade. In cold climates, mint roots should be mulched for protection. We all know the spreading habit of mint. It can be contained by planting in a bottomless bucket (plastic is best) and burying the bucket in the garden. More about this in a minute. ❧ I have found that mint varieties must be separated from each other. If not, and if allowed to grow together, they lose their individual identities as far as aroma and leaf form are concerned. They will tend to revert to a parent plant, probably spearmint (*M. spicata*) or peppermint (*M. piperita*). If you are a mint lover, and wish to grow several varieties, I suggest a bed large enough to accommodate the varieties you choose. Let's suppose you wish to grow 6 varieties of mint in this bed. Bury 6 bottomless plastic buckets (remove handles) in the garden — they need to be deep buckets, like 5-gallon size. Leave 3 or 4 feet of space on all sides of each bucket. In bucket No.1, plant 1 or 2 mints of the same variety. Continue with bucket No. 2 and another variety; and so on with the other 4 buckets. At the end of the first summer, you should have 6 beautiful mounds of 6 varieties of mint. In the fall, take a spade and cut around each bucket rim to cut any stray spreading roots. Mulch the area well. In the spring, push mulch away from the plants and soon new mint leaves will appear.

In Morocco, N. Africa, as well as Turkey and other countries, mint tea seems to be the national drink. If visiting in those countries, drinking a cup of mint tea with the natives is the hospitable thing to do. As you know, on many tours, the bus will stop for a coffee break, or a soft drink break, but in Morocco, you stop for a mint tea break! The tea is almost always served in clear glass cups and it's brewed a little stronger than I like. They will offer you raw brown sugar to sweeten it. In Moroccan cuisine, many salads are flavored with mint leaves. Back in the United States, and particularly in northwestern Indiana, it is a treat to drive the country roads, adjacent to the mint fields, in summer during mint harvest. The aroma of fresh mint is absolutely overwhelming. The mint oil from these fields is distilled (a complicated process too technical for me to explain) and shipped to chewing gum manufacturers, candy makers, and pharmaceutical companies. Through the centuries, mint has been used as a digestive aid and as an antiseptic and cleanser. In ancient times, it was used as a strewing herb to freshen the floors of homes, churches and temples.

As people walked on the floor, the wonderful mint aroma perfumed the entire room. In medicine, besides being used as a digestive aid, mint was and still is used to make cold and flu medicines. It is a great masker added to bad-tasting medicine! ❦ The mints are very easy to dry. Hang harvested stems upside down just before the plant flowers and dry in a warm, shaded area in low humidity if possible. You also may strip fresh leaves from the stems and lay them on clean screens to dry in a warm, dry place. Store dried leaves in airtight containers away from heat and light. Another nice way to preserve leaves is to freeze individual leaves in ice cube trays — a pleasant addition to iced tea, lemonade, and numerous other drinks. ❦ Some popular varieties to grow: 1. *M. spicata* — commonly called garden mint or spearmint. It has bright green leaves with saw-tooth leaf edges and grows 2 to 3 feet tall. 2. *M. piperita* — commonly called peppermint, is a sterile hybrid that does not produce seeds. Contains the oil menthol. It has pointed oval leaves. The oil is widely used in mouthwash, toothpaste, chewing gum, and many medicines. Grows about 2 feet tall. 3. *M. piperita*, 'Crispa' variety — wonderful curly, dark green leaves that is a variety of black peppermint. Has a very strong peppermint scent. Grows about $2\frac{1}{2}$ feet tall. 4. *M. gentilis* 'Variegata' — commonly called ginger mint. Has gold and green leaves, grows about $1\frac{1}{2}$ feet tall. I use this mint to make a wonderful vinegar. 5. *M. suaveolens* — commonly called apple mint. Has hairy, bright green leaves and grows about 2 feet tall. 6. *M. suaveolens* 'Variegata' variety — commonly called pineapple mint. It has beautiful cream and green leaves and has a distinct pineapple aroma. It grows about 2 feet tall. 7. *M. citrata* — commonly called orange mint. Has dark green, round leaves and grows $1\frac{1}{2}$ to 2 feet tall. ❦ This barely scratches the surface of the mint world. Look for other wonderful and interesting varieties at your nursery or your favorite herb farm. ❦

How do I use mint?

- with chicken
- with lamb, veal, beef
- with fish
- in jelly
- with duck
- in some soups, especially split pea
- in tea
- in vinegar
- in liqueurs
- in dessert syrups
- in candy making
- in cakes
- in cookies
- in desserts
- in dessert sauces
- with cream cheese dishes

- in making potpourris
- with chocolate
- in oil infusions
- with peas and other vegetables such as carrots, cabbage, green beans, potatoes, celery, onions
- in numerous drinks and punches
- in applesauce
- chopped in fruit salads
- in yogurt dishes
- toss with salad greens
- to flavor melons
- in breads and muffins
- with orange slices
- in salad dressings
- to flavor rice

INDEX

Mint Recipes

MENU

A Hint of Mint

Green Salad

Orange Balsamic Vinaigrette (p. 317)

Roasted Marinated Salmon Steaks (p. 351)

Apricot-Pine Nut Pilaf with Fresh Mint (p. 111) *

Fresh Green Beans

Wilma Clark's Raspberry-Mint Muffins (p. 114) *

Lime Sherbet

Chocolate-Covered Raisin Cookies (p. 390)

Minted Lemonade (p. 109) *

Recipe contains mint

I am forever looking for good drink recipes. The following tea and punch recipes are among some of the best I've tried. I've collected some and friends throughout the country have sent me some. All these recipes are flavored with mint.

Pineapple-Orange-Mint Iced Tea

4   orange pekoe regular-size tea bags
1/2 cup fresh mint leaves (pineapple mint or orange mint if available)
3   cups boiling water
1/3 cup sugar
1   cup pineapple juice
1   cup orange juice
    Fresh mint sprigs for garnish

Place tea bags and mint in a tea pot. Add boiling water. Cover and steep for 5 minutes. Strain mixture into a large pitcher. Discard tea bags and mint leaves. Add sugar and juices. Stir well. Serve in ice-filled glasses. Garnish with a sprig of mint. Makes 4 servings.

FOR A DELICIOUS PARTY PUNCH, TRIPLE RECIPE AND ADD 1/2 TO 1 CUP DARK RUM.

Raspberry-Mint Iced Tea

4   cups boiling water
6   orange pekoe regular-size tea bags
1/2 cup fresh mint leaves (spearmint or peppermint)
1   12-ounce package frozen unsweetened red raspberries
1/3 cup sugar
    Fresh red raspberries for garnish

Pour boiling water over tea bags and mint in a teapot. Cover and let steep for 5 minutes. Remove tea bags and mint leaves and discard. Purée raspberries in blender or food processor. Combine tea, puréed raspberries and sugar in a pitcher. Stir well. Strain through a fine strainer or sieve. Pour into ice-filled glasses. Drop a few berries into each glass. Serves 4.

Minted Peach Iced Tea

8 cups water
¼ cup sugar
3 regular-size English breakfast tea bags
5 regular-size peach herbal tea bags
5 fresh mint sprigs
8 cups ice cubes
2 peaches, washed but not peeled
Fresh mint sprigs

Combine water and sugar in a large saucepan. Bring to a boil, lower heat and simmer until sugar has dissolved, stirring frequently. Simmer 3 or 4 minutes. Remove from heat. Immediately add tea bags and mint. Let steep 25 minutes. Remove tea bags and mint. Add the 8 cups of ice cubes. Cover and let stand to melt ice cubes, then refrigerate. Fill 12 iced tea glasses with ice. Pour tea over ice. Cut ½-inch wedges of the peaches and place 1 wedge of peach and 1 sprig of mint in each glass. This is delicious. Serves 12.

---

some thoughts on
TEAS AND TISANES

tea is a drink that contains leaves from a tea plant. A tisane is a drink that contains leaves from herb plants only. A drink such as "Minted Peach Iced Tea" can be called a tea because it contains leaves from both the tea plant and from herb leaves. A drink such as "Hot Mint Tisane" can only be called a tisane because it contains herb leaves exclusively.

Hot Mint Tisane

Fresh mint
Place 1 tablespoon **fresh mint** leaves in a teapot. Add 2 cups boiling **water**. Let steep for 3 to 5 minutes. Pour through a strainer into 2 serving cups. If you like stronger mint flavor, add more mint; if you like weaker mint flavor, add less.

Dried mint
Place 1 teaspoon **dried mint leaves** in a teapot and proceed with directions above.

CHOOSE THE MINT LEAVES OF YOUR CHOICE. ANY MINT YOU WOULD COOK WITH WILL MAKE A DELICIOUS TISANE.

Minted Lemonade

Make your own **fresh lemonade**, or use a package of the powdered variety. Set aside. Place 2 cups fresh clean **mint sprigs** (lemon mint, orange mint, spearmint or peppermint would be good choices) in a saucepan. Boil 4 cups water and pour over the mint. Cover pan and steep for 15 minutes. Discard mint sprigs and strain concentrate through a coffee filter into a pitcher. You now have mint concentrate to use to flavor lemonade or other drinks. **Sugar** may be added if desired. Use 1 teaspoon of mint concentrate per 8 ounces of prepared lemonade. Serve with ice and mint sprigs. You may wish to add a little more concentrate or even a little less. Cover and refrigerate leftover concentrate. Will be good for a week in the refrigerator.

Summer Punch

4 cups cranberry juice or cranberry juice cocktail
4 cups apple juice
$^1/_2$ cup orange juice
1 cup mint concentrate (see Minted Lemonade recipe, above, on how to make concentrate)
1 quart ginger ale
  Pineapple spears for garnish
  Fresh mint sprigs for garnish

Combine the juices and the mint concentrate in a punch bowl. Just before serving, add ginger ale and ice or an ice ring to the bowl. Garnish each cup with pineapple and mint. Makes about 25 punch cup servings.

Pineapple-Mint Punch

Pick 25 sprigs of **fresh mint**. Wash leaves and place in a saucepan. Cover mint with water. Bring to a boil and set off stove to steep, about 20 minutes, covered. Strain and discard leaves. Add 1$^1/_2$ cups **sugar** and stir to dissolve. Place mint syrup in a punch bowl. Add one 48-ounce can of **pineapple juice**, one 6-ounce can **frozen lemonade concentrate** and one 6-ounce can **frozen orange juice concentrate**. Add 1 to 1$^1/_2$ quarts **water**. Add ice ring to bowl and serve very cold. Makes about 1 gallon. Garnish with **fresh mint sprigs**.

Orange-Mint Salad Dressing

THIS DRESSING IS SO GOOD ON FRESH GREENS. ADD SOME FRESH ORANGE SLICES TO THE SALAD FOR A SPECIAL TREAT.

3 tablespoons orange juice concentrate (from a can of frozen)
$^1/_4$ cup balsamic vinegar*
$^1/_2$ cup extra virgin olive oil
Salt and pepper
Fresh mint leaves (orange mint, if available), finely chopped

Combine all ingredients in a jar with a screw-on top. Shake well. Refrigerate if not using now. When ready to serve, shake well and pour over salad. Toss and serve.

*Balsamic vinegar is a rich, brown vinegar that has been aged in oak barrels. The longer it's aged, the more mellow it is and the more expensive it is. It is a product of the Modena, Italy, area.

Mint Vinegar

USE THIS VINEGAR IN SALAD DRESSINGS, SPLASH ON SLICED TOMATOES OR SEASON A DISH OF PEAS AND CARROTS WITH A SPLASH OF IT. DEGLAZE THE LAMB ROASTING PAN TO ADD EXTRA FLAVOR TO THE SAUCE OR GRAVY.

3 cups cider vinegar
2 tablespoons sugar
3 cups mint, cleaned and dried (no moisture on leaves)

Heat vinegar, sugar and 2 cups mint in a large nonreactive saucepan to just below the boiling point. Turn off heat, cover and steep until the mixture has cooled to room temperature. Remove and discard mint. Place the other 1 cup mint in a sterilized container. Fill with the steeped vinegar. Let stand in a cool, dark place for about 3 weeks. Discard mint. Strain vinegar through a coffee filter into a sterilized bottle. Cork or seal.

Roasted Sweet Onions with Mint

3 sweet onions
2 tablespoons extra virgin olive oil
3 or 4 cloves garlic, finely minced
1 teaspoon salt
$^1/_2$ teaspoon pepper
$^1/_2$ cup fresh mint leaves
$^1/_4$ cup balsamic vinegar

Peel onions. Cut them in half from top to bottom. In a medium bowl, combine olive oil, garlic, salt, pepper and mint. Smear mixture all over the onions and place them in a small roasting pan. Bake in a 350° oven for 30 minutes. Baste with the juices. Continue roasting for another 20 to 30 minutes, or until onions are tender when pierced with a fork. Remove from oven. Place onions on a serving platter and drizzle with the balsamic vinegar. Serves 4.

SWEET ONIONS ARE A WONDERFUL INVENTION! WHETHER YOU USE VIDALIA (GEORGIA) SWEET ONIONS, THE SWEET FLORIDA ONIONS, THE TEXAS SWEET ONIONS OR THE WALLA WALLA (WASHINGTON) SWEET ONIONS, IT DOESN'T MATTER. EACH IS GREAT AND I'M FINDING THEM IN OUR MARKETS ALMOST YEAR-ROUND. THIS IS A SPECIAL SIDE DISH.

Apricot-Pine Nut Pilaf with Fresh Mint

$^1/_4$ cup pine nuts
$^1/_4$ cup butter
1 medium onion, chopped
1 cup long grain white rice
$1^3/_4$ cups chicken broth
2 to 3 teaspoons fresh mint, finely chopped
$^1/_2$ cup dried apricots, chopped

In a heavy skillet, toast pine nuts in butter to a golden brown. Stir frequently. Remove nuts with a slotted spoon and set aside. Use same skillet and sauté onion until soft. Add rice. Sauté 1 to 2 minutes, stirring all the time. Add chicken broth. Bring to a boil. Reduce heat and simmer, covered, for 20 minutes or until broth is just absorbed. Stir in mint, apricots and the reserved pine nuts. Cook over low heat another 10 minutes. Serves 4.

SERVE THIS TERRIFIC PILAF WITH LAMB, PORK OR BEEF. THE PINE NUTS GIVE THE DISH SOME CRUNCH AND THE DRIED APRICOTS GIVE IT SOME TANG. A GREAT COMBINATION.

Fresh Fruit with Honey and Mint

The Honey-Mint Syrup

2   cups water
1   cup fresh mint leaves
$^1/_3$ cup honey
1   6-ounce can frozen lemonade concentrate

Combine water, mint and honey in a saucepan. Bring to a boil. Quickly reduce heat, stir well, cover and simmer for 8 to 10 minutes. Discard mint leaves. Stir in the lemonade concentrate and mix well. Set aside to cool.

The Fruit

A combination of the following is good, but substitute your favorite if it isn't listed here.

2   cups fresh nectarines or peaches, peeled and sliced
2   cups fresh pineapple (see box at right), cut in chunks
2   cups fresh blueberries
1   cup red seedless grapes, cut in half
1   cup green seedless grapes, cut in half
1   cup fresh red or black raspberries
1   cup banana slices (do not add until nearly ready to serve)

Wash, peel and prepare all fruits, except bananas. Place fruit in a large glass or crystal bowl. Mix gently with your hands so as not to bruise or damage fruits. Pour mint syrup mixture over the fruit. Cover bowl with plastic wrap and refrigerate for several hours before serving. When ready to serve, gently fold in banana slices. This is a wonderful cold fruit salad. There should be enough fruit and syrup to serve 12 or more.

I don't usually mention brand names, but if I find something wonderful, such as Del Monte Gold Pineapple, I have to tell you or you might not stumble across it yourself! Del Monte has developed the best pineapple I've ever tasted. Del Monte Gold is gold and ripe all the way through and as sweet as sugar. It will cost a little more, but you'll forget all about the cost with the first bite.

We recently entertained some "herb" friends for a weekend. Dick grilled thick steaks while I prepared fresh asparagus and tossed a salad with purple ruffles basil vinaigrette. Just before the steaks were done, I sautéed Del Monte Gold pineapple slices (see recipe below) and served one or two per person beside the steak. Apple cream pie finished the meal. I think Chuck and Pat would come back for another visit if we promised them the same menu!

Sautéed Pineapple Slices with Mint

¾-inch-thick slices of pineapple (one or two per serving)
2 tablespoons butter
2 tablespoons light brown sugar
   Fresh mint leaves, chopped

Prepare pineapple slices. Melt butter in a large skillet. Add brown sugar and cook until bubbly and thickened a little. Add pineapple slices and sauté on both sides to a golden brown. Sprinkle mint on pineapple and cook another 2 or 3 minutes to release the mint flavor. Serve immediately. Garnish plates with fresh mint sprigs. Serves 4.

Wilma Clark
AND CLARK'S GREENHOUSE AND HERBAL COUNTRY

Wilma is a friend I met through the Illinois Herb Association. She is one of the hardest workers I know and will tackle anything from serving as president of the above association, to sponsoring back-to-back herb festivals, to tending 40 (yes, 40!) herb plots on her farm. Her business is called Clark's Greenhouse and Herbal Country and she is located just outside San Jose, Illinois. If you're looking for quality plants and some unusual varieties, Wilma's is the place to go in central Illinois. She possibly has the largest selection of scented geraniums in the state. This great recipe, below, appeared in one of Wilma's newsletters.

Wilma Clark's Raspberry-Mint Muffins

2	cups flour
2	teaspoons baking powder
1/2	teaspoon salt
1/2	cup butter, softened
3/4	cup granulated sugar
1/2	cup brown sugar
2	eggs
1	teaspoon vanilla
1/2	cup milk
2 1/2	cups fresh raspberries, or frozen, thawed and drained berries
1/4	cup fresh mint leaves, finely chopped

In a large mixing bowl, combine flour, baking powder and salt. Set aside. In a separate mixing bowl, cream the butter. Add both sugars to the butter and cream at high speed. Add eggs, one at a time, creaming after each addition. Add vanilla and beat again. Add half the milk, then half the dry ingredients and mix. Add remainder of milk and remainder of dry ingredients. Mix after each addition, but only enough to wet the dry ingredients. Mash 2 cups of the berries and mix them into the batter. Fold in the remaining whole berries and the chopped mint leaves. Grease 18 medium muffin cups. Spoon batter into cups and fill 2/3 full. Bake at 375° for 25 to 35 minutes, or until a toothpick inserted in the middle of a muffin comes out clean. Cool for 10 minutes in the pan. Remove muffins and serve warm or cool. Makes 18 muffins.

Orange-Mint Muffins

Zest from 3 oranges
$^1/_4$ cup sugar
$^1/_4$ cup water
$^1/_2$ cup sugar
$^1/_4$ cup butter or margarine
1 egg, well beaten
$2^1/_4$ cups flour
3 teaspoons baking powder
$^1/_4$ teaspoon baking soda
$^1/_2$ teaspoon salt
1 tablespoon fresh chopped mint (orange mint if you have it)
1 cup orange juice, squeezed from 3 oranges above

Combine zest, the $^1/_4$ cup of sugar and the $^1/_4$ cup of water in a small saucepan and simmer over low heat for about 5 minutes until mixture is golden brown and bubbly. Watch closely so mixture doesn't stick and burn. Remove from heat and cool. In mixing bowl, combine the $^1/_2$ cup of sugar and butter. Add the egg and mix well. Add cooled zest mixture to egg mixture. Sift flour, baking powder, baking soda and salt together. Stir in the chopped mint leaves. Alternately add the dry ingredients and the orange juice to the first mixture. Do not overmix. Grease 16 muffin cups. Fill cups about $^2/_3$ full with the batter. Bake in a 350° oven 20 to 30 minutes or until tops are firm and muffins are lightly browned. Wonderful served warm. Makes 16 muffins.

Chocolate Mint Cake

Buy a box of your favorite **chocolate** or **devil's food cake mix**. Mix as directed, except replace the liquid called for with **mint-infused water** (see below). Bake as directed. Frost with **chocolate icing**, again using the mint-infused water for the liquid in the icing.

Mint-Infused Water
2 cups water
1 cup mint leaves (spearmint, peppermint or chocolate mint)

Bring water and mint leaves to a boil. Reduce heat and simmer about 5 minutes. Remove from heat, cover and cool. Strain out and discard mint. Use this water in the cake and icing recipes.

THESE ORANGE MUFFINS ARE BETTER THAN USUAL BECAUSE THE ZEST IS CARAMELIZED BEFORE ADDING TO THE BATTER. I LOVE THE HINT OF MINT IN THESE MUFFINS.

WE CAN'T ALWAYS PREPARE EVERYTHING FROM SCRATCH, WE JUST HAVE TO HAVE A FEW SHORTCUTS HERE AND THERE. THE TRICK IS TO MAKE THE SHORTCUT VERSION TASTE JUST AS GOOD AS THE REGULAR VERSION. ACTUALLY, WHO NEEDS TO KNOW?! ONE SHORTCUT THAT RATES AN "A" IS MY CHOCOLATE MINT CAKE RECIPE.

Kim's Orange Slices Marinated in Mint Syrup

Mint Syrup

    3   cups water
    1   cup fresh mint leaves, or $\frac{1}{2}$ cup dried
    2   cups sugar

Boil water and pour over the mint. Cover and let steep for 2 hours or longer. Strain liquid and discard mint. Place liquid into a saucepan. Add sugar. Boil over medium heat, stirring until sugar dissolves. Remove from heat and let cool. Cover and refrigerate.

Orange Slices

    2   large navel oranges
        Fresh mint sprigs

Peel the oranges carefully and remove the white part. Slice oranges crosswise into thin slices. Place slices in a serving bowl. Snip the fresh mint over the oranges. Cover oranges with the mint syrup. Cover bowl and refrigerate overnight. Kim serves these orange slices with the syrup over ice cream or pound cake. Delicious! Serves 4.

Lime-Mint Marinade

    $\frac{1}{2}$ cup chicken broth
    $\frac{1}{3}$ cup fresh lime juice
    2   tablespoons olive oil, or other vegetable oil
    1   tablespoon brown sugar
    2   or 3 cloves garlic, finely chopped
    $\frac{1}{4}$ teaspoon dried red pepper flakes
    3   teaspoons chopped fresh mint, or 1 teaspoon dried mint (fresh is best)

Combine all ingredients and mix well. Makes about 1 cup marinade for about 2 pounds of meat.

Ginger-Mint Vinegar

4   cups fresh mint leaves, cleaned and dried (no moisture on leaves)
1   1-inch piece of fresh gingerroot, peeled and coarsely chopped
2   quarts white distilled vinegar, or cider vinegar

Wash and dry mint leaves (by all means use ginger mint here if you have it). Place in a sterilized glass or plastic jar. Add chopped ginger root. Pour vinegar over leaves and root. Seal with a non-metallic lid. Let set in a cool, dry place for about 3 weeks. Discard leaves and root. Strain vinegar through a coffee filter. Pour into a pretty sterilized bottle. Cork or seal.

I USE THIS FLAVORFUL VINEGAR IN ORIENTAL COOKING, PARTICULARLY WITH THE WOK. STIR A BIT INTO RICE DISHES TO PEP THEM UP, OR SEASON MEAT OR VEGETABLE DISHES WITH IT.

Fresh Mint Jelly

1³/₄   cups Mint Infusion (see below)
2¹/₂   cups water
2   tablespoons fresh lemon juice
     Green food coloring
3¹/₂   cups sugar
¹/₂   bottle liquid fruit pectin (Certo)

Mint Infusion
Wash 1¹/₂ to 2 cups firmly packed mint leaves and stems. Place in a large pan and crush with a potato masher. Add 2¹/₂ cups water and quickly bring to a boil. Remove from heat. Cover and let stand for 10 minutes. Discard mint. Strain mint liquid through a coffee filter.

To make jelly, measure Mint Infusion into a large pan. Add lemon juice and a few drops of green food coloring — add drop by drop until you have the color you want. Add sugar and mix well. Place over high heat and bring to a boil, stirring constantly. Add liquid fruit pectin. Bring to a full rolling boil and boil hard for 1 minute, stirring constantly. Remove from heat. Skim off foam and pour into prepared and sterilized jelly glasses. Cover at once with a layer of hot paraffin.

NO CHAPTER ON MINT WOULD BE COMPLETE WITHOUT A RECIPE FOR MINT JELLY. USE THIS JELLY WITH LAMB, ADD A LITTLE TO FRUIT SALADS OR, OF COURSE, IT'S WONDERFUL ON HOT BISCUITS OR TOAST.

Oregano
&
Marjoram

ORIGANUM SPECIES

Oregano & Marjoram

ORIGANUM SPECIES

I tried to separate these two herbs, but found that I simply couldn't! There has always been a lot of controversy surrounding this group of plants and the more I researched, the more I got caught up in the controversy. The oregano that I grow in my garden is a perennial plant about 12 inches tall. It likes full sun and well-drained soil. It has small, pointed oval, gray-green leaves and white flowers. Most authorities, by the way, agree that the best oregano to cook with is white flowering. There are many species and varieties that all seem to be very similar, and yet they grow from 6 to 24 inches tall, are upright, creeping or prostrate in form. So with this information about the oregano growing in my garden, let's try to sort out these oregano/marjoram varieties — it isn't easy! The following discussion is on oreganos, even though some are called marjorams! 1. *Origanum heracleoticum* — or Greek oregano, also called winter marjoram by some. It is a native plant of Greece and the Greek islands. It has dark green, oval leaves and grows 10 to 12 inches tall. It has pale pink to white flowers and is a fairly hardy perennial. I have seen it growing wild on Greek islands and in hot climates of North Africa. In Greece, oregano is called *oros ganos* and means "joy of the mountain." The aroma as one drives through the countryside is incredible — spicy and sharp. This is a wonderful culinary herb. This is the variety that I grow in my garden. Set plants 12 to 15 inches apart and keep the soil moist to establish them. Once they're growing and covering the ground, they don't mind being on the dry side. Mulch well for winter, and oregano will re-appear in the spring. 2. *Origanum onites* — also called pot marjoram, or some call it French marjoram. It is a hardy perennial that can become very invasive if allowed to spread. The plant has pinkish purple flowers on stems growing 2 feet tall. This plant's leaves taste harsh and robust. It is native to the Mediterranean. Even though it is widely used as a culinary herb, it is not my favorite. It is often sold as "Greek oregano," but believe me, there is a great deal of difference between the two! Actually, I treat pot marjoram as (forgive me) a weed. It's a good spreader and the pink to light purple blooms are lovely dried for wreaths and potpourri, but I don't cook with it. 3. *Origanum vulgare* — or wild marjoram. This hardy Mediterranean perennial grows abundantly in the south of England, other parts of Europe, Asia, North Africa, and North America. This plant looks a lot like pot marjoram. Most novices (and that includes me) would have difficulty telling them apart. Wild marjoram is mainly used for medicinal or decorative, and not culinary purposes. 4. *Origanum dictamnus* — or Dittany of Crete. I haven't read this, but I'm assuming this plant is native to the Greek isle, Crete. It is not culinary, but it makes a beautiful decorative border or low hedge. ❦ The flavors between the oregano varieties are markedly different. It's all a bit confusing, but if you find a sharp-tasting, almost tongue-numbing oregano that blooms white, I believe you've found **the** oregano to cook with! ❦ Concerning oregano, I buy seeds or plants from nurseries or seed houses who will tell me about the plant's taste and about its flowers. In my lectures, I say oregano is one plant that **must** be tasted before bringing home. Nip off a small bit of leaf and taste it. If it reminds you of all good things Greek or Italian, and if it's sharp- and peppery-tasting to the tongue, then it's probably an oregano you'd want to cook with. ❦ Oregano is widely used in medicines. The oil of oregano is said to aid an aching tooth. It also is used to treat stomach and gallbladder disorders. ❦

And finally to sweet marjoram, also in this complex family of plants. *Origanum majorana*, or sweet marjoram (also called knotted marjoram), is native to Sicily and Portugal. It is a perennial there, but otherwise it is treated in most areas as an annual. It is a symbol of youth, beauty, and happiness — who wouldn't love this herb? ❦ I love sweet marjoram — truly one of my favorite culinary herbs. When someone asks me how sweet marjoram smells, the word that immediately comes to mind is "soft." It has a soft, spicy, sweet, and wonderful aroma and taste. This is the most delicately flavored plant in the oregano/ marjoram family. Sweet marjoram grows 10 to 12 inches tall, and has pale green oval leaves on rather woody stems. The seed is slow to germinate and needs to be sown after all danger of frost is past. Better yet, start the seed in a greenhouse, or greenhouse-type environment in March or April and set out plants in May. Sweet marjoram also is called knotted marjoram because of the round whorls of leaves that form near the top of the stem. These whorls of flowers and leaves appear in midsummer. The best time to harvest the leaves is just before the flower whorls appear. Cut back the first growth to within 2 or 3 inches of the ground. With rain and sun, a vigorous second growth will appear. Be sure to plant some sweet marjoram in your bee or butterfly gardens — they love this plant. ❦ Fortunately, sweet marjoram retains most of its flavor when dried. Dry in a cool, dark, moisture-free place for a week or two. Lay the sprigs on clean screens to dry, or hang upside down in bunches. Strip the dried leaves from the stems and store in a cool, dark place in airtight containers. ❦ As for medicinal uses, oil of sweet marjoram is used in compounds to treat sprains and bruises. A tisane made from the leaves is said to aid in calming nerves and to settle the stomach. The English in particular used the oil in a polish to clean and shine furniture. ❦ There are at least two other varieties of marjoram worth considering in your garden. One is called *O.v. 'Variegatum'* — or gold variegated marjoram. It has beautiful gold-splotched green leaves that have a nice mild flavor. Another is *O.v. 'Aureum'* — or golden marjoram. This variety has beautiful golden leaves with a mild flavor. This plant must have some midday shade to protect the leaves from sunburn. ❦ Three important things I've learned about sweet marjoram are: 1. It absolutely will not live in standing water, so make sure your growing area is well drained.   2. It is a great plant for the container gardener to become acquainted with. It droops over the side of the container in a gorgeous mound of aromatic leaves.   3. When cooking with fresh sweet marjoram (or Greek oregano for that matter), add only the last 3 to 5 minutes of cooking time to preserve the delicate flavor. Overcooking will destroy the flavor.

❦ I hope this discussion has at least partially clarified the differences between the oreganos/marjorams. It really is impossible to discuss one and not the other. ❦

How do I use oregano and sweet marjoram?

These are interchangeable — however, sweet marjoram is not as robust as oregano.

- in spaghetti sauces
- in other pasta dishes
- to flavor pizza and pizza sauces
- to flavor tomato dishes
- with beef
- in salads
- in soups
- in stews
- with lamb
- with chicken and turkey
- with sausages
- with veal
- with pork
- with zucchini, broccoli, peas, carrots, onions, beans, potatoes, eggplant, sweet corn, spinach
- in salad dressings
- with cheeses, particularly cream cheese

- in oil
- in vinegar
- in chili and other Mexican foods
- in cheese dishes
- in some egg dishes, such as soufflés and omelettes
- with fish and seafood
- in bouquet garnis
- in dried seasoning blends
- in potpourris (the flowers)
- in cream sauces
- in cheese sauces
- with mushrooms
- in marinades
- with onion dishes
- with garlic
- in breads and muffins

Oregano Recipes

Sweet Marjoram Recipes

Mediterranean Inspired

Appetizer Pepperoni and Cheese Tartlets (p. 128) *

Asparagus with Bleu Cheese Vinaigrette (p. 132) **

Grilled or Broiled Steak with Mediterranean Herb Rub (p. 140) *

Baked Tomatoes with Oregano (p. 137) *

Sweet Marjoram Breadsticks (p. 142) **

Pears Poached in Red Wine (p. 399)

* Recipe contains Greek oregano

** Recipe contains sweet marjoram

Appetizer Pepperoni and Cheese Tartlets

USING OREGANO

MAKE THE FILLING AND THE TARTLET SHELLS THE DAY BEFORE THE PARTY. REFRIGERATE. THE NEXT DAY, ADD FILLING TO THE SHELLS AND BAKE. THIS IS THE TYPE OF PARTY RECIPE WE ALL NEED!

Cream Cheese Pastry

1 cup unsalted butter, melted
2 cups flour
6 ounces cream cheese, melted

Blend butter, flour and cream cheese to make a soft dough. Form into forty-eight 1-inch balls. Grease tiny muffin pans with nonstick vegetable spray. Place a ball in each muffin cup and with your thumb, mold each into a tiny crust. Cover and refrigerate tartlet shells.

Pepperoni and Cheese Filling

3 eggs
1 cup half-and-half cream
½ teaspoon salt
4 ounces Swiss cheese, shredded
¼ pound pepperoni, finely chopped
½ teaspoon dried oregano

Beat eggs. Add cream and salt. Mix in cheese, pepperoni and oregano and blend well. Cover and refrigerate filling. When ready to bake, bring crusts and filling to room temperature. Add filling to each crust and bake at 350° for about 30 minutes. Serve warm. Makes 48 appetizers.

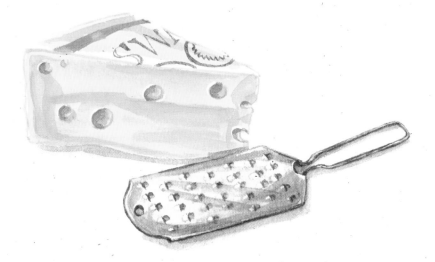

Bacon-Wrapped Shrimps
USING SWEET MARJORAM

12	large shrimps
$^3/_4$	cup teriyaki sauce
1	teaspoon fresh sweet marjoram, chopped, or $^1/_2$ teaspoon dried and crumbled Toothpicks
2	medium onions
12	large mushroom caps (use stems for another recipe)
12	strips bacon

Marinate shrimps in teriyaki sauce and chopped sweet marjoram for 30 minutes. Slice onions in quarters and peel off 3 layers. Roll each shrimp, onion piece and mushroom cap in a bacon slice and secure with toothpicks. Heat broiler. Broil until bacon is crisp, turning once or twice. Drain on paper towels and serve hot. Makes 12 appetizers.

HERE IS AN EASY AND DELICIOUS APPETIZER. IT'S A GREAT CHANGE FROM THE COLD SHRIMPS USUALLY SERVED. SURE TO BECOME A FAVORITE.

Mexican Appetizer
USING OREGANO

1	pound ground beef
1	teaspoon dried oregano
$^1/_2$	small onion, diced
$^1/_2$	clove garlic, crushed
1	small red bell pepper, cored, seeded and diced
3	8-ounce jars Mexican processed cheese, or similar nacho processed cheese, either mild or hot (whatever your crowd likes)
$1^1/_2$	teaspoons nacho seasoning blend, chili spice blend or a spicy seasoned salt blend*
1	1-pound bag tortilla chips

Brown ground beef, oregano, onion, garlic and bell pepper in a medium skillet. Drain fat and cook another 8 or 10 minutes. In a medium microwave-safe bowl, microwave cheese on medium power until cheese melts, about 1 minute. Mix in ground beef and seasonings blend. Pour into a serving bowl and serve with the tortilla chips. Makes 8 or 10 appetizer servings.

There is an explosion of seasoning blends on the spice shelves today. The day of plain salt and plain pepper is over!

THIS RECIPE MAY SOUND LIKE ONE THAT EVERYONE ELSE HAS, BUT WE ALL NEED A FEW PUT-TOGETHER-FAST RECIPES. THE BEAUTY OF THIS ONE IS IT'S SO GOOD! THIS IS ANOTHER ONE THE KIDS IN THE HOUSE WILL LOVE.

Salsa with Oregano

7 medium-size ripe tomatoes, seeded and diced
$^1/_2$ cup tomato sauce
$^1/_2$ cup chopped red onion
3 cloves garlic, minced
2 jalapeno peppers, seeded and minced
2 tablespoons chopped fresh cilantro
$1^1/_2$ tablespoons chopped fresh oregano
$2^1/_2$ tablespoons fresh lime juice
1 to $1^1/_2$ teaspoons salt

Combine all ingredients. Cover and refrigerate several hours before serving. Makes about 3 cups.

Cream of Broccoli Soup with Sweet Marjoram

1 large head broccoli
1 medium to large potato, peeled
1 medium onion, chopped
1 clove garlic, finely chopped
2 tablespoons butter
$^1/_2$ teaspoon curry powder
2 cups chicken broth
$^1/_2$ to 1 cup water
$^1/_2$ teaspoon salt
1 teaspoon fresh sweet marjoram, or $^1/_3$ teaspoon dried
1 cup half-and-half cream
2 cups cheddar cheese, grated

Trim broccoli and separate into flowerets. Cut stems into $^1/_2$-inch pieces. Cut potato into $^1/_2$-inch cubes. Sauté onion and garlic in butter in a large soup pot until tender, but not brown. Add curry powder, chicken broth, water and salt to the pot. Bring to a boil. Add broccoli and potato pieces. Return to a boil, reduce heat and simmer, covered, 20 minutes. Purée mixture, a little at a time, in food processor or blender. Return blended mixture to the soup pot and heat over low heat, stirring often. Add sweet marjoram, half-and-half cream and cheese. Taste for seasoning. Heat until hot, but do not boil. Serves 6.

Cream of Pea Soup with Sweet Marjoram

4   cups water

1   ham bone, with meat and any fat left on

2   cups chicken broth

2   cups dried split peas, picked over and rinsed

$^2/_3$ cup rinsed and chopped leeks (if unavailable, use large green onions)

$^1/_2$ cup carrots, finely chopped

$^1/_2$ cup celery, finely chopped

$^1/_2$ teaspoon sugar

1   teaspoon fresh sweet marjoram, or $^1/_3$ teaspoon dried and crumbled
     Black pepper and salt to taste

1   cup chopped ham (from the ham bone)

$2^1/_2$ cups milk

1   cup whipping cream

IF YOU THOUGHT YOU DIDN'T LIKE CREAM OF PEA SOUP, THINK AGAIN. THIS ONE IS THE BEST I'VE TASTED. NEXT TIME YOU HAVE A HAM BONE AVAILABLE, DO MAKE THIS SOUP. IT IS REAL COMFORT FOOD FOR A COLD WINTER NIGHT.

In a large soup pot, bring water, ham bone, broth and peas to a boil. Reduce heat to low and simmer, uncovered, for 30 minutes. Stir occasionally. Skim off any foam that forms. Add leeks or onions, carrots, celery, sugar, marjoram and pepper. Taste and add salt if needed. Simmer slowly for about 30 minutes, stirring occasionally. Remove ham bone and let cool a little. Dice meat to make at least 1 cup, or more if meat is available. Add ham pieces back to soup. Slowly stir in milk and cream. Barely simmer for 10 minutes. Do not boil or soup may curdle. Serves 8.

Oregano Vinaigrette

$^1/_2$ cup vegetable oil, not olive oil

6   tablespoons mixed herb vinegar or cider vinegar

2   tablespoons sugar

2   teaspoons dried oregano

$^1/_4$ teaspoon salt

1   clove garlic, minced

Combine in a jar with a screw-on lid. Shake well to combine. Before serving, shake well again. Makes a wonderful dressing for 4 green salads.

Asparagus with Bleu Cheese Vinaigrette

USING SWEET MARJORAM

1   pound fresh asparagus
2   tablespoons bleu cheese
¼   cup olive oil
2   teaspoons fresh lemon juice
     Salt and pepper
1   tablespoon fresh sweet marjoram, chopped, or 1 teaspoon dried and crumbled

Trim tough ends of asparagus. Cook spears in a skillet in 1 inch of boiling water until tender, 8 to 14 minutes depending on how thick asparagus is. Do **not** overcook. Drain well. Divide spears between 4 salad plates. Mash bleu cheese in a small bowl. Add olive oil, lemon juice, salt, pepper and sweet marjoram. Spoon dressing over asparagus. Serve warm or at room temperature to 4.

Marinated Vegetables with Shrimps

USING OREGANO

The Vegetables and Shrimps

2   medium red onions, thinly sliced
1   pound fresh mushroom caps, cleaned and dried
1   head broccoli, broken into flowerets
1   head cauliflower, broken into flowerets
1   6-ounce can pitted, drained black olives
2   pounds cooked, shelled, deveined shrimps, cut into pieces

Combine all the above in a large bowl and set aside.

The Marinade

1⅓	cups vinegar	2	teaspoons dried oregano
⅔	cup vegetable oil	1	teaspoon salt
3	tablespoons fresh lemon juice	¼	teaspoon pepper
½	cup sugar		Dash or 2 of Tabasco sauce

Combine marinade ingredients and stir until sugar is dissolved. Add marinade to the vegetables and shrimps bowl. Toss gently to coat well. Refrigerate for several hours or overnight, stirring occasionally. To serve, drain and arrange vegetables and shrimps on a large lettuce-lined platter. Serves 8.

Mediterranean Chicken Breast Rolls

USING SWEET MARJORAM

 ¹/₂ cup red onion, finely chopped

  2   tablespoons olive oil

1¹/₂ teaspoons garlic, minced

 ¹/₂ cup pitted Kalamato olives, or other brine-cured black olives, cut into thin strips

 ¹/₄ cup pine nuts, lightly toasted

 ¹/₂ cup drained oil-packed sun-dried tomatoes (rinse, dry and cut into thin strips)

  1   cup feta cheese, crumbled

  2   tablespoons Parmesan cheese, grated

  1   tablespoon fresh sweet marjoram, chopped, or 1 teaspoon dried and crumbled
      Salt and pepper

  4   boneless chicken breast halves
      Toothpicks

 ¹/₄ cup flour

In a large ovenproof skillet, cook onion in 1 tablespoon of the olive oil over moderate heat, stirring until softened but not brown. Add garlic and cook 1 more minute. Place in a bowl and set aside to cool. Stir in olives, pine nuts, tomatoes, the cheeses, sweet marjoram and salt and pepper to season. Stir well to blend. Set aside. Lay chicken breast pieces on a waxed paper-covered chopping board. Lay more waxed paper on top and flatten breasts to ¹/₄-inch thick with a meat mallet. Remove waxed paper. Cover each breast piece with one-fourth of the above mixture. Roll up tightly and secure with toothpicks. In another large skillet, heat the remaining 1 tablespoon olive oil. Lightly flour the chicken rolls and quickly sauté them on all sides. Transfer the skillet to the oven and bake at 350° for about 15 minutes, or until chicken is done. Serves 4.
Delicious.

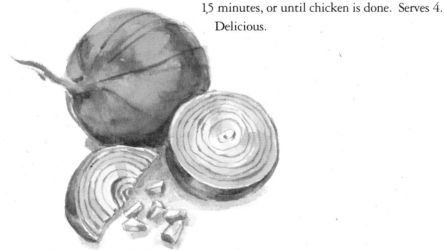

THERE ARE SOME WHO SAY THE MEDITERRANEAN-INSPIRED FOOD CRAZE WILL FADE AWAY. HOW CAN IT POSSIBLY FADE AWAY WHEN WE'RE TALKING ABOUT OLIVE OIL, KALAMATO OLIVES, PINE NUTS, SUN-DRIED TOMATOES, FETA CHEESE AND FRESH SWEET MARJORAM. BY THE WAY, ALL THOSE THINGS ARE IN THIS RECIPE!

Chicken Breasts with Morel Cream Sauce

USING SWEET MARJORAM

THIS IS A DISH TO HERALD THE ARRIVAL OF SPRING. WHEN MY HUSBAND MAKES HIS FIRST TRIP TO THE WOODS TO HUNT MUSHROOMS, HE USUALLY COMES BACK WITH ONLY A HANDFUL. THERE IS NO BETTER WAY TO USE THAT HANDFUL THAN IN THIS RECIPE! IF MORELS AREN'T AVAILABLE, USE CHOPPED PORTOBELLOS. A FRIEND FROM MICHIGAN (REAL MUSHROOM COUNTRY) SENT THIS RECIPE. IF YOU GOT THE GARDEN PLANTED SOON ENOUGH, SERVE THIS DELICIOUS DISH WITH A FRESH SPINACH SALAD.

4 chicken breast halves, skinless and boneless
$^1/_4$ cup flour
Salt and pepper to season
1 teaspoon fresh sweet marjoram, or $^1/_3$ teaspoon dried and crumbled
3 tablespoons butter or margarine
Up to 1 cup (or whatever came in from the woods!) fresh morels, or fresh portobellos from the grocery, coarsely chopped
2 tablespoons onion, chopped
1 small clove garlic, minced
2 tablespoons flour
$1^2/_3$ cups half-and-half cream or whole milk
$^1/_4$ teaspoon salt
1 tablespoon dry sherry

Place breast halves between waxed paper or plastic wrap. Pound to $^1/_4$-inch thickness. Discard the wrap. Combine $^1/_4$ cup flour, salt, pepper and sweet marjoram. Coat chicken with flour mixture. In a large skillet, melt butter and sauté chicken until it is done. Place on a platter and keep warm. Chop the mushrooms and place them, the onion and garlic in the skillet and cook 3 or 4 minutes, stirring often. Place 2 tablespoons flour in a small bowl. Add just enough milk or cream to make a paste. Slowly whisk in remaining milk or cream. Add salt, if needed. Add to the skillet mixture and cook and stir until thickened and smooth. Add the sherry. Cook and stir 2 more minutes. Spoon sauce over the chicken and serve to 4.

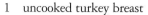

Turkey Breast Scallopini
USING SWEET MARJORAM

1   uncooked turkey breast
1   tablespoon butter
¹/₄   cup fresh lemon juice
4   green onions, chopped
1   cup chicken broth
2   cloves garlic, chopped
1   cup heavy cream
2   teaspoons smooth Dijon mustard
1   teaspoon fresh sweet marjoram, chopped, or ¹/₃ teaspoon dried and crumbled
1   teaspoon fresh parsley, chopped
     Salt and pepper

Cut down center of turkey breast with a sharp knife. (Reserve other half of breast for another recipe, or if preparing for a large crowd, use both breast halves and double the sauce recipe). Cut the breast into thin slices (scallops). Heat butter in a large skillet. Sauté the turkey scallops, a few at a time, in hot butter on both sides. Lay turkey scallops in a large baking dish, overlapping the scallops. In the same skillet, add all other ingredients and cook until cream thickens and cooks down a little. Pour sauce evenly over the scallops. Add salt and pepper, if necessary. Bake scallopini, uncovered, at 350° for 10 minutes. If not done, cover loosely with foil and bake a few more minutes until turkey is done. Do not cover tightly — you do not want to steam the turkey. Serves 8 or more.

THIS IS A VERY GOOD PARTY DISH USING A TURKEY BREAST, EITHER FRESH OR FROZEN, THEN THAWED. THE SAUCE IS DELICIOUS.

Oregano Butter

¹/₂   cup butter, softened
¹/₄   cup grated Parmesan cheese
1   tablespoon fresh oregano, chopped, or 1 teaspoon dried
1   tablespoon fresh parsley, chopped, or 1 teaspoon dried
¹/₄   teaspoon garlic powder

Mix all ingredients thoroughly. Cover and keep refrigerated. Makes about ¹/₂ cup.

SPREAD THIS BUTTER ON THICK SLICES OF FRENCH BREAD AND TOAST UNDER THE BROILER. GREAT WITH ANY GRILLED MEATS.

Grilled Lemon Chicken with Oregano

2   pounds uncooked chicken breasts, cubed
³/₄ pound mushrooms, cleaned and halved
¹/₂ cup white wine
¹/₃ cup fresh lemon juice
¹/₄ cup vegetable oil
3   teaspoons fresh oregano, or 1 teaspoon dried
2   cloves garlic, minced

Place chicken and mushrooms in a shallow baking dish. Place wine, lemon juice, oil, oregano and garlic in a container with a lid. Shake to combine. Pour marinade over chicken and mushrooms. Refrigerate for 2 hours. Skewer chicken and mushrooms on 4 skewers, alternating pieces of chicken with a mushroom half. Grill for 10 to 15 minutes, turning once or twice. Serves 4 to 6.

Roast Pork with Oregano

1   4-pound pork loin
2   teaspoons salt
1   teaspoon ground pepper
3   cloves garlic
2   tablespoons fresh oregano, or 2 to 3 teaspoons dried
4   teaspoons cider vinegar or mixed herb vinegar
2   tablespoons vegetable oil

Place pork in a foil-lined roasting pan (for easy clean-up). Use a sharp paring knife and poke holes all over sides and top of roast. Place remaining ingredients in food processor bowl or blender and process until smooth. Spread and rub seasonings all over the roast, being sure to rub it into the holes you made. Let roast stand with seasonings for 15 or 20 minutes. Now place roast in a 400° oven and bake for 10 minutes. Lower heat to 350° and bake for 1 hour and 15 minutes, or until a meat thermometer registers 160°. Remove from oven. Let rest 15 minutes before slicing. Serves 10.

Italian Sausage, Chicken, Peppers and Potatoes

USING OREGANO

2 pounds sweet or hot Italian sausage, your choice
4 boneless, skinless chicken breasts, sliced
1/4 cup olive oil
2 cups diced potatoes (medium dice)
2 cups sliced green bell peppers
1 cup sliced onions
1 tablespoon chopped fresh oregano, or 1 teaspoon dried
1 tablespoon chopped fresh parsley, or 1 teaspoon dried
1/4 to 1/2 teaspoon hot red pepper flakes
Salt and pepper

Rinse a large skillet, but do not dry it. Place sausage in the wet skillet and sauté until sausage is browned. Remove sausage and set aside in a bowl. Do not drain fat. Place chicken pieces in the same skillet. Turn heat to low and sauté, covered, until chicken pieces are very tender. Place in the bowl with sausage. In the same skillet, heat the olive oil. Add the potatoes, peppers and onions. Brown vegetables over low heat. Stir in herbs, hot red pepper flakes and salt and pepper. Cook until vegetables are tender. Add sausage and chicken to the vegetables and sauté until all the flavors are mixed together. Serves 6 to 8.

I LOVE THIS ALL-IN-ONE MEAL AND IN-ONE-SKILLET DISH. THIS IS SO MUCH LIKE A DISH SERVED IN GERMAN AND AUSTRIAN RESTAURANTS WHERE LOCALS EAT, EXCEPT THEY WOULD USE ONE OF THEIR GOOD GERMAN OR AUSTRIAN SAUSAGES. IT'S A HEARTY COLD-WEATHER DISH. BY THE WAY, TO TASTE TRUE REGIONAL COOKING WHEN TRAVELING, EAT SOME OF YOUR MEALS IN RESTAURANTS OR CAFÉS WHERE THE LOCAL PEOPLE EAT! USUALLY NOT FANCY — JUST GOOD.

Baked Tomatoes with Oregano

4 medium tomatoes, or enough slices to cover bottom of pan
1/4 cup butter or margarine, melted
1 clove garlic, minced
1/2 teaspoon salt
1/2 teaspoon pepper
1 tablespoon chopped fresh oregano, or 1 teaspoon dried

Cut tomatoes into 1/2-inch slices. Place in a 13x9x2-inch baking dish in a single layer. Combine butter with remainder of ingredients. Spoon over the tomato slices. Bake at 350° for about 25 minutes. Serves 6.

HERE IS A SPLENDID VEGETABLE DISH THAT'S EASY TO PREPARE AND CAN BE SERVED FROM THE SAME DISH IT'S BAKED IN. CAN ALSO BE PREPARED EARLY IN THE DAY, REFRIGERATED AND BAKED LATER.

Roast Beef Roll-Ups
USING OREGANO

Horseradish Sauce (recipe follows)
Lahvosh or flour tortillas
Thinly sliced deli roast beef
Thinly sliced tomatoes
Fresh oregano, chopped
Salt and pepper

IF YOU CAN FIND
CRACKER BREAD (OR LAHVOSH),
USE IT FOR THIS RECIPE.
(AVAILABLE AT GOURMET FOOD
SHOPS AND SOME LARGE
SUPERMARKETS). IF NOT, USE
SOFT FLOUR TORTILLAS.

Place a thin layer of Horseradish Sauce on bread or tortilla — spread evenly. Add a layer of roast beef, then a layer of tomato slices. Sprinkle with oregano, salt and pepper. Roll up. Trim ends and slice into $1/4$-inch-thick slices for appetizers or $1/2$-inch-thick slices for sandwiches.

Horseradish Sauce

2   cups sour cream
$1/2$ cup bottled horseradish, well drained
2   teaspoons Dijon-style mustard
$1/2$ teaspoon salt
     Dash of pepper

Combine all sauce ingredients in a small bowl and refrigerate, covered. Leftover sauce can be used on beef, pork or ham sandwiches. Makes 2 cups.

Zucchini Parmesan with Oregano

2   tablespoons olive oil
2   medium zucchini, cut into $1/4$-inch-thick slices
2   tablespoons chopped fresh oregano, or 2 teaspoons dried
1   medium fresh tomato, seeded and diced
$1/4$ cup shredded Parmesan cheese

This dish has a real Italian flavor. Use green or yellow zucchini or a combination of the two. The trick here is to not overcook the squash.

In a fairly large skillet, heat the olive oil and add the zucchini slices and the chopped oregano. Stir gently over medium heat until zucchini is almost tender. Stir in the diced tomato and cook and stir another 2 or 3 minutes only. Sprinkle Parmesan cheese on top. Turn off heat. Place a lid on skillet and let skillet stand until cheese melts, a minute or so. Serve right out of the skillet to 4.

Pasta Pie

USING OREGANO

For one 9-inch pie:

2½   cups hot cooked pasta (such as elbow macaroni, rigatoni, penne)
½   cup grated Parmesan cheese*
2   tablespoons butter
1¼   cups shredded mozzarella cheese
1   pound lean ground beef
1¼   to 1½ cups store-bought spaghetti sauce**
½   teaspoon dried oregano
     Salt and pepper

Combine pasta, ¼ cup Parmesan cheese and butter. Toss. Press into a buttered 9-inch pie plate. Top with ¾ cup of the mozzarella cheese. In a medium skillet over medium heat, brown ground beef and drain. Add spaghetti sauce and oregano. Add salt and pepper to taste. Mix well. Spoon over the pasta. Sprinkle with the remaining Parmesan cheese. Bake in a 350° oven for 20 to 30 minutes until thoroughly heated. Sprinkle with remaining mozzarella cheese. Return to the oven just to melt the cheese. Cut into wedges. Serves 5 to 6.

Parmesan cheese — By now, you know that Parmigiano Reggiano is the best Parmesan cheese, but if unavailable, check the deli of your favorite grocery for shredded or grated Parmesan cheese. It is also available in resealable plastic bags and hangs in the display with other shredded cheeses. Either of these is so much better than what comes off the grocery shelf.

**Spaghetti sauce — When you don't have time to make your own pasta sauces, there is a wonderful array of them on grocery shelves. They are in glass quart jars and there are many varieties — basil, ripe olive, red hot pepper, mushrooms, and more.... These are all excellent. My favorite brand remains Classico.*

WE ALL NEED A FEW RECIPES
LIKE THIS ONE. IT'S VERY
SIMPLE, HAS ONLY A FEW
INGREDIENTS AND GOES
TOGETHER VERY QUICKLY AFTER
A LONG DAY AT THE OFFICE OR
SHOPPING. CHILDREN AND
TEENAGERS LOVE THIS, SO
MAKE PLENTY.

Sausage and Pasta Bake

WHAT A WONDERFUL DISH TO TAKE TO THE NEXT CARRY-IN SUPPER. EVERYONE LOVES THIS CASSEROLE. MAKE IT IN THE MORNING, REFRIGERATE, AND BAKE IT LATER IN THE DAY. LET IT COME TO ROOM TEMPERATURE BEFORE BAKING.

8	ounces pasta (rotelli, rigatoni or mostaccioli)
1½	pounds bulk pork sausage
½	cup chopped onion
¼	cup chopped green pepper
1	clove garlic, minced
1	16-ounce can tomatoes, cut up, undrained
1	6-ounce can tomato paste
½	cup water
½	to 1 teaspoon dried oregano, to your taste
⅛	teaspoon pepper
1½	cups shredded American or mild cheddar cheese, divided

Cook pasta according to package directions. Drain and set aside. In a large skillet, cook sausage, onion, green pepper and garlic until meat is browned. Drain off fat. Stir in the undrained tomatoes, tomato paste, water, oregano and pepper into the skillet mixture. Stir in the cooked pasta. Spoon half the pasta mixture into a greased 3-quart casserole. Sprinkle with half the cheese. Top with remaining pasta mixture. Bake in a 350° oven for about 40 minutes. Sprinkle with remainder of cheese and bake another 5 minutes to melt cheese. Serves 8.

Mediterranean Herb Rub for Steaks or Chops

RUB THESE SEASONINGS ON STEAKS OR PORK CHOPS BEFORE GRILLING OR BROILING. NOTICE HOW LITTLE SALT IS NECESSARY WHEN THESE STRONG-FLAVORED HERBS ARE INVOLVED.

3	cloves garlic, minced
1	tablespoon vegetable oil
2	teaspoons dried oregano, crushed
2	teaspoons dried basil, crushed
1	teaspoon dried thyme, crushed
¼	teaspoon salt
¼	teaspoon pepper

Mix all ingredients together in a small bowl. Spread mixture on both sides of meat. Cover and refrigerate 2 to 4 hours. Grill over hot coals or broil. Makes about ¼ cup seasonings.

Vegetable–Herb Lasagna
USING OREGANO

4   tablespoons butter

3   cups chopped zucchini

2   cups broccoli flowerets

    Salt to taste

2   cups cleaned and dried spinach leaves

2   teaspoons fresh oregano leaves or $^1/_2$ teaspoon dried

1   pound package ricotta cheese

2   eggs

12   lasagna noodles

3   tablespoons butter

$^1/_4$ cup flour

$^1/_4$ teaspoon salt

$2^1/_2$ cups milk

$^1/_2$ cup grated Parmesan cheese

2   cups shredded mozzarella cheese

THIS LASAGNA IS PREPARED WITHOUT MEAT OR TOMATO SAUCE. LADIES LOVE THIS FOR LUNCHEON. FOR A HEARTIER MEAL, SERVE WITH GRILLED OR BROILED CHICKEN, STEAK OR CHOPS. ADD A GOOD CRUSTY BREAD, A BOTTLE OF WINE AND YOU'RE READY TO SIT DOWN TO A FINE SUMMER MEAL.

In a large sauté pan, melt 4 tablespoons butter. Sauté zucchini and broccoli and a little salt until vegetables are tender-crisp, 3 or 4 minutes. Add spinach leaves and fresh oregano and stir until spinach is wilted. In a small bowl, mix together ricotta cheese and eggs; set aside. Prepare lasagna noodles as label directs. Drain. In a saucepan, melt 3 tablespoons butter. Stir in flour and $^1/_4$ teaspoon salt until smooth. Gradually stir in milk. Cook, stirring constantly, until sauce boils and thickens. Remove pan from heat and stir in Parmesan cheese. In a large, greased baking pan (at least 13x9x2) lay 6 lasagna noodles. Spread half of ricotta mixture on noodles, half of vegetable mixture and half of the mozzarella. Top with half the sauce, then remainder of noodles, ricotta and vegetables. Spread with the remainder of the sauce, then sprinkle remainder of mozzarella on top. Bake lasagna at 350° for 45 minutes until hot and bubbly. Let lasagna stand for 10 minutes before cutting into squares. Will serve about 8.

Sweet Marjoram Breadsticks

1	package active dry yeast
$1/4$	cup warm water
$1/2$	teaspoon sugar
4	cups flour
$1/8$	teaspoon salt
1	egg
3	tablespoons salad oil
1	cup warm milk
$1/2$	cup fresh sweet marjoram, chopped
3	tablespoons Parmesan cheese, grated
$1/4$	cup coarse salt

Proof yeast in $1/4$ cup warm water and $1/2$ teaspoon sugar in a small bowl. In another bowl, combine flour and salt. When yeast is frothy, add yeast mixture, egg, oil and milk to the flour. Make a soft dough. Turn dough out of bowl and knead for about 5 minutes. Place dough in a greased bowl, cover with a clean towel and let rise for 30 to 40 minutes, or until doubled. Turn out dough. Scatter sweet marjoram and Parmesan cheese over dough and knead to incorporate into the mixture. Divide dough into 18 equal pieces. Shape into a breadstick form. Sprinkle breadsticks with coarse salt. Let rise until doubled, 20 to 30 minutes. Bake on a lightly greased baking sheet at 350° for 15 minutes, or until browned. Makes 18 delicious breadsticks. Another time, shape dough into small buns. Place on lightly greased sheet and bake.

Herbs and Spices Vinegar

USING SWEET MARJORAM

1	cup fresh sweet marjoram leaves and tender stems
4	sprigs fresh rosemary, each 6 inches long
4	sprigs fresh lemon thyme, each 6 inches long
8	fresh sage leaves
1	large sprig fresh green basil
1	large bay leaf
1	teaspoon mustard seeds
$^1/_2$	teaspoon ground cinnamon
$^1/_2$	teaspoon ground cloves
$^1/_2$	teaspoon ground allspice
$^1/_4$	teaspoon hot red pepper flakes
1	to 2 quarts white wine vinegar or cider vinegar to cover

Wash and dry herbs. Place in a half gallon, or larger, glass or plastic container. Bruise herbs with a wooden spoon to release some of their oils. In a nonreactive pan, place remainder of ingredients. Add vinegar and heat just to boiling. Remove from heat. Let stand 10 minutes, then pour hot vinegar over the herbs. Stir or shake well. If you didn't heat enough vinegar to cover the herbs, just add a little more from the vinegar jug. Cool vinegar, then cover with a nonmetallic lid or covering. Store in a cool, dark place for 3 to 5 weeks to develop the flavors. Strain herbs and spices and discard. Strain vinegar through a coffee filter into a sterilized bottle.
Cork and seal. A wonderful vinegar.

YOU COULDN'T GUESS THAT VINEGAR — PLAIN OLD VINEGAR — COULD RISE TO SUCH HEIGHTS. USE THIS TASTY VINEGAR TO SEASON SAUTÉED CABBAGE, TO SPLASH ON COLD COOKED VEGETABLES AND, OF COURSE, TO MAKE SALAD DRESSINGS AND MARINADES. A SECRET OF CLEAR, UNCLOUDY VINEGAR IS TO START WITH DRY INGREDIENTS. BE SURE HERB LEAVES AND SPRIGS HAVE NO CLINGING DROPS OF WATER ON THEM.

Parsley

PETROSELINUM SPECIES

Parsley

PETROSELINUM SPECIES

Most of us are pretty blasé about parsley. After all, the curly variety is available in most grocery stores most anytime of the year. But we really need to think about parsley as more than that green sprig to decorate the dinner plate. It is an herb that is very rich in vitamins and minerals so that sprig actually should be eaten! Parsley is native to the eastern Mediterranean area and still grows wild in Greece, Turkey, and other countries of the area. It is cultivated throughout the world today and has been grown for thousands of years. Parsley is associated with festivity, due no doubt to ancient times when the Greeks crowned victors of games with wreaths of parsley. Parsley is a biennial, but I treat it as an annual. The first year, the plant has beautiful green curly or flat (depending on variety) leaves. The plant will grow about 18 inches tall the first year. The second year, the plant sends up long stems with umbels of greenish-yellow small flowers. These stems can be as tall as 3 feet. If you allow the plant to grow its second year, it will readily reseed. I think parsley tastes best its first year. The leaves of second-year parsley can be bitter. Sow parsley seeds in rich soil in a sunny location, but it likes a little afternoon shade also. Thin the seedlings to 6 to 8 inches apart. Parsley has a rather long taproot, but even so, I successfully set out small plants — the bigger the plant, the more difficult it is to transplant. ❧ No living creature loves parsley more than rabbits. I would be happy to plant a row somewhere just for them if I could train them to eat theirs and leave the plants in my herb garden alone! ❧ Some varieties to consider are: 1. *P. crispum crispum* — there are many varieties of crispum. They all have close, tightly curled leaves that have saw-toothed edges. Parsley grows on tender green stems. 2. **Italian** (*P. crispum neapolitanum*) — Italian flat leaf is the common name. Also referred to as celery-leaved parsley because of its wide, flat leaves. This variety is less bitter than the curly varieties and therefore is best to use in green salads, or to eat raw. 3. **Hamburg** (*P. crispum tuberosum*) — also called turnip-rooted parsley because the root tastes like turnip when cooked. The leaves do not taste like parsley as we know it. ❧ Parsley is an important culinary herb. It blends with almost any food. It is always one of the herbs in the classic **Bouquet Garni**.

MY FAVORITE GARNI

1 bay leaf
1 tablespoon dried French tarragon
1 tablespoon dried parsley

1 teaspoon dried rosemary
1 teaspoon dried thyme
6 whole peppercorns

Place herbs in the middle of a coffee filter. Gather up into a bag and tie with white kitchen string. Use to flavor soups and stews.

If using fresh parsley in cooking, as with most fresh herbs, add toward the end of cooking time to keep from destroying the flavor. Parsley keeps well in the refrigerator. Bring in a handful, place in a glass of water, and keep in the refrigerator to use as needed. It will keep for several days. Parsley is easy to dry and retains much of its dark green color and flavor if dried properly. I gather 8 or 10 stems of Italian parsley and suspend them in a brown grocery bag to dry — bunch top of bag and tie with the stems. Punch a few holes in the sides of the bag. After 10 days or 2 weeks, the leaves will be crispy dry and beautifully green. Store these leaves whole in airtight glass or plastic containers out of heat and light. I crumble the leaves as I need them.

I don't bring many pots of herbs inside — I don't have a lot of success growing them indoors (probably because I'm gone so much they are neglected!), but one pot I bring in is parsley. I keep it in a sunny window, water and lightly fertilize it occasionally, and harvest leaves most of the winter. True, the bottom leaves may turn yellow, but I remove them. Medicinally, since parsley is so rich in nutrients, it isn't surprising that it's used widely as a treatment for anemia, as an aid to digestion, as an antiseptic, as a breath freshener, and much more.

How do I use parsley?

- with most meats
- in dried herb seasoning mixes, such as bouquet garnis
- in rice dishes
- in salads
- in salad dressings
- in vinegars
- in marinades
- in cheese sauces
- in cream sauces
- in butters
- in soups
- with most vegetables (carrots, potatoes, onions, tomatoes, etc.)
- in bread stuffings
- in stews
- with eggs
- in mayonnaise
- in pesto to replace some of the basil
- with cottage cheese, cream cheese, sour cream
- with fish and seafood, especially with shrimps
- with chicken and turkey
- with pasta dishes
- in appetizers
- in breads, muffins, biscuits

Parsley Recipes

More Than a Sprig of Parsley

Cream of Fresh Mushroom Soup (p. 154) *

Wonderful Rib Eye Roast (p. 340)

Baked Tomatoes Provençal (p. 162) *

Persian Rice (p. 162) *

Buttermilk Batter Bread (p. 324)

Heavenly Lemon Pie (p. 379)

* Recipe contains parsley

Fried Parsley Bundles

Pick parsley — leave stems on. Wash and dry parsley — it **must** be moisture-free. Heat vegetable oil 1 inch deep in a heavy pan. Tie small, short bunches of parsley together with white kitchen string and drop the bundle carefully into the hot fat. When parsley turns bright green (only a few seconds), remove bundle and drain on paper towels. Sprinkle with a little salt and serve immediately.

THIS METHOD WORKS
WELL WITH SAGE ALSO.
DELICIOUS LITTLE APPETIZERS
BEFORE DINNER. CRUNCHY
AND BEAUTIFUL.

Honey — Mustard Dressing

1¼   cups mayonnaise
⅓   cup honey
⅔   cup vegetable oil, not olive oil
1   tablespoon vinegar
2   tablespoons fresh parsley, chopped
2   tablespoons dried onion flakes
2   tablespoons prepared yellow mustard

Combine all ingredients. Cover and refrigerate a day or two before using to blend flavors.
Makes about 2 cups.

HONEY-MUSTARD DRESSINGS
HAVE BEEN THE RAGE
RECENTLY. I DO HOPE THIS
RECIPE DOESN'T GO "OUT OF
STYLE" ANYTIME SOON. IT IS
REALLY GOOD!

YELLOW
MUSTARD

Cream of Fresh Mushroom Soup

¹/₂ pound fresh mushrooms (see below), cleaned and chopped
1   tablespoon onion, finely chopped
¹/₂ to 1 cup cooked ham, diced (optional)
¹/₄ cup butter
¹/₃ cup flour
3¹/₂ cups chicken broth
¹/₂ cup water
¹/₂ teaspoon salt, or more to taste
     Dash of pepper
1   tablespoon fresh parsley, chopped, or 1 teaspoon dried
1   cup half-and-half cream

Sauté mushrooms, onion and ham in butter for 3 or 4 minutes. Stir occasionally. Stir in flour and cook until bubbly. Add broth, water, salt and pepper and cook, stirring constantly, until mixture thickens. Add parsley and half-and-half and heat thoroughly, but do not boil. Serves 5 or 6.

---

some thoughts on
MUSHROOMS

Regular grocery store button mushrooms are of course fine, but a combination of varieties is really good in this soup. Some varieties to consider are:

1. Cepes or Porcini — a large mushroom that is wonderful grilled.

2. Oyster — these grow on or under trees. Mild-tasting.

3. Portobello — superb for grilling or broiling. They are very large, dark in color and absolutely delicious.

4. Cremini — related to the button mushroom but darker in color and more flavorful.

5. Shiitake — native to Japan. Very heavy mushroom flavor, especially good in soups.

6. Morels — there is no mushroom in America (the French have their truffles) better than the fresh morel. We know spring has indeed arrived when we find the morel in our woods. The pointed top looks like a honey comb and it's golden brown in color.

Turkey-Apple Salad

2   small tart apples, washed but not peeled
8   cups (or the meat from a breast) cooked turkey, cut into $\frac{1}{2}$-inch cubes
1   cup celery, finely chopped
$\frac{1}{2}$ cup green onions, finely chopped
$\frac{2}{3}$ cup toasted pecans*, coarsely chopped
6   slices bacon, fried crisp, drained and crumbled
3   tablespoons fresh Italian parsley, chopped and divided
     Maple-Mustard Mayonnaise (recipe follows)
     Lettuce leaves

Cut apples into thin slices. Place apples, turkey, celery, green onions, pecans, bacon and 2 tablespoons parsley in a large bowl. Mix gently. Set aside.

Maple-Mustard Mayonnaise

1   cup light or regular mayonnaise
$\frac{1}{4}$ cup Dijon mustard (grainy)
$\frac{1}{4}$ cup maple syrup
2   teaspoons prepared horseradish

Combine dressing ingredients in a small bowl. Blend well. Dressing can be made a day or two ahead of time. Cover and refrigerate. When ready to serve, pour dressing over salad. Add salt and pepper to taste and mix well. Line a large bowl with lettuce leaves. Mound salad in the middle and sprinkle remaining 1 tablespoon of parsley on top.

To toast pecans, place pecans in a medium skillet over medium-high heat. Shake skillet while toasting nuts 5 minutes or so to lightly brown them. Let nuts cool, chop and add to salad.

THIS GOOD SALAD RECIPE WAS SENT TO ME BY A FRIEND IN ILLINOIS. SHE RAVED ABOUT THE DRESSING FOR THE SALAD. I COOKED A TURKEY BREAST FOR THE RECIPE AND SERVED THE SALAD TO 8. EVERYONE LOVED IT. AND YES, THE DRESSING IS WONDERFUL.

Oven Beef Stew with Fresh Parsley

$1^1/_2$ to 2 pounds chuck roast, cut into 1-inch chunks

2 medium onions, cut into chunks

3 medium potatoes, peeled and cut into chunks

4 or 5 medium carrots, scraped and cut into chunks

1 clove garlic, minced

1 $14^1/_2$-ounce can beef broth

1 cup dry red wine or water

2 tablespoons tomato paste

1 large bay leaf

2 or 3 whole cloves

Salt and pepper

1 10-ounce package frozen peas

$^1/_2$ cup fresh parsley, finely chopped

Place meat, prepared vegetables and garlic in a large casserole with a tight-fitting lid. Pour beef broth and wine or water over all. Add tomato paste, bay leaf, cloves, salt and pepper and stir gently. Cover casserole with the lid. Place casserole in a 300° oven for $2^1/_2$ to 3 hours, or a 275° oven for 3 to 4 hours. If possible, check stew occasionally and add more broth, wine or water if necessary. About $^1/_2$ hour before serving, remove and discard the bay leaf. Stir in the frozen peas and add more liquid, if necessary. Re-cover and continue baking for about 30 minutes. Just before serving, stir in the chopped parsley. Serves 6 to 8.

Italian Meat Loaf

2 slices rye bread
2 slices firm white bread
1 cup water
1 pound lean ground beef
1 small onion, finely chopped
1 egg, slightly beaten
3 tablespoons Parmesan cheese, grated
2 tablespoons fresh parsley, minced
1 teaspoon salt
1/4 teaspoon pepper
1 8-ounce can tomato sauce
1 teaspoon dried oregano, crumbled

REMEMBER THIS RECIPE WHEN YOU HAVE A COUPLE OF LEFT-OVER SLICES OF RYE BREAD. THIS MEAT LOAF GOES TOGETHER QUICKLY AND IS DELICIOUS.

Grease a 9x5-inch loaf pan. Place breads in a large bowl. Pour 1 cup water over bread and let soak for 5 minutes. Drain off excess water. Mash bread finely with your fingers. Add beef, onion, egg, cheese, parsley, salt and pepper. Mix well. Place in greased pan. Cover and refrigerate if not baking now. Remove meat loaf from refrigerator 45 minutes before baking. Uncover meat loaf and bake at 375° for 30 to 40 minutes. Combine tomato sauce and oregano. Pour over meat loaf and bake another 15 to 20 minutes. Let stand a few minutes, then serve. Serves 4. Recipe can easily be doubled.

Lemon-Parsley Beef Roast

1   5- to 6-pound best quality beef roast (a rib-eye roast is best)
1/2 cup fresh parsley, finely chopped
1   tablespoon olive oil
4   cloves garlic, minced
1   teaspoon fresh lemon peel, grated (no white)
1   teaspoon salt
1/4 teaspoon pepper

Place roast on a rack in a shallow roasting pan. Combine parsley, olive oil, garlic, lemon zest, salt and pepper. Press this mixture evenly over the roast. Insert a meat thermometer. Do not add water. Do not cover. Roast at 325° for medium, or 155° on the thermometer. For rare, roast to 135° on the thermometer. The roast will continue to bake for about 5 minutes after it's out of the oven. Remove roast from the oven. Tent with foil and let stand for 15 minutes. Carve roast into thin slices. Serves 8 to 10.

THE SEASONING MIXTURE FOR THIS ROAST IS SUPERB. IT WOULD BE EQUALLY GOOD ON A PORK ROAST.

Ham and Cheese Frittata

2   tablespoons butter or margarine
1/2 cup fresh mushrooms, cleaned and sliced
1/2 cup sweet red pepper, seeded and chopped
1/4 cup green onions, sliced
6   eggs
2   tablespoons water
1/2 cup cooked ham, diced
1   tablespoon fresh parsley, finely chopped
1   cup cheddar cheese, shredded

In a skillet, melt butter over medium heat. Sauté mushrooms, pepper and onion until tender. Set aside. In a mixing bowl, beat eggs with water until foamy. Stir in the diced ham and the chopped parsley. Pour egg-ham mixture over mushroom mixture. Do not stir. Cook over medium heat until eggs are set on the bottom. Lift edges of frittata to allow any uncooked egg to flow underneath. Cover and cook over low heat until the eggs are set, about 3 minutes. Sprinkle with cheese. Cut into 4 wedges and serve immediately.

A FRITTATA IS THE ITALIAN VERSION OF AN OMELETTE. THE MAIN DIFFERENCE BETWEEN THE TWO — THE FRITTATA HAS THE FILLING INGREDIENTS MIXED INTO THE EGGS BEFORE THEY ARE COOKED. THEN THE FRITTATA IS OFTEN FINISHED IN THE OVEN. THE OMELETTE IS USUALLY COOKED, THE FILLING ADDED ON TOP AND THE OMELETTE FOLDED OVER THE FILLING. REGARDLESS OF WHETHER IT'S AN OMELETTE OR A FRITTATA, HERE IS A GOOD "EGG" DISH.

Chicken Fettuccine Alfredo

1 12-ounce package fettuccine
1 tablespoon canola or olive oil
4 4-ounce boneless, skinless chicken breasts, cut into strips
$1/2$ cup onion, chopped
1 teaspoon minced garlic
1 cup dry white wine
2 tablespoons chicken base (look for this in the herbs and spices section of your grocery)
3 cups heavy cream, or 3 cups evaporated skim milk
1 pound grated Parmesan cheese
$1/2$ teaspoon pepper
$1/4$ cup fresh Italian flat leaf parsley, chopped

Cook pasta in a large pot of boiling water.* Cook according to package directions.
When pasta reaches al dente stage, remove pan from heat; drain pasta. Place pasta back
in cooking pot. Cover to keep warm. Add oil to a large skillet. Add chicken strips and
brown quickly on all sides, about 2 minutes per side. Do not overcook. Remove chicken
and place it in the pot with the pasta. Cover pot again. To the same skillet, add onion and
garlic and sauté until tender. Reduce heat to low and stir in the wine. Add chicken base
and simmer 1 minute. Stir in cream or milk. Add Parmesan cheese, pepper and fresh
parsley. Simmer 2 minutes, stirring constantly. Pour hot sauce over pasta and chicken.
Quickly toss to coat pasta. Serve immediately to 4 people.

* If desired, add a teaspoon of olive oil to the boiling water. Helps to keep pot from boiling over and
  helps to keep pasta from sticking. The purist will tell you **not** to do this — the sauce won't adhere
  to the pasta as well.

impressions of
THE MILANO INN

There is an old, but wonderful Italian restaurant in Indianapolis called The Milano Inn.
The walls are decorated with World War I murals, painted by a man in exchange for room
and board. A true Sunday treat is to attend a matinée performance at the Indiana Repertory
Theater, then hustle off to the Milano Inn for dinner, especially a dinner that includes their
Chicken Fettuccine Alfredo. It is very, very rich, so you may want to share with a friend.
Above is a slightly adapted recipe.

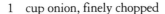

Sensational Seafood Casserole

1   cup onion, finely chopped
1   cup celery, finely chopped
2   cloves garlic, finely chopped
1   stick butter or margarine
1   $10^{1}/_{2}$-ounce can cream of mushroom soup
1   $10^{1}/_{2}$-ounce can cheddar cheese soup
1   4-ounce jar diced pimiento
4   cups seafood (shrimp, crab, lobster or, better yet, a combination)
1   teaspoon salt
2   tablespoons fresh parsley, chopped
2   tablespoons fresh green onion-tops, chopped
2   cups cooked white rice
$^{1}/_{2}$ cup soft bread crumbs
$^{1}/_{3}$ cup almonds, sliced
1   to 2 tablespoons butter, melted

I LOVE THIS RECIPE FOR
PARTIES BECAUSE IT CAN BE
MADE AHEAD OF TIME AND
REFRIGERATED, IT IS
PRACTICALLY A MEAL IN ONE
DISH, AND IT IS DELICIOUS. I
OFTEN SERVE THIS FOR
CHRISTMAS BUFFETS —
IT'S A BIG HIT.

Cook onion, celery and garlic to the 1 stick butter until tender. Add soups, pimiento, seafood, salt, parsley and onion tops. Simmer for a couple of minutes, stirring constantly. Add rice and stir. Pour into a 13x9x2-inch greased casserole. Top with bread crumbs and almonds. Drizzle melted butter over the top. Cover and refrigerate if not baking now. Bake casserole (let come to room temperature first) at 325° for 30 to 45 minutes, or until hot and bubbly. Serves 8 to 10.

Baked Cheddar Fondue

11 ¹/₂-inch-thick slices of French bread
   Softened butter
1 medium onion, coarsely chopped
2 green onions with tops, finely chopped
¹/₄ cup fresh parsley, finely chopped
2 teaspoons fresh thyme, chopped, or ¹/₂ teaspoon dried
2 teaspoons fresh basil, chopped, or ¹/₂ teaspoon dried
¹/₂ pound sharp cheddar cheese, coarsely grated
4 eggs
2¹/₂ cups milk
2 tablespoons Dijon mustard
1 teaspoon Worcestershire sauce
   Dash of Tabasco sauce
¹/₂ teaspoon salt

Spread 10 slices of bread with butter and cut into 1-inch cubes. Place half the bread cubes in a greased 2-quart soufflé dish. Sprinkle with half the vegetables, half the herbs and half the cheese. Repeat with second half of ingredients. Butter and cube the last slice of bread and mound in the center. Beat eggs with milk, mustard, Worcestershire, Tabasco and salt. Pour over mixture in casserole. Refrigerate overnight. Remove from refrigerator and let stand at room temperature for 45 minutes. Bake at 350° for 1 hour. Serve immediately. Serves 4 to 6.

THIS IS A WONDERFUL DISH TO
SERVE FOR BRUNCH OR SUPPER.
SERVE WITH BACON, HAM OR
CANADIAN BACON, A FRUIT
DESSERT AND MUFFINS.

Parsley Butter

1 cup unsalted butter, softened
1 cup fresh parsley leaves, finely chopped
  Fresh grated black pepper to taste
1 tablespoon fresh lemon juice
1 or 2 cloves garlic, minced

Combine all ingredients thoroughly. Cover tightly and refrigerate up to 2 weeks. To freeze, wrap butter very well and freeze. Good for several weeks. Let thaw in the refrigerator, if possible, before using. Use this butter with meat, fish, chicken, bread or vegetables.

THIS BUTTER CAN BE MADE
YEAR-ROUND BECAUSE PARSLEY
IS AVAILABLE NEARLY
EVERYWHERE YEAR-ROUND.

Persian Rice

2 tablespoon butter
1¹/₃ cups uncooked white rice
1 teaspoon salt
³/₄ cup light raisins
2 cups chicken broth
1 cup orange juice
¹/₂ teaspoon orange rind, grated
1 tablespoon fresh parsley, chopped
¹/₄ cup toasted slivered almonds

Melt butter. Add rice. Cook, stirring constantly until rice is lightly browned. Add salt, raisins, chicken broth and orange juice. Bring to a boil. Reduce heat. Cover and simmer 20 minutes, stirring occasionally. Remove from heat. Let stand, covered, 5 minutes. Stir in the orange rind, the parsley and the almonds. Serves 6 or 8.

Baked Tomatoes Provençal

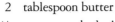

4 large tomatoes, each sliced into 4 equal slices
³/₄ teaspoon salt, divided
3 slices white bread, torn into pieces
¹/₄ cup Parmesan cheese, grated
2 tablespoons fresh parley, chopped
1 tablespoon olive oil
1 clove garlic, finely chopped
1¹/₂ teaspoons fresh oregano, chopped, or ¹/₂ teaspoon dried
¹/₂ teaspoon pepper

Place tomato slices in a single layer on a large, ungreased baking sheet with sides. Sprinkle slices with ¹/₂ teaspoon salt. Place bread in food processor and pulse on/off to form soft fine crumbs. Combine bread crumbs, Parmesan cheese, parsley, olive oil, garlic, oregano, pepper and remaining ¹/₄ teaspoon salt in a small bowl. Sprinkle evenly over the tomato slices. Bake at 475° for 15 minutes or until crumb topping is golden brown. Serve warm. Serves 8.

Glazed Carrots with Fresh Parsley

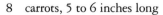

8   carrots, 5 to 6 inches long
4   tablespoons butter
2   tablespoons honey
1/4 teaspoon grated orange rind (no white)
1   tablespoon orange juice
1   tablespoon brown sugar
1   tablespoon fresh parsley, chopped

Clean carrots and boil them until they are tender. Do not overcook. Drain and set aside.
Melt butter in a small skillet. Add honey, orange rind, orange juice and brown sugar.
Blend well. Add the carrots and cook gently over low heat until well glazed. Shake skillet
to glaze carrots evenly. Sprinkle carrots with parsley. Serves 4.

THE HONEY-ORANGE
GLAZE ON THESE CARROTS IS
REALLY SPECIAL. YOU WON'T
HAVE TROUBLE GETTING
THE CHILDREN TO EAT
THESE CARROTS!

Garlic and Parsley Red Wine Vinegar

3¹/₂ cups red wine vinegar
6   cloves garlic, peeled and cut in half
2   large sprigs fresh parsley
1   bay leaf
10 whole peppercorns
¹/₂ teaspoon crushed red pepper flakes

Scald a 1-quart bottle with a tight-fitting top. Let bottle dry completely. Heat vinegar in
a medium saucepan, just to boiling. Let cool slightly, then pour into the bottle. Add
garlic, parsley, bay leaf, peppercorns and pepper flakes. Let cool. Seal bottle with cork or a
rubber gasket — no metal. Let stand at room temperature for 2 to 3 weeks, shaking
occasionally. Strain and discard herbs and spices.

AN UNBELIEVABLY GOOD
VINEGAR AND THE TASTE AND
AROMA OF PARSLEY ARE
DOMINANT. MAKE GREAT
SALAD DRESSINGS AND
MARINADES WITH THIS
VINEGAR. ANYTIME ONE OF
YOUR RECIPES CALLS FOR
DE-GLAZING THE PAN, REACH
FOR THIS VINEGAR.

Rosemary

ROSMARINUS OFFICINALIS

Rosemary

ROSMARINUS OFFICINALIS

Rosemary, wonderful rosemary. It is the herb of remembrance. It is an important wedding herb — it is the emblem of fidelity. Every bride should carry a sprig tucked into her bouquet. Wreaths of pliable rosemary sprigs make delightful headdresses for bridesmaids. But rosemary is especially an herb for Christmas. More about that later. ❦ In Latin, rosemary means "dew of the sea," so it is not surprising it is native to the misty hills surrounding the Mediterranean Sea. I have seen it in Spain, France, and Italy growing six feet tall and used as shrubbery around people's homes. I have seen it in parts of what used to be called Yugoslavia where it was nearly weedlike. It was everywhere! And of course, rosemary does well in California and other southwestern states. Obviously in these climates, rosemary is a perennial. In my Indiana garden, I treat it as an annual. It seldom reaches great heights, but I can count on a new plant being about 2 feet tall by the end of summer. Even the newer varieties developed for colder climates won't make it on the cold and windy hill I live on. ❦ Rosemary does especially well for me in containers. I like to use soilless mix or a mixture of potting soil and soilless mix in the pots. Give the pot good drainage and as the plant grows, keep placing it in a larger pot. It seems to love to have plenty of room. I water and lightly fertilize my rosemary plants frequently. Never overfertilize because that could lead to interfering with the volatile oil of the plant, but I am yet to be convinced that herbs don't like a shot of fertilizer once in a while! They do. ❦ When there is a threat of frost, I gather the pots I can't bear to see freeze and take them to a friend who has a greenhouse. It is worth the price of a gift certificate to be able to go back in April and bring home my wonderful rosemaries! ❦ Rosemary is woody-stemmed, pinelike scented, with needlelike leaves. Most varieties have blue flowers. But I have seen the "Alba" variety, which blooms white, and even a pink blooming variety called "Majorca Pink." The prostrate form is gorgeous in large pots or in hanging baskets. ❦ Named here are a few varieties I particularly like. 1. *R.o.* **'Arp'** — said to be hardy to -10°F. Has very pale blue flowers. Grows as much as 4 feet tall. For me, this is the best variety to bring indoors. It isn't quite as fussy and difficult to keep alive indoors as most of the others are. 2. *R.o.* **'Blue Spire'** — grows 2 feet tall with very beautiful dark blue flowers. 3. *R.o.* **'Gorizia'** — I have only seen this variety from Italy for sale in one place — Nik Alwerdt's Garden in Altamont, Illinois. The leaves on this plant are twice the size of common rosemary leaves. It's an interesting plant to add to your rosemary collection. 4. *R.o.* **'Huntington Carpet'** — a beautiful prostrate form that blooms almost constantly in warm weather or in the greenhouse. The blooms are medium blue. To see this plant in bloom is incredible! 5. *R.o.* **'Majorca Pink'** — grows about 2 feet tall and has lovely pink flowers. 6. *R.o.* **'Lockewood de Forest'** — a creeping prostrate variety that is a vigorous grower. Has beautiful soft blue flowers. 7. *R.o.* **'Shish-Kabob'** — a rare form from California growing straight up. Named because the heavy woody stems make good kabob holders. 8. *R.o.* **'Alba'** — this 4 foot plant has wide leaves.

It is a vigorous grower with white flowers. 9. *R.o.* '**Tuscan Blue**' — this may become your favorite rosemary. It reaches 4 feet in height, has dark blue flowers, has large fat leaves, and grows like mad! It also has a very favorable pine aroma. Wonderful to cook with. 10. *R.o.* '**Joyce DiBaggio**' often sold as Golden Rain — this plant has beautiful golden foliage. It can grow to 4 or 5 feet tall. ❦ Topiaries or pots of rosemary are special for Christmas time. The aroma mingles with the pine and other scents of Christmas — it belongs. It has many significant symbolisms with Christmas and religion. A legend says that when Mary draped her blue cloak over a white-blooming rosemary bush during the flight into Egypt, the rosemary has bloomed the color of her cloak ever since. It is also believed to be one of the manger herbs. I have found no verification of this, but it seems likely considering the part of the world where the Child was born. ❦ Medicinally, rosemary is said to be good for arthritis and rheumatism. A strong brew of rosemary and water is said to be a good gargle for a sore throat. ❦ Rosemary dries easily for culinary use and retains its taste and aroma for a very long time. I hang bunches of rosemary upside down in a brown grocery bag, poke a few holes in the bag, tie the bag top and stems together, and set the bag in a cool, dark place for 10 to 14 days. Then the leaves are ready to strip and store whole in glass or plastic containers out of heat and light. ❦ A discussion of rosemary would not be complete without bringing in the culinary aspect. Rosemary is a delicious but powerful herb to be used sparingly. I like it in hearty dishes like stews, marinades, and red meat dishes, but it is wonderful with chicken also. You'll find it in many of my recipes, not only in this chapter, but throughout the book. ❦

How do I use rosemary?

- with chicken and turkey
- with lamb, pork, beef
- with coarse fish, such as cod or haddock
- with salmon
- in hearty stews
- in egg dishes
- with potatoes and some green vegetables, especially spinach and peas; also with squash, eggplant and mushrooms
- with lemons, limes, oranges, grapefruit, pineapple
- in soups
- on or in breads
- on or in pizza dough
- in cookies
- in drinks and punches
- in tea
- in salad dressings
- in marinades
- in olive oil
- with dried tomatoes
- in honey
- with walnuts
- with cheese, such as mozzarella
- in vinegars
- in mustards
- in butters
- in bouquet garnis
- in herbal seasoning mixes
- with garlic

MENU

*A Rosemary Affair
to Remember*

Broiled Rosemary-Skewered Pineapple Kabobs (p. 182) *

Green Salad with Bleu Cheese-Sour Cream Dressing (p. 318)

Pork Tenderloin with Orange-Rosemary Butter (p. 177) *

Fresh Asparagus or other green vegetable

Walnut Bread (p. 325)

Rosemary Lemonade (p. 173) *

Vanilla Ice Cream with Brandied Pear Sauce (p. 403)

Rosemary Cookies (p. 181) *

* Recipe contains rosemary

Rosemary Walnuts

- 2 cups blanched, toasted English walnut halves or large pieces
- 3 tablespoons extra virgin olive oil
- 2 teaspoons dried rosemary, slightly crushed
- $^1/_2$ to 1 teaspoon sea salt, to your taste (or other coarse salt)
- $^1/_2$ teaspoon ground red pepper

Drop shelled walnuts into boiling water. Cook 2 minutes after water returns to a boil. Drain nuts in a colander. Rinse well with cold water. Spread nuts on paper towels. Let dry. Spread dried nuts on a baking sheet and toast in a 350° oven for 10 or 12 minutes, stirring once or twice.

Line a large baking sheet with foil. Gently heat olive oil, rosemary, salt and red pepper in a small pan, stirring to mix well. Spread nuts on the baking sheet. Pour the oil mixture over them and stir gently to coat all the nuts evenly. Toast in a 350° oven for 10 to 15 minutes, stirring once or twice. Cool. If storing nuts, wrap and refrigerate. To reheat, place in a 350° oven for about 5 minutes. Best if served slightly warm. If you have any left over (doubtful), toss a few in your green salad. Makes 12 or more appetizer servings.

BLANCHING, THEN TOASTING, WALNUTS BRINGS OUT THE BEST IN THIS VERSATILE NUT. THAT DYNAMIC DUO OF OLIVE OIL AND ROSEMARY SHOWS UP AGAIN IN THIS RECIPE. THESE ARE GREAT APPETIZER MUNCHIES.

Rosemary Lemonade

Wash a handful (about 1 cup) of fresh **rosemary leaves** and tender stems. Place in a medium-size pan. Add **water** to cover and bring to a boil. Turn off heat, cover pan and let mixture cool completely. Discard rosemary and strain liquid through a coffee filter. This mixture will be grassy green and not very pretty! Make your favorite **lemonade** (real or otherwise), adding the steeped rosemary water a little at a time to your taste. Serve with fresh **lemon slices** and small sprigs of **fresh rosemary**. Any leftover rosemary water can be refrigerated to use within a few days. This is also a great seasoner for hot tea, cold tea or punches. It's potent, so go slowly and don't overdo.

ROSEMARY AND LEMONS COMPLIMENT EACH OTHER, AS THEY DO IN THIS REFRESHING SUMMER DRINK.

Red Wine Vinegar with Rosemary and Garlic

6 to 10 sprigs fresh rosemary, each about 6 inches long
1 quart red wine vinegar
1 large clove garlic, coarsely chopped

Wash and pat dry the rosemary sprigs. Adjust the rosemary flavor by adding more or less rosemary. Heat vinegar to almost a boil. Sterilize a fairly large glass or plastic jar. Pour hot vinegar over garlic and rosemary. Let cool. Cover with a nonmetallic lid. Set in a cool dark place for about 3 weeks. Discard herb and garlic. Strain vinegar through a coffee filter into a sterilized bottle. Seal or cork. Makes 1 quart.

Butterflied Leg of Lamb with Rosemary

2 cloves garlic, finely minced
2 tablespoons fresh rosemary, minced
2 tablespoons olive oil
4 teaspoons white wine vinegar
4 teaspoons Dijon mustard
1 teaspoon salt
   Butterflied leg of lamb (ask your butcher to do this)
   Fresh ground black pepper

This is great either on the grill or baked in a hot oven. Line a jellyroll pan with foil. Combine garlic, rosemary, oil, vinegar, mustard and salt in a small bowl. Rub over the entire surface of lamb. Best if this is done early in morning before grilling that evening. Cover and refrigerate. About 1 hour before grilling or baking, take lamb out of the refrigerator. Place lamb on grill or baking sheet and sprinkle with pepper. Grill or bake at 450° until a meat thermometer registers 120° for rare, or about 35 to 40 minutes. Roast longer if desired, but don't overcook. Let rest a few minutes before slicing. Serves 6 to 8.

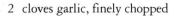

Grilled Rosemary Chicken

2 cloves garlic, finely chopped

¹/₂ cup olive oil

2 tablespoons fresh lemon juice

2 tablespoons balsamic or red wine vinegar

1¹/₂ tablespoons Worcestershire sauce

1 tablespoon dried rosemary, or 2 tablespoons fresh

2 teaspoons Dijon mustard

1 teaspoon salt

1 teaspoon dried basil, or 1 tablespoon fresh

1 teaspoon crushed red pepper flakes

2 frying chickens, cut into serving pieces

Combine all ingredients except chicken pieces. Mix well. Place chicken pieces in a large plastic bag. Pour marinade over chicken. Seal bag. Refrigerate for 2 or 3 hours. Grill or broil chicken until juices run clear, about 15 minutes per side. You may find it takes a little more time or a little less. Just don't overcook. Serves 6 to 8.

COOK THIS ON THE GRILL
OR UNDER THE BROILER.
EITHER WAY, IT'S SPLENDID.

Roast Chicken with Rosemary and Lemon

1 6-pound roasting chicken, or two 3-pound whole fryers
  Salt and pepper
1/2 cup extra virgin olive oil
3 large cloves garlic, coarsely chopped
8 or 10 sprigs of rosemary, 6 inches long
2 lemons, thinly sliced
  Fresh rosemary sprigs for garnish

Prepare chicken. Remove giblets and wash chicken inside and out. Pat skin dry with paper towels. Salt and pepper cavity and outside of bird. Place chicken in a large, shallow pan. Set aside.

Heat olive oil over medium-high heat. Add garlic and rosemary and cook until rosemary is crisp, 2 or 3 minutes. Remove and discard rosemary and garlic pieces and let oil cool. Rub about half the oil over surface of chicken. Roast in a 425° oven about 20 minutes.

Reduce oven heat to 350°. Remove pan from oven and rub more rosemary-garlic oil over the chicken. Scatter lemon slices over the chicken and return chicken to oven. Continue to roast about 45 more minutes or until a meat thermometer registers 160°. Baste a time or two with pan drippings during the last roasting period. Sprinkle a little chopped fresh rosemary over the chicken the last 5 minutes of roasting time. Can you imagine how your kitchen smells by now?!

Carve chicken. Spoon some of the drippings around chicken, if desired. Serve with fresh lemon slices and fresh rosemary sprigs as garnish. Will serve 6.

HERE IS ROAST CHICKEN AT ITS BEST. THE MEAT IS JUICY AND SUCCULENT AND FLAVORED JUST RIGHT WITH ROSEMARY AND A HINT OF LEMON. THE BEST CHICKEN FOR THIS RECIPE IS A ROASTING CHICKEN, BUT I HAVE USED 2 THREE-POUND FRYERS WITH SUCCESS. A MARVELOUS CHICKEN RECIPE.

Pork Tenderloin with Orange-Rosemary Butter

Make the butter first. Combine 1 stick softened **butter**, 2 tablespoons frozen **orange juice concentrate**, 1 tablespoon grated **orange peel**, 1½ tablespoons fresh **rosemary**, finely chopped (or 2 teaspoons crushed dried rosemary), and a little **salt** and **pepper**. Best if made a day or two ahead of use to blend flavors. Refrigerate butter until ready to use, but bring to room temperature before using.

THE ORANGE-ROSEMARY BUTTER CAN BE USED WITH OTHER MEATS. I HAVE BRUSHED IT ON PORK CHOPS OR STEAKS HOT OFF THE GRILL. IT'S WONDERFUL.

4	pork tenderloins (12 to 14 ounces each)
16	thin slivers of orange peel
16	thin slivers of garlic
	Salt and pepper
1	cup canned chicken broth

With a sharp knife, make 8 slits in each tenderloin, about ½ inch to ¾ inch deep. Alternately insert orange and garlic slivers into each slit.

Melt 2 or 3 tablespoons of the orange-rosemary butter in a large skillet. Brown tenderloins evenly, about 5 to 8 minutes. Place tenderloins on a rack in a roasting pan. Pour pan drippings into the roaster. Season meat with a little salt and pepper and drizzle about 1 teaspoon of melted orange-rosemary butter over each tenderloin. Add broth to pan. Roast, uncovered, at 350° for 20 minutes. Drizzle another teaspoon of melted butter over each tenderloin, return to oven and bake 15 or 20 minutes more, or to 155° on a meat thermometer. Do not overbake. If roasted properly, this meat will melt in your mouth! Place loins on a large platter, cover with foil and let stand for 10 minutes. Pour pan juices into a small saucepan, bring to a boil and quickly reduce by half. Stir remaining orange-rosemary butter into liquid and simmer for about 3 minutes, stirring constantly. To serve, slice pork and drizzle the sauce over the slices. This is fantastic. Serves 8.

Rosemary Brushes

Tie three 6-inch sprigs of rosemary together and use as a basting brush for barbecue sauce, melted butter and marinades. Adds lots of flavor to the liquid.

Bruschetta with Rosemary and Mozzarella

1	1-pound loaf Italian crusty bread
$1/3$	cup olive oil
1	clove garlic, finely minced
$1/2$	teaspoon salt
$1/4$	teaspoon coarsely ground black pepper
$1/2$	cup green onions, thinly sliced
$3/4$	cup chopped tomato
1	tablespoon chopped fresh rosemary
$1 1/2$	cups shredded low-moisture part-skim milk mozzarella cheese

Cut bread in half lengthwise. Place cut sides up on a foil-lined baking sheet. Combine oil, garlic, salt and pepper. Drizzle over bread. Sprinkle with green onions, tomato and rosemary. Top with mozzarella cheese. Bake at 500° in upper half of the oven for 5 to 7 minutes, or until cheese melts and bread edges are brown. Cut into 1-inch serving pieces. Delicious and easy. Everyone will rave about this bread!

Focaccia

The Dough

2 ¼   cups flour
      Dash of salt
¼   cup olive oil
1   package dry yeast, dissolved in ¼ cup warm water
½   to ¾ cup warm water

In food processor or electric mixer, combine flour and salt. With processor running, add olive oil slowly. Add the yeast dissolved in the ¼ cup water. Start adding the ½ to ¾ cup warm water. Add until dough forms a ball and leaves the sides of the processor bowl. Continue to mix only until ball is soft and satiny. Place dough in a lightly greased bowl. Cover and let rise for about 1½ hours. Punch down dough and roll into two 9-inch rounds or into a 12-inch round for a pizza pan. Grease pan or pans and place dough in pans. Now make the topping.

Rosemary and Onion Topping

1   large onion, chopped or thinly sliced
1   to 2 teaspoons dried rosemary, crushed
3   tablespoons olive oil

In a skillet, cook onion and rosemary in the olive oil until onion is tender, but do not brown. With fingertips, press indentations every inch or so in the dough round or rounds. Top dough evenly with the onion-rosemary mixture. Cover and let rise until doubled, about 30 minutes. Bake in a 375° oven for 15 to 20 minutes. Cool and serve in wedges or squares.

Another Rosemary Topping Minus the Onion

      Olive oil
      Coarsely ground salt
¼   cup fresh rosemary leaves, chopped
2   or 3 cloves garlic, finely chopped

Make the dough. Roll and fill well-greased (with olive oil) pan or pans. Drizzle olive oil over the dough in the pans — two tablespoons per 9-inch pan. Sprinkle lightly with coarsely ground salt. Mix the rosemary and chopped garlic together. Push the mixture into the dough, making indentations all over the surface. Pierce dough all over with a fork. Cover pans with plastic wrap and let rise until doubled, about 1 hour. Bake in a 400° oven about 25 minutes. Remove from oven. Slice and serve warm. Wonderful with pasta.

FOCACCIA IS THE TRUE FLAT BREAD OF ITALY. IT IS A SLIGHTLY CHEWY, FLAT, BUT PUFFY, BREAD REMINISCENT OF PIZZA. A NICE CHANGE FROM ORDINARY ITALIAN BREAD. FOCACCIA (FO-KA-CHA) IS DEFINITELY A SOUTHERN ITALIAN CONCOCTION. ALL FOCACCIA IS FLAVORED WITH OLIVE OIL AND MOST RECIPES WILL CALL FOR ROSEMARY, BUT OTHER ITALIAN HERBS ALSO CAN BE USED. AFTER THE DOUGH IS MADE, YOU CAN CREATE MANY TOPPINGS TO ADD TO THE DOUGH. ONE OF MY FAVORITES IS THIS ROSEMARY AND ONION MIXTURE.

Rosemary Rye Bread

2 packages active dry yeast

$^{1}/_{2}$ cup warm water

$2^{1}/_{2}$ cups beer, at room temperature

$^{1}/_{2}$ cup shortening

1 cup dark molasses

2 teaspoons salt

1 tablespoon caraway seeds

2 teaspoons chopped rosemary, either fresh or dried

5 cups rye flour

4 cups bread flour

1 egg

1 tablespoon water

Add yeast to warm water. Stir until dissolved. Heat beer until it starts to bubble. Remove from heat and add shortening. Add molasses, salt, caraway seeds and rosemary to beer mixture. Stir. Cool to lukewarm, then stir in the yeast. Mix in rye flour, then bread flour until you can no longer stir the dough with a heavy spoon (may not need all the flour). Turn mass onto a floured board and knead until smooth and elastic, 5 or 6 minutes. Place in a greased bowl and butter or grease top of dough. Cover and let rise in a warm place until doubled, 1 to $1^{1}/_{2}$ hours. On a lightly floured board, knead until smooth. Shape into 2 large round loaves. Slash tops with a sharp knife. Combine the egg with 1 tablespoon water. Brush mixture on top of loaves. Let loaves rise until doubled, 45 minutes to 1 hour. Brush again with the egg mixture. Bake at 350° for 45 minutes or until loaves are baked through and sound hollow when tapped. Makes 2 delicious loaves.

Rosemary Butter

1 cup butter, softened

3 cloves garlic, finely chopped

2 tablespoons chopped fresh rosemary, or 2 teaspoons dried

1 tablespoon chopped fresh Italian parsley, or 1 teaspoon dried (regular curly parsley will do)

2 teaspoons grated lemon peel

Salt and pepper

Combine all ingredients in a mixing bowl. Makes 1 cup.

Pineapple-Rosemary Muffins

- 2 cups flour
- 2 teaspoons baking powder
- $1/2$ teaspoon baking soda
- $1/2$ teaspoon salt
- $1/2$ teaspoon fresh or dried, crumbled rosemary
- $1/2$ cup light brown sugar
- 1 egg
- 1 8-ounce carton sour cream
- 1 8-ounce can crushed pineapple, undrained
- $1/3$ cup shortening, melted
- $1/2$ cup pecans, chopped

Combine flour, baking powder, baking soda, salt, rosemary and brown sugar in a medium bowl. In another bowl, combine the egg, sour cream, pineapple, shortening and nuts. Add second mixture to the flour mixture, but do not overmix. Spoon into greased muffin cups, filling two-thirds full. Bake at 400° for 20 to 25 minutes. Makes about 1 dozen.

Rosemary Cookies

- 1 cup butter
- 1 cup oil
- 1 cup sugar
- 1 cup confectioner's sugar
- 2 eggs
- 1 teaspoon vanilla
- 1 teaspoon baking soda
- 1 teaspoon cream of tartar
- 4 cups flour
- 2 tablespoons chopped fresh rosemary, or 2 teaspoons dried

Combine all ingredients, except rosemary, in mixer bowl. Mix thoroughly. You may need to add a little more flour if dough appears sticky — add a tablespoon at a time. Add rosemary and gently mix into the batter. Form into small balls and place on an ungreased cookie sheet. Flatten with the bottom of a glass dipped in sugar. Bake at 375°. Check after 6 minutes. Turn pan and bake another 2 to 4 minutes until cookies are pale golden brown and firm to the touch. Baking time depends on how large you form the cookies. Makes 6 to 8 dozen.

MOTHER PASSED THIS RECIPE ON TO ME. I HAVE ADDED THE ROSEMARY. IT COMBINES NICELY WITH THE SWEETNESS OF THE PINEAPPLE.

A WONDERFUL COOKIE RECIPE ON ITS OWN. ADD THE CHOPPED ROSEMARY AND IT'S SPECIAL. DO NOT OVERBAKE. THESE COOKIES LITERALLY MELT IN YOUR MOUTH!

Rosemary Steak Rub

1 teaspoon dried crushed rosemary leaves
1¹/₂ teaspoons grated lemon peel
¹/₄ teaspoon dried thyme
¹/₄ teaspoon ground pepper
2 garlic cloves, peeled and minced

Combine all ingredients. Rub over steaks. Grill or broil to desired doneness. Enough to season about 2 pounds of steaks.

Shish Kabob Skewers

Here is a terrific idea for flavorful skewers. Strip the leaves from the woody stems of **rosemary** — you must avoid the new green growth, use only woody stems — and cut into 6- to 8-inch lengths. Soak these stems in **water** or a **citrus fruit juice** for an hour or so. Thread pieces of **meat, vegetables** or **fruit** onto skewers and grill or broil. The rosemary flavor transfers to the food.

Bertha Reppert
AND THE ROSEMARY HOUSE

Bertha Reppert has been writing about herbs for many years. I consider her one of the foremost authorities on herbs today. I have been fortunate to hear Bertha lecture and I love her down-to-earth, homey approach that we all enjoy sitting back and listening to. Bertha, her husband and their four daughters are all involved with the family business — herbs. The world-famous shop, The Rosemary House at 120 S. Market Street, Mechanicsburg, PA 17055, is a treasure trove of every herbal goodie imaginable. When I told Bertha I was writing a chapter about rosemary that included rosemary recipes, I also told her no rosemary chapter would be complete without something from her! She graciously submitted 2 wonderful recipes — Roasted Veggies Rosemary and Rosemary Punch.

Bertha Reppert's Roasted Veggies Rosemary

(Recipe in Bertha's words)

Eggplant, chunked
Sweet potato, chunked
Onion, chunked
Carrot, smaller pieces
Celery, small pieces
White potato, chunked
Zucchini, chunked
Summer squash, chunked

Use your choice of vegetables, cubed, chunked, diced or sliced. Use whatever is available, but use a good variety. Prepare at least 1 cup per person. Makes a lot, but there is shrinkage.

Choose a large baking or roasting pan. Toss veggies with 1 teaspoon **olive oil**, ¹/₂ teaspoon chopped **fresh rosemary** and ¹/₂ **clove garlic**, smashed, **per cup or per person**. Toss and cover the bottom of the pan with the veggies. Do not crowd pan and do not cover pan. They are to be roasted and **not** steamed! They should be crispy and slightly browned. Bake at 400° for about 30 minutes or until done inside and crusted outside. Toss occasionally. Serve about 1 cup per person and garnish with fresh sprigs of rosemary.

Bertha adds that she does not use salt, but it is optional.

Bertha Reppert's Rosemary Punch

IN BERTHA'S WORDS, THIS
PUNCH IS "DELICIOUS AND
REFRESHING! AND NO SUGAR!"

2   cups water
1   cup fresh rosemary, or 1/2 cup dried
1   46-ounce can unsweetened pineapple juice
1   2-liter bottle of lemon-lime soda (7-Up)
1   1-liter bottle of ginger ale

Heat the water and rosemary to a boil. Remove from heat, cover and steep for 30 minutes. Strain and discard rosemary. Chill. Add to chilled juice and sodas. Makes 20 to 25 punch cup servings.

Sage

SALVIA OFFICINALIS

Sage

SALVIA OFFICINALIS AND OTHER VARIETIES

Generally speaking, sages can be divided into two groups — those used for culinary purposes and those used as ornamentals. I will mention two or three of my favorite ornamentals, but my discussion on sage will mainly deal with six culinary sages. Sage is an old-fashioned, long-lasting plant that grows profusely in the Mediterranean area along with so many other herbs. It is the herb of immortality, domestic virtue, and health. There are literally hundreds of varieties of sage throughout the world and sages have been recorded for thousands of years. I have learned a very important thing about my culinary sages — they do not like to stand in water — so be sure to grow sage in well-drained soil and in a sunny location. For me, the hardiest of the culinary sages is the old standby, *Salvia officinalis,* or garden sage. It is a woody-stemmed, hardy perennial that grows $1^{1}/_{2}$ to $2^{1}/_{2}$ feet tall. The leaves are gray-green, long, oval, and rough-textured. The bloom is pale purple. Some say sage should be replaced every 3 or 4 years because the stems get so woody and also the flavor diminishes. I'm sure this is true, but I have had productive sage plants longer than 4 years if I cut out all the dead wood and cut the plant back to half size in early spring. Also in the spring, I either cut through the plant with a spade, or divide it. This encourages new growth. But I agree that when the plant slows down putting on new growth, or just plain isn't as vigorous as it once was, then it's time to replace it. There is a fairly new garden sage called *S. o. 'Berggarten,'* or round leaf sage. This is a terrific plant! It is by far the best culinary sage I cook with. It grows about 1¹/₂ feet tall and stays low to the ground and forms a beautiful mound of round leaves. It seldom blooms (actually none of my Berggarten plants have ever bloomed). The leaves are grayish-silver green, are nearly round, and are also rough-textured. This plant is potent in flavor, but it has become my favorite culinary sage. I have to mulch this sage very well in my Indiana garden. It is not as hardy as the *officinalis* (which usually doesn't get mulched and comes up anyway!), but if you can grow it in your area, you'll love not only how it looks in the garden, but how it tastes in your food! 🖤 Even though the next four sages I will talk about are culinary, I actually grow them for their beautiful foliage or flowers. 1. The sage I like best in this group is ***Salvia elegans*, or pineapple sage** — although it is a tender perennial, I treat it as an annual. Even after considerable mulching, I've never had one live through the winter. Hummingbirds love pineapple sage because of the beautiful red trumpet-shaped flowers that appear in late summer into fall. Bringing hummingbirds to the garden is reason enough to plant pineapple sage! This plant has dark green serrated leaves and grows 3 to 4 feet tall and branches profusely. Many cooks use pineapple sage to flavor drinks and breads, but frankly (in my opinion) the scent and taste are not that pronounced. Perhaps it's my soil or growing conditions. I have friends who grow this plant and rave about the pineapple flavor. At any rate, it's a gorgeous plant that I wouldn't want to do without in my garden. 2. ***S. o. 'purpurea,'* or purple sage** — is also a beauty. It is a tender perennial, but seldom will it winter over for me. It grows 2¹/₂ to 3 feet tall and has lovely purple-green leaves. This is a beautiful border or accent plant in the garden.

3. ***S. o. 'Tri-color,'* or tri-colored sage** — is another beautiful plant. It is a tender

perennial, but again, I've had no luck with it wintering over. I resign myself to buy a new plant (or plants) each spring and enjoy it throughout the growing season. It only gets 15 to 18 inches tall and makes a spectacular border plant with pink, green and pale yellow splotches on the leaves. Set out some pink zinnias behind tri-color sage — gorgeous!

4. The last culinary sage I plant is *S. o. 'Aurea,'* **or golden sage** — It is a tender perennial that grows 12 inches tall. It makes a nice golden mound in the garden. Some of the leaves have green markings. It too seldom comes back for me in the spring, but it is a very interesting and fragrant plant in the herb garden.   Three special ornamental sages I grow are clary sage, Mexican bush sage, and beautiful mealycup sage. 1. *Salvia sclarea*, **or clary sage** — is a biennial plant that grows about 3 feet tall. In order to have one in bloom every summer, be sure to plant a new one each year. This plant has large leaves that are long and wide with serrated edges. The surface is rough and pebbly. In its second summer, clary sage sends up tall spikes with lilac-colored flowers and makes quite a display for a long time. It's a wonderful garden plant. 2. *Salvia leucantha*, **or Mexican bush sage** — is a beautiful big 4-foot-tall plant. It is a tender perennial and therefore doesn't winter well for me. It has long, narrow, silvery-gray leaves on tall stems. Bright purple flowers appear in mid-summer and last for weeks. This is a superb background plant. It is quite spectacular planted in front of a white picket fence. This plant, as well as most sages, prefers lots of sun. 3. One of my favorite cutting flowers for summer bouquets is *Salvia farinacea*, **or commonly called mealycup sage** — I treat this plant as an annual, but occassionally a stray plant or two will come up in the spring. It has dark green, narrow, smooth leaves and grows $1\frac{1}{2}$ to 2 feet tall. The variety I have grown for years and love the best is called 'Victoria.' 'Victoria' has a lovely blue-violet flower head

that starts blooming in June and doesn't quit until a hard freeze knocks it down. Plant in full sun and keep new seedlings moist until they're established, then ignore it — it will thrive in almost any condition. I use this plant in most of my summer flower and herb bouquets. It looks especially good with rosemary, lemon verbena, and scented geraniums. Add some white daisies and pink geraniums and you've created a winner! Sage is supposed to enhance mental powers, hence a "sage" is a wise person. The Latin meaning for sage is "to save" or "to cure." With this in mind, it is easy to see why sage has been such an important medicinal herb. It is used as an aid to digestion. It supposedly is a blood cleanser. It also is used as a disinfectant, a fumigant, and a deodorizer. It has many uses indeed. Sage is very easy to dry. Harvest leaves in late summer or early fall and wash and dry them. I lay the leaves on a clean window screen in a cool, dark room and let them dry naturally for about 2 weeks. Store them in jars or plastic bags, but be sure to store them out of heat and light. I crumble the leaves as I need them. They will stay pungent for a long time. Since sage is a powerful and pungent herb, it must be used sparingly in cooking. A little goes a long way. Many cooks spoil the turkey dressing with too much sage! Sage is particularly used to flavor sausages, stuffings, and cheeses. With the hundreds of varieties of culinary and ornamental sages available to the gardener, you're sure to find a few you'll love to grow and use.

How do I use sage?

- in soups
- in stews
- in breads
- in muffins
- in biscuits
- in bread dressings and stuffings for fish and poultry
- with chicken
- with turkey
- to season vegetables, especially tomatoes, eggplant, carrots, peas, green beans, onions

- in cheese dishes
- in vinegar
- with pork
- with veal
- with beef
- with lamb
- in pâtés
- in egg dishes, especially scrambled eggs and omelettes
- in tea
- in meat sauces and gravies

INDEX

Sage Recipes

MENU

Sage Advice...
Try This Menu

French-Fried Sage Leaves (p. 194) *

Green Salad with Karen's Honey-Mustard Dressing (p. 320)

Autumn Pork Chops with Apples and Sage (p. 196) *

Fresh Corn Pudding (p. 355)

Sour Cream-Sage Bread (p. 201) *

Brown Sugar-Pumpkin Pie (p. 377)

* Recipe contains sage

French-Fried Sage Leaves

Pick unblemished **sage leaves**. Wash and dry. The leaves **must** be dry. Heat **vegetable oil** (not olive oil) at least 1 inch deep in a heavy pan. Drop the sage leaves, a few at a time, into the bubbling oil. Fry only a few seconds until leaves are crisp. Remove from oil and drain on paper towels. Sprinkle with a little salt. Serve immediately.

My Turkey Soup

2	cups diced, cooked turkey
4	cups chicken broth, or part turkey broth if available
$1/4$	cup butter or margarine
2	tablespoons chopped onion
1	teaspoon curry powder
1	cup diced potatoes
$1/2$	cup diced carrots
$1/2$	cup diced celery
	Salt and pepper
1	cup frozen peas
$1/2$	to 1 teaspoon dried, crumbled sage
1	tablespoon dried parsley
2	tablespoons flour
$1/2$	cup water
2	cups half-and-half cream

Combine first 8 ingredients. Salt and pepper to taste. Simmer until vegetables are tender. May need to add more broth. Add peas, sage and parsley. Make a paste with the 2 tablespoons flour and the $1/2$ cup water and slowly add to the simmering soup, stirring vigorously. Slowly add the half-and-half cream. Add more salt and pepper, if necessary. Heat thoroughly, but do not boil. Serves 6.

Mother's Scalloped Chicken

Cover a **whole hen (or 2 fryers)** with salted water. Add an **onion**, a **carrot**, a rib of **celery with leaves** and cook until chicken is tender. Remove chicken from broth and let meat cool. You should have 2 quarts of broth. (Save 1 quart to cook down for the gravy.) Beat 3 **eggs**. Add 1 quart broth (skim fat off top of broth and discard) to the eggs. Tear a 1-pound loaf of **white bread** into small pieces and place them in a large bowl. Season with **salt and pepper**. Dice the cooled chicken and add to the broth. Pour egg-broth mixture over bread and mix gently. Add $^1/_2$ to 1 teaspoon ground **sage** (depending on your taste). Place in a greased 13x9x2-inch pan. Bake at 350° for 1 to 1$^1/_2$ hours. The last 10 to 15 minutes, sprinkle a few **buttered bread crumbs** on top of casserole and return to the oven to brown. Cook down the other quart of broth to $^1/_2$ volume and thicken with a little flour and water to make a thin gravy. Serve in squares and top each square with a ladle of gravy and a sprinkling of chopped fresh **parsley**. Serves 8 to 12 depending on how large you cut the squares.

THIS IS GOOD OLD-FASHIONED COOKING AT ITS BEST. A BIG PAN OF SCALLOPED CHICKEN WAS POPULAR AT CHURCH SUPPERS AND ELECTION DINNERS.

Chicken with Sage

2	oranges
2	lemons
$^1/_4$	cup fresh sage leaves, coarsely chopped
2	tablespoons olive oil
1	teaspoon salt
3	to 3$^1/_2$ pounds chicken (breasts, legs and thighs)
	Fresh sage sprigs for garnish

Grate 1 tablespoon orange peel and 1 tablepoon lemon peel (no white). Squeeze oranges and lemons separately. Set aside. In a large bowl, combine the 2 tablespoons grated peel, 3 tablespoons orange juice and 3 tablespoons lemon juice. Add sage, olive oil and salt. Mix well. Add chicken pieces to juice mixture and coat all pieces with the marinade. Refrigerate 2 or 3 hours. Heat grill* to medium and cook chicken about 20 minutes on first side. Turn and cook about 15 minutes longer. Juices must run clear when pierced with a fork. Garnish completed dish with fresh sage sprigs. Serves 6 to 8.

* Chicken can be broiled, if desired. If broiling, do not place chicken too close to the broiler element.

THERE IS A WONDERFUL ORANGE AND LEMON MARINADE HERE. THIS IS A VERY GOOD DISH FOR A SUMMER MEAL ON THE GRILL.

Autumn Pork Chops with Apples and Sage

PUT A PUMPKIN PIE IN THE
OVEN AND BAKE THESE PORK
CHOPS FOR A MEMORABLE FALL
DINNER. THERE IS A GREAT
PORK AND APPLE FESTIVAL IN
CLINTON, ILLINOIS, EVERY YEAR
IN LATE SEPTEMBER. SOMEONE
GAVE THIS RECIPE TO ME AT
THAT FESTIVAL.

3 tablespoons oil
6 thick pork chops
1/2 teaspoon salt
 Dash of pepper
1/2 teaspoon dried ground or rubbed* sage
2 apples, peeled and sliced
2 tablespoons lemon juice
1 small onion, finely chopped
1/4 cup dark molasses
3 tablespoons flour
3 cups water
1 tablespoon vinegar, or Sage-Caraway Vinegar (see p. 201)

Heat oil in large skillet. Season chops with salt, pepper and sage. Brown chops in hot oil then place them in a large, flat baking dish. Reserve oil. Scatter apple slices over the chops. Sprinkle apples with the lemon juice. Scatter chopped onion over apples. Drizzle molasses over apples. Set aside. Add flour to the fat in the skillet. Cook and stir until flour browns slightly. Add water and stir until gravy thickens. Stir in vinegar and pour over meat and apples. Cover with foil and bake at 350° for 1 hour. Remove foil the last 5 minutes of baking. Serves 6.

*Rubbed sage is sage that has been
ground to a powder.*

Sausage, Sage and Parsley Stuffing

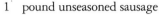

1 pound unseasoned sausage

1 large onion, finely chopped

6 to 8 ounces fresh mushrooms, cleaned and sliced

1 cup celery, sliced

2 apples, peeled and sliced

$^1/_2$ cup walnuts, coarsely chopped

$^1/_2$ cup raisins

3 cups chicken broth

3 eggs, slightly beaten

2 sticks butter or margarine, melted

1 to $1^1/_4$-pound loaf plain firm white bread

2 teaspoons rubbed sage

2 teaspoons dried parsley flakes

Salt and pepper

THIS IS A LONG RECIPE, BUT
TRULY, IT'S NOT DIFFICULT.
ONE OF THE BEST STUFFINGS
I'VE EVER PREPARED.

Sauté sausage. Drain, but leave 2 tablespoons fat in skillet. Sauté onion, mushrooms, celery and apple slices until soft, but not brown. Stir in walnuts and raisins. Add onion-walnut mixture to sausage. Stir to combine. Set aside. Combine chicken broth, eggs and melted butter. Set aside. Cut crusts from bread slices. Cut bread into croutons. Spread croutons on a baking sheet and dry in a 275° oven until lightly browned. Remove from oven. Mix sage and parsley together and sprinkle over the croutons. Place croutons and sausage mixture in a very large mixing bowl. Pour broth mixture over croutons to moisten. Toss and mix well. Season with salt and pepper. Spoon into a lightly greased 13x9x2-inch baking pan. Refrigerate until ready to bake (can be made day before). Heat oven to 350°. Bake 45 minutes or until golden brown. May need to pour a little broth over the top. Toward the end of baking, may need to loosely cover with foil to prevent overbrowning. Serves 10 to 12.

Thanksgiving
IN GRANDMOTHER'S KITCHEN ·

I remember watching my Grandmother and then my Mother put this dressing together on Thanksgiving morning. It couldn't be made ahead of time, because they liked to use the hot turkey broth straight from the oven. If you have ever seen the painting by Doris Lee (I love her style) called "Thanksgiving Morning," I'm sure she was painting my Grandmother Clem's kitchen — women bustling around, children underfoot, pies cooling on the old wooden table, and someone checking the turkey in the wood stove oven. Enough reminiscing — here's the recipe.

Grandma's Sage Dressing for the Turkey

3¹/₂	cups cornbread crumbs
3¹/₂	cups soft bread crumbs
2¹/₂	cups hot turkey or chicken broth
1	cup chopped celery
3	tablespoons chopped onion
¹/₄	cup butter or margarine
1¹/₂	teaspoons salt
2	teaspoons rubbed sage
¹/₂	teaspoon pepper
2	eggs, slightly beaten

Combine both crumbs in a very large bowl. Pour chicken broth over crumbs. Stir well. Sauté celery and onion in butter until tender. Add to crumb mixture and stir well. Stir in remaining ingredients. Spoon into a lightly greased shallow 2-quart baking dish. Cover loosely with foil. Bake at 350° for about 40 minutes. Uncover and bake 5 to 10 minutes more. Enough for 8 servings.

Broccoli-Cheese Soufflé

1   20-ounce package frozen chopped broccoli, thawed and well drained
4   cups cottage cheese
6   tablespoons flour
½   cup melted butter
1   8-ounce package shredded cheddar cheese
¼   teaspoon rubbed sage
    Salt and pepper
6   eggs, slightly beaten

Place broccoli in a large bowl. In another bowl, combine all other ingredients. Gently fold broccoli into egg mixture. Bake in a greased 13x9x2-inch pan at 350° for 1 hour. Can make and refrigerate 1 day before using. If refrigerated, bring to room temperature 30 minutes, then bake as above. Serves 12. Can easily be cut in half to serve 6.

I DON'T OFTEN USE SAGE TO SEASON VEGETABLES, BUT HERE IS ONE RECIPE WHERE IT IS PUT TO GOOD USE. IT ADDS JUST THE RIGHT TOUCH TO THIS BROCCOLI SOUFFLÉ.

Scalloped Cabbage and Cheese

4   cups shredded cabbage
2   tablespoons butter or margarine, melted
1½ tablespoons flour
½   teaspoon salt
1   cup milk
¼   teaspoon ground sage
1   cup shredded cheddar cheese
2   cups soft bread crumbs
¼   cup butter or margarine, melted

Boil cabbage for 5 minutes. Drain well and set aside. Combine 2 tablespoons melted butter, flour and salt in a saucepan. Cook over low heat, stirring constantly, until bubbly. Gradually add milk. Cook, stirring constantly, until smooth and thick. Place a layer of cooked cabbage in the bottom of a greased 1½-quart baking dish. Sprinkle the sage evenly over the cabbage. Sprinkle the cheese over the cabbage. Pour the white sauce over the cheese. Combine bread crumbs and ¼ cup melted butter. Sprinkle crumbs over casserole. Bake at 350° for 30 minutes. Do not brown. Serves 6.

I REALLY LOVE THIS DISH WITH ROAST PORK, OR FRIED CHICKEN, OR EVEN HAMBURGERS. IT IS A GOOD CHANGE OF PACE FROM POTATOES. IT GOES TOGETHER QUICKLY, CAN BE MADE AHEAD OF TIME AND HELD IN THE REFRIGERATOR UNTIL TIME TO BAKE — IT HAS A LOT GOING FOR IT. BUT THE BEST THING ABOUT IT IS IT IS DELICIOUS.

Cheese and Sage Biscuits

2   cups flour
1   tablespoon baking powder
$^1/_2$ teaspoon rubbed sage
1   teaspoon caraway seeds
$^1/_2$ teaspoon salt
$^1/_4$ cup cold butter, cut into small pieces
$^1/_2$ cup grated cheddar cheese
$^2/_3$ cup milk

Use an ungreased cookie sheet. Fit steel blade in the food processor. Combine flour, baking powder, sage, caraway seeds and salt in the work bowl. Add butter and pulse on/off until mixture is crumbly, about 12 or 15 seconds. Add cheese and pulse to blend. With machine running, add milk through feed tube and blend for 5 or 6 seconds only. Do not overmix. Turn dough out onto a floured surface and press into a $^1/_2$-inch-thick circle, working dough as little as possible. Cut out biscuits with a 2-inch cutter. Place on baking sheet and bake at 425° for 10 to 15 minutes, or until brown. Makes 12 wonderful biscuits. Serve hot with butter.

Sour Cream–Sage Bread

4³/₄ cups flour, sifted
2 tablespoons sugar
2 teaspoons salt
1 package active dry yeast
1 cup warm sour cream
6 tablespoons soft butter
1 teaspoon rubbed or ground sage
¹/₂ teaspoon dried parsley
¹/₂ cup warm water (120°)
2 eggs

Combine 1 cup flour, sugar, salt, yeast, sour cream, butter, herbs and water in a large bowl. Beat 2 minutes at medium speed. Add eggs and ¹/₂ cup flour. Beat 2 minutes at high speed. Stir in remainder of flour to make a soft dough. Cover and let rise until doubled, about 45 minutes. Stir down and turn into 2 well-greased 1-quart casserole dishes. Cover and let rise until doubled, about 1 hour. Bake at 375° for 35 minutes. Makes 2 loaves.

Sage–Caraway Vinegar

For 1 quart of vinegar:

1 quart cider vinegar
1 cup cleaned, bruised, chopped fresh sage leaves
1 teaspoon caraway seeds

Heat vinegar in a nonreactive pan to nearly the boiling point. Pour vinegar over the sage leaves and caraway seeds. Let cool, then pour into a sterilized jar. Seal or cork jar and set in a cool, dark place for about 3 weeks to develop flavors. Discard sage leaves. Strain vinegar through a coffee filter into a sterilized bottle. Seal or cork.

AS YOU CAN SEE BY READING OTHER RECIPES, SAGE AND PARSLEY MARRY VERY WELL. SOUR CREAM MAKES THIS BREAD MOIST AND TENDER. IF YOU'RE LOOKING FOR A DELICIOUS QUICK BREAD, BUT MADE WITH YEAST, HERE IS THE RECIPE. IT IS A CASSEROLE BREAD, SO NO NEED TO KNEAD!

SPLASH A LITTLE OF THIS SAVORY VINEGAR OVER A PORK ROAST OR PORK CHOPS. ADD A TABLESPOON OR TWO THE NEXT TIME YOU COOK CABBAGE. USE TO FLAVOR MEAT MARINADES.

Scented Geraniums

PELARGONIUMS

Lynde Hurwart

Scented Geraniums

PELARGONIUMS

When we were in South Africa a few years ago (and before I knew much about herbs), I saw wonderful plants growing wild near the sea. They looked like geraniums, but had insignificant blooms on them, so I thought they surely couldn't be geraniums. When I asked what they were, I was told by everyone I asked they were pelargoniums. That didn't mean much to me at the time, but since then I have come to know and love these fragrant plants as scented geraniums. I have also learned their origin is the Cape of Good Hope, where the Indian and Atlantic Oceans come crashing together, where the climate is remarkable, and where natural beauty abounds. In the last 200-plus years, pelargoniums have been transplanted to Europe, and eventually throughout the world. Pelargoniums became very important in France where they were and still are cultivated for the perfume industry around Grasse. There are literally hundreds of varieties with many leaf shapes, sizes, aromas, textures, and colors. Brush against the leaves, or rub them to release their aromas. They grow from about 1 foot tall to 3 feet tall. All are considered perennial, but frost certainly kills them so they must be treated as annuals in cold climates. Fortunately, scented geraniums do quite well as houseplants, so bring some in before frost. Pot in a fairly large pot, trim back $^1/_3$ of the growth, and water sparingly inside. Later in this article, I mention a few varieties that are splendid in hanging baskets for either outside or inside. 🐚 Scented geraniums like a sunny location in compost-rich soil. They need good air circulation and require well-drained, but adequate moisture. These plants are relatively insect-free. When Japanese beetles attacked this summer, they didn't go near the pelargoniums, but they sure loved the basil bed! 🐚 All scented geraniums are easy to propagate through stem tip cuttings. Cut and root in moist sand. In just a few days, transplant to pots or the garden. Besides potting some for fragrant house plants, I love these plants in large containers on the patio or deck. 🐚 More and more cooks are learning that scented geraniums have much to offer in the way of flavorings. I always use fresh leaves if they are available, but I like to have some dried or frozen for winter use. To dry the leaves, lay them on clean screens in a dark room and in a couple of weeks or less, they'll be crispy dry. Store them whole in glass jars away from any light. Crumble them as you use them in your recipes. Another method of preserving is freezing. I cut 4-inch squares of waxed paper, lay a clean leaf on one square, lay a paper square on leaf, another geranium leaf, and so forth, until I have a stack of paper and leaves 5 or 6 leaves high. I slip those into a sealable plastic bag and freeze them. They are ready to use for my cakes and punches. 🐚 Besides being valuable in the perfume-making industry, the essential oil (particularly of the rose-scented varieties) is important in aromatherapy. The oil also is used in the making of certain lotions and balms for the skin. 🐚 As I said before, there are many varieties of scented geraniums. One of the most popular is certainly the *P. graveolens*, or rose-scented geraniums. This variety has at least 50 members.

They all smell like roses and grow from $1^{1}/_{2}$ to 3 feet tall. Most have medium to large gray-green leaves that are deeply lobed. The flowers in the *graveolens* family are pink, lavender, red, or shades of these colors. Remember, however, that the blooms on all scented geraniums are insignificant! These plants are grown mainly for their leaves. Following is a short list of some of my favorite *graveolens* varieties. Remember these are all rose-scented. 1. **P. graveolens 'True Rose'** — this plant has the true deep rose aroma. It has lavender blooms. 2. **P. graveolens 'Attar of Roses'** — has pretty pink flowers and beautiful fernlike foliage. Very good rose scent. 3. **P. graveolens 'Red Flowering Rose'** — has crimson blooms, deeply notched leaves, good rose scent.

4. **P. graveolens 'Rober's Lemon Rose'** — the leaves look like oak leaves. Flowers are pinkish lavender. Leaves have a wonderful lemon-rose fragrance. 5. **P. graveolens 'Old-Fashioned Rose'** — a large plant with deep-lobed leaves and pink flowers. A very heady rose aroma. 6. **P. graveolens 'Grey Lady Plymouth'** — the leaves are deeply lobed and are variegated silvery grey. The flowers are pink. This is a showy plant. 7. **P. graveolens 'Snowflake'** — this is one of my favorites. It smells of roses and lemons. The leaves are large and round with white margins. The flowers are pinkish lavender. This is a beautiful plant to bring inside. I also have used it in a hanging basket — just keep it trimmed. 8. **P. graveolens 'Dr. Livingston'** — deeply lobed leaves that are very fragrant of rose and a hint of lemon. There are small pink to dark pink blooms. This is one of the best rose-scented geraniums to cook with — intense flavor and aroma. ❦ There are many lemon-scented geraniums also. I will mention four that I grow — there are many, many more, but the home gardener can,

will, and does run out of space! 1. *P. crispum* 'Lemon Crispum' or 'Fingerbowl Lemon' — in Victorian times, the leaves used to be added to finger bowls to scent the water. This is a small plant, with tiny green leaves that are very crinkled. Has pink flowers and an intense lemon aroma. A favorite of mine. Set a pot of Lemon Crispum in a sunny dining room window. 2. *P. crispum* 'Prince Rupert' or 'French Lace' — small, variegated, ruffled leaves that have creamy edges. The blooms are pink. Leaves are very lemon-scented. A lovely small, compact plant. Good for indoors. 3. *P. cucullatum* 'Spanish Lavender' — this is a gorgeous upright plant with large fan-shaped leaves. The flowers are purple and the scent is very lemon. A different and showy plant. 4. *P. citrosum* 'Mabel Grey' — I find this plant difficult to locate, but if you find one, hang on to it. It's special with large fan-shaped leaves. Has pale purple flowers and smells intensely of lemon. Wonderful to cook with. ❤ Here are a few more scented geraniums I grow for beauty and fragrance. Just remember, there are many more for you to choose from. 1. *P. denticulatumor* or 'Apricot' — this is a rather large, beautiful plant with fine-cut, shiny leaves. The bloom is coral-colored. There is a distinct aroma of fresh apricots if the leaves are bruised. 2. *P. quercifolium* or 'Chocolate Mint' — the leaves feel like velvet, are dark green with a darker "chocolate" center vein. The bloom is pink. The aroma is mostly mint, with a hint of chocolate. 3. *P. glutinosum* or 'Pheasant Foot' — this plant gets rather large with narrow, deep-lobed leaves. The aroma is pungent. I grow it for its beauty, not good flavor. 4. *P. odoratissimum* or 'Apple' — I love this trailing variety along the edge of the garden. It has small, round, smooth leaves with a distinct apple aroma. A good hanging basket plant.   5. *P. x nervosum* or **'Pink Champagne'** — a pretty name for a pretty plant. Has dark green serrated leaves with a hint of ginger aroma. The beauty of this plant is the large pink single bloom.   6. *P. fragrans* or **'Nutmeg'** — another small, slightly trailing plant that is lovely in a hanging basket. The leaves are small, gray-green, and smell of freshly grated nutmeg. The flowers are tiny and white. Another favorite of mine.   7. *P. tomentosum* or **'Peppermint'** — this is one of the first scented geraniums I grew and I still grow it today. The leaves are large, rather round, dark green, and feel like velvet. The aroma is strongly mint. The flowers are tiny and white. Use this in a hanging basket but keep it trimmed so it doesn't get scraggly.   8. *P. tomentosum x graveolens* or **'Joy Lucille'** — the botanical name tells us this should smell like roses and mint. It does and it's a true "Joy." These leaves are large and velvety and deeply lobed. There are pink flowers. It is beautiful. 9. *P. quercifolium* or **'Village Hill Oak'** — this name is as close to Oak Hill as I can get, so I had to have one for my Oak Hill garden. The leaves are oak leaf-shaped and deeply lobed, and the aroma is pungent. The flowers are dark pink and they last a long time. This is the newest variety in my garden and I like it a lot.   Scented geraniums — what a wonderful world of aroma awaits you when you plant your first one. You'll never be satisfied with just one. Plan a bed and enjoy many varieties — each is truly unique.

How do I use scented geraniums?

- in dessert sauces
- in breads and biscuits
- in cakes
- in pies
- in jellies and jams
- in punches and other drinks
- in teas
- in custards

- flowers can be tossed in green salads
- in butters
- in potpourris
- with fruits (chop finely and add to fruit salads)
- in sorbets and ices
- to scent sugar (especially the rose varieties)

Scented Geranium Recipes

A Summer
Scented Geranium Tea

Rose Geranium Punch (p. 213) *

Tea

Quick Scented Geranium Biscuits (p. 214) *

Susan's Rose Geranium Thumbprint Cookies (p. 219) *

Beulah's Strawberry-Lemon-Geranium Cake (p. 215) *

Beulah's Rose-Scented Geranium Pound Cake (p. 216) *

Carolee's Scented Geranium Chiffon Pie Filling (p. 217) *
in tiny tart shells (your favorite pastry recipe)

Cucumber and Cream Cheese Open-Faced Sandwiches

Asparagus Roll-Ups (p. 298)

* Recipe contains scented geranium leaves

Rose Geranium Punch

2 cups rose geranium leaves, washed and dried
4 cups cold water

Place in a medium saucepan. Bring just to a boil. Remove pan from heat and cover. Let cool. Strain into a large punch bowl. Discard the leaves. Add to the punch bowl:

1 cup super-fine sugar
8 cups cranberry juice cocktail
4 cups orange juice

Mix gently in the punch bowl. Cover until ready to serve. At serving time, add:

1 2-liter bottle lemon-lime soda (7-Up)

Stir together gently. Add an ice ring made with orange slices and rose geranium leaves frozen into it. Serves about 15.

WHAT A GORGEOUS, ROSE-SCENTED SUMMER PUNCH! OR IF YOU BRING SCENTED GERANIUMS INTO THE HOUSE BEFORE THE COLD WEATHER SETS IN, MAKE THIS PUNCH FOR A VERY SPECIAL HOLIDAY PARTY. ANYTIME OF THE YEAR, IT'S DELICIOUS.

Scented Geranium Salad Dressing

6 to 8 large rose-scented geranium, or lemon-scented geranium leaves
3 tablespoons red raspberry vinegar
1 tablespoon sugar
$^1/_2$ cup olive oil

Wash and dry geranium leaves. Cut out and discard the heavy center vein. Coarsely chop the leaves and place them, the vinegar and the sugar in bowl of food processor. Purée mixture. With motor running, slowly add the olive oil. Make early in the day and use dressing the same day it's made. Wonderful over bibb or other tender lettuces. Makes about $^2/_3$ cup.

THIS IS A SUPERB FRESH DRESSING. USE YOUR FOOD PROCESSOR TO MAKE A SMOOTH DRESSING.

Quick Scented Geranium Biscuits

THESE GO TOGETHER SO
QUICKLY. THEY ARE PERFECT
WITH A CUP OF TEA IN THE
AFTERNOON. USE ONLY FRESH
LEAVES IN THIS RECIPE, AND USE
ONLY ONE "FLAVOR"
PER RECIPE.

12 to 14 scented geranium leaves (any of the rose varieties, lemon varieties, or the fruit or spice varieties)

¼ cup butter or margarine

¼ cup light brown sugar, packed

1 tube refrigerated buttermilk buscuits (8 to 10 per tube)

Wash geranium leaves and pat dry. Cut out heavy center vein of each leaf and discard. Finely chop the tender portions of the leaves. Place butter or margarine in a 9-inch cake pan or pie plate. Place in oven to melt butter, but don't let it burn. Add brown sugar to pan and stir to combine with melted butter. Return pan to oven to melt sugar and allow mixture to bubble. Again, watch closely so it doesn't burn. Remove pan from oven and sprinkle the chopped geranium leaves over the butter-sugar mixture. Separate biscuits and place on top of chopped geranium leaves. Bake at 400° for 10 to 15 minutes, or until lightly browned. Remove pan from oven and immediately invert bisuits onto serving platter. Serve warm.

Beulah Hargrove
AND THE GRAND OAK HERB FARM

Grand Oak Herb Farm is located at 2877 Miller Road, Bancroft, MI 48414, midway between Lansing and Flint. I am proud to call Beulah Hargrove, the owner of the farm, a good friend. I have presented several lectures and programs for her and she always sends me back to Indiana with a carload of wonderful plants — especially scented geranium plants. The farm has grown and flourished due to Beulah's love of herbs and flowers. She is a skilled floral designer, herbalist, horticulturalist, teacher and, if that isn't enough, a gourmet cook.

The farm is named for a 350-year-old (or more) white oak tree located in Beulah's front yard. This historical tree is registered as Michigan's largest white oak tree. The herb farm began in 1980 and has grown into one of Michigan's most interesting and largest herb businesses. Visitors are welcome to view more than 20 gardens designed by theme. There are two gift shops, a dried flower operation where nearly 20,000 bunches of herbs and everlastings are dried, and a Tea Room where special teas, workshops, and group meetings are held. Also located at Grand Oak is H & H Botanicals, owned by son, John, and his wife, Lea Ann. H & H Botanicals is a greenhouse operation dealing with more than a thousand varieties of herbs, alpines, and perennials.

When I told Beulah I needed a recipe or two for my scented geranium chapter, she sent two fine recipes — one for Strawberry-Lemon-Geranium Cake (p. 215) and one for Rose-Scented Geranium Pound Cake (p. 216). She has used both these recipes many times for herbal teas or luncheons at Grand Oak Herb Farm.

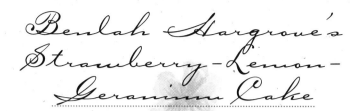

Beulah Hargrove's Strawberry-Lemon-Geranium Cake

1	cup sugar	1	teaspoon baking soda
6	fresh large-leaf, lemon-scented geranium leaves	2	cups all-purpose flour
1/2	cup butter or margarine	1	cup buttermilk
2	egg yolks	1	cup strawberry jam
1	teaspoon ground cinnamon	2	egg whites, stiffly beaten
1	teaspoon baking powder	1	cup heavy cream, whipped

Grease and dust with flour a 13x9x2-inch baking pan. Combine sugar and lemon geranium leaves in a food processor. Process until leaves are tiny green specks throughout the sugar. Reserve 1 tablespoon of the geranium sugar for the whipped cream topping.

Cream butter and remaining geranium sugar, beating until fluffy. Add egg yolks, beating well after each addition. Combine all dry ingredients in a separate bowl. Add alternately with buttermilk to margarine and sugar mixture. Mix well. Fold in strawberry jam. In a small bowl, beat egg whites until stiff peaks form. Fold the whites into the strawberry mixture. Spoon batter into prepared pan. Bake at 350° for 35 to 45 minutes, or until center tests clean. Cool cake thoroughly. Whip cream with 1 tablespoon of the reserved geranium sugar. Top cake with whipped cream. Garnish with lemon-scented geranium blossoms and leaves. Will serve 12 to 15.

FOR THIS CAKE, BEULAH'S FAVORITE SCENTED GERANIUM IS MABEL GREY, BUT ANY LEMON-SCENTED GERANIUM WILL DO.

My Scented Geranium Cake

Grease a 13x9x2-inch baking pan or a 9- or 10-inch springform pan. Lay clean and dry fresh **scented geranium leaves** to cover the bottom of the pan. Prepare your favorite **white or yellow cake mix** and pour the batter over the geranium leaves.

Bake cake according to package directions. Let cake cool a few minutes, then turn cake out onto tray or cake stand. Peel off geranium leaves and discard. The flavor from the leaves will go into the batter as it bakes. Quick and very good.

If you have some **Rose Geranium Sugar** prepared (p. 220), sprinkle a little on top of cake before slicing, or drizzle with a little **confectioner's sugar icing**.

TOO BUSY TO MAKE A CAKE FROM SCRATCH? THEN TRY THIS SHORTCUT.

Beulah Hargrove's Rose-Scented Geranium Pound Cake

2³/₄   cups sugar

1   cup butter or margarine

6   egg yolks

2   teaspoons vanilla

3   cups all-purpose flour

¹/₂   teaspoon salt

¹/₂   teaspoon ground nutmeg

¹/₂   teaspoon baking soda

1   cup buttermilk

6   egg whites

¹/₂   cup brandy or Grand Marnier

About 40 fresh rose geranium leaves (20 for each loaf)

Grease and flour two 9x5x3-inch loaf pans. (Or you may bake in a greased and floured 10-inch tube pan.) In a large electric mixing bowl, cream sugar and butter. Add egg yolks, one at a time, beating well after each addition. Beat in vanilla. Sift together flour, salt and nutmeg. Dissolve baking soda in buttermilk. Gradually add flour mixture to creamed mixture, alternating with buttermilk. Beat on medium speed until mixture is smooth. In a separate bowl, beat egg whites until stiff peaks form. Gently fold whites into batter and spoon into prepared pans. Bake at 350° for about 1 hour, or until top is firm and a cake tester comes out clean. Cool for 30 minutes in pan or pans, then remove from pan.

Place cooled cakes on a large sheet of plastic wrap. With a pastry brush, gently brush the brandy or Grand Marnier on one side of the loaf. Press on scented geranium leaves to cover that side of the cake. Gently bruise the leaves while applying them to the cake. Repeat the other side. Apply leaves immediately after brushing with brandy or Grand Marnier — the alcohol will absorb the rose flavor and hold it to the cake. As soon as sides are completed, wrap cake in plastic wrap. Let cake or cakes stand at room temperature for 18 to 24 hours. Unwrap and slice thin. A wonderful cake that's moist and delicious. Will serve 16 to 20, depending on size of slices.

Carolee's Scented Geranium Chiffon Pie

One week before baking pie, layer the scented geranium leaves of your choice (rose geranium, any of the lemon varieties, or lime or ginger) with sugar (see method in Rose Geranium Sugar recipe, p. 220).

For the crust

- 10 Pecan Sandie cookies
- 3 tablespoons margarine, melted

Gently crush cookies with a rolling pin. Place crumbs in a small bowl. Add melted margarine and press mixture into a 9-inch pie plate. Set aside.

For the geranium water

- 6 scented geranium leaves (use corresponding leaves as used for sugar)
- $^1/_2$ cup water

Place the 6 leaves and the $^1/_2$ cup water in a microwave-safe bowl. Cover and microwave for 30 seconds. Let steep, covered, until cool. Remove and discard leaves. Set bowl of geranium water aside.

For the filling

- $^1/_3$ cup scented geranium sugar
- 1 envelope unflavored gelatin
- 4 egg yolks
- $^1/_2$ cup cooled geranium water (from above)
- 4 egg whites
- $^1/_3$ cup scented geranium sugar
  Whipped cream (optional)

In a saucepan, blend $^1/_3$ cup scented geranium sugar and the unflavored gelatin. Set aside. In a small bowl, whisk together the egg yolks and $^1/_2$ cup of the cooled geranium water. Stir egg mixture into sugar mixture. Place saucepan on medium heat. Cook and stir until mixture thickens and coats a spoon. Beat 4 egg whites until foamy. On high speed, beat and gradually add $^1/_3$ cup rose geranium sugar until stiff peaks form. Gently fold pudding mixture into egg whites and fold until blended. Pour into crust and chill. Top with dollops of whipped cream, if desired, and sprinkle scented geranium sugar around outside edge of pie. Garnish with fresh leaves and blooms, if desired. Serves 6.

I MET CAROLEE SNYDER THROUGH THE INTERNATIONAL HERB ASSOCIATION. I HAVE GREAT ADMIRATION FOR THIS YOUNG WOMAN. SHE MOVED EVERY PLANT FROM HER HERB GARDEN IN SOUTHERN INDIANA TO HER NEW LOCATION IN NORTHERN INDIANA, DOING MOST OF THE WORK HERSELF, AND SAVED NEARLY ALL THE PLANTS! AND I COMPLAIN ABOUT DIVIDING AND TRANSPLANTING THE PEONIES — ALL IN THE SAME GARDEN! IF IN THE HARTFORD CITY AREA, VISIT CAROLEE'S GARDENS AND SHOP AT CAROLEE'S HERB FARM, 33055 100 W, HARTFORD CITY, IN 47348. CAROLEE SENT THIS RECIPE FOR SCENTED GERANIUM CHIFFON PIE. IT IS DELICIOUS.

Scented Geranium Tisane

For 1 cup, pour 6 to 8 ounces **boiling water** over 2 or 3 (add more or less to your taste) coarsely chopped fresh **scented geranium leaves**. (Amount used will also depend on size of leaves.) Let steep 5 minutes. Strain and discard leaves. Sweeten, if desired.

Susan Wittig Albert
AND HER BOOK, "THYME OF DEATH"

*O*ne evening I received a call from a friend in a neighboring town asking if I knew my book, It's About Thyme! *was mentioned in an herbal mystery book called* Thyme of Death *by Susan Wittig Albert. Well no, I didn't know that and decided to get to the bottom of this mystery! I located Susan in Bertram, Texas, called her and we became instant friends.*

Susan had created a sleuth (I like to think of her as a very modern Miss Marple) called China Bayles. China, a lawyer-turned-herbalist, lives in Pecan Springs, Texas, and is proprietor of an herb shop there called Thyme and Seasons Herb Company. It seems that lots of strange and mysterious things happen in Pecan Springs and China and her friends are very busy solving crimes. One of the books China sells in her shop is It's About Thyme!, *and according to China, "With almost every order, I sold a copy of* It's About Thyme!, *a great book by Marge Clark."*

When I talked with Susan, she mentioned she would be coming through the Midwest on a book promotion tour and I immediately suggested we plan a tea for her. I would invite all my herbal friends within driving distance. On the day of the tea, they came from as far away as southern Indiana and St. Louis, Missouri, to meet this fine and talented author.

So finally, Susan and I met and now we carry on our friendship through long-distance calls. Since Thyme of Death, *Susan has written more China Bayles mysteries. They are* Witches Bane, Hangman's Root, Rosemary Remembered, *and her newest offering,* Rueful Death. Love Lies Bleeding *will be published in 1997. You can tell by the names of her books that herbs play a big role in the stories. Susan's herbal mysteries are a must-read for anyone interested in herbs and who loves a good mystery. Her books are available nationwide, but if you order them from Susan, she'll sign them! Her address is Thyme and Seasons Books, PO Drawer M, Bertram, TX 78605.*

Since Susan and I met at the tea I gave for her, I thought it only appropriate to use one of her Tea Thyme Sweets recipes from her booklet, Herbal Teas. *She kindly gave permission to use the following recipe. Her Rose Geranium Jelly recipe is first, then the cookie recipe follows.*

Susan Wittig Albert's Rose Geranium Jelly

3   pounds tart apples
3¾ cups sugar
     Red food coloring (optional)
12 rose geranium leaves, cleaned and dried of moisture

Wash and slice the apples. Cover with water in a large heavy pan. Cook about 15 minutes, or until apples are soft. Strain juice without squeezing. Measure 5 cups of juice into the pan. Bring juice to a rolling boil, then gradually add the sugar, stirring constantly. Add 2 or 3 drops of red food coloring, if desired, for a pretty pink jelly, but this is optional. Boil to 222° on a candy thermometer. Skim foam. Place 1 rose geranium leaf in each of 6 hot sterilized jelly glasses. Pour hot jelly over leaves. Add another leaf on top of jelly and immediately seal. Cool. Store in refrigerator.

Susan Wittig Albert's Rose Geranium Thumbprint Cookies

1   cup shortening, at room temperature
½   cup brown sugar, packed
2   egg yolks
1   teaspoon vanilla
2   cups flour, sifted
½   teaspoon salt
2   egg whites, slightly beaten
1½ cups pecans, finely chopped
     Rose Geranium Jelly (recipe above)

Cream shortening, sugar, egg yolks and vanilla. Sift flour with salt and stir into creamed mixture. Roll cookies into small balls. Dip in egg whites, then roll in the chopped nuts. Bake at 375° on a greased cookie sheet for 4 to 5 minutes. Remove from oven and thumbprint each cookie. Return to oven for 5 minutes. Fill depression (the thumbprint) with rose geranium jelly. Makes 3 to 3½ dozen beautiful little cookies — delicious, too!

Scented Geranium Sorbet

$^1/_2$ cup super-fine sugar

1   cup water

$^1/_4$ cup scented geranium leaves, chopped

  Juice of 1 lemon

1   egg white

Place sugar and water in a small heavy saucepan. Bring water to a boil and stir until sugar is dissolved. Add chopped geranium leaves to the pan. Cover and remove from heat. Let stand for 30 minutes. Strain the liquid. Add lemon juice to liquid. Transfer to an ice cube tray and freeze for 2$^1/_2$ to 3 hours. When sorbet is semifrozen, beat egg white until stiff and fold it into the mixture. Return to the freezer for 3 to 4 hours. Serve in pretty glass or crystal dishes to 4.

SERVE BETWEEN COURSES,
OR FOR A COLD, SWEET TREAT
AFTER A HEAVY MEAL, SERVE
THIS REFRESHING SORBET WITH
COOKIES OR POUND CAKE.

Rose Geranium Sugar

Rose-scented geranium leaves

Granulated sugar

Flat container with a lid that seals tightly, or a wide-mouth canning jar with lid

Pick, wash and thoroughly dry geranium leaves. No moisture must be on leaves. Place a thin layer of sugar in the bottom of your container, slightly bruise the leaves and lay on the sugar. Sift sugar over leaves to cover them, add another layer of bruised leaves, and so on until your container is full. After a week to 10 days, remove the leaves and discard. Cover the scented sugar tightly and store away from heat and light. The sugar stays fragrant for a long time.

I USE THIS SUGAR TO FLAVOR
TEA, PUNCHES AND OTHER
DRINKS. SPRINKLE A LITTLE
OVER THE TOPS OF YOUR
FAVORITE SUGAR COOKIES. CAN
BE USED TO SWEETEN DESSERTS,
ESPECIALLY FRUITS.

Rose-Scented Geranium Butter

4	to 6 fresh rose-scented geranium leaves, clean and dry, coarsely chopped
1	cup butter, at room temperature
4	to 6 drops rose water, if available

Remove heavy vein from leaves and discard. Place coarsely chopped leaves in bowl of food processor and pulse on/off until leaves are finely minced. Add butter and blend with leaves. Add rose water, if using, and blend well. The rose water (available at gourmet food stores, many herb shops and from food specialty catalogs) enhances the rose flavor of the leaves.

USE THIS BUTTER ON BISCUITS,
TOAST OR WITH DESSERTS.
SPREAD SOME ON THIN SLICES OF
QUICK FRUIT BREADS. ONLY
FRESH SCENTED GERANIUM
LEAVES WILL WORK FOR
THIS RECIPE.

Thyme

THYMUS SPECIES

Thyme

There are literally hundreds of species of thyme throughout the world. Thyme is the symbol for courage and bravery. *Thymus vulgaris* species, also called "common" thyme, are the ones we usually cook with. In my opinion, the best culinary thymes are French thyme (*T. v* '**narrow-leaf French**') and lemon thyme (*T. x citriodorus*). French thyme is sweet and spicy and contains the oil thymol (this oil is present in many medicines). In my Midwest garden, French thyme is the hardiest I grow. Lemon thyme is a great culinary thyme with good lemon flavor. Its leaves vary from green to yellow-green variegated to a full yellow.   ❦   Thyme, native to the Mediterranean region and Asia, is a lovely low-growing hardy perennial. In warm climates it is an evergreen shrub. Thyme planted in warm, dry soil is more potent in flavor than thyme planted in cooler, wetter, northern areas. White or pinkish purple flowers adorn most thyme plants, but there are so many varieties that I have seen white-, red-, and yellow-blooming thymes as well. The leaves are narrow, oval-shaped, and most are gray-green to dark green in color. The stems are woody. For culinary purposes, thyme is best picked just before it blooms. Thyme likes to grow in full sun in well-drained soil. The varieties grow from 1 to 15 inches tall. There are numerous growth habits including upright, compact, prostrate, and creeping.   ❦   Some other varieties that I grow are: 1. *T.* **'Argenteus' or silver thyme** — has silvery green leaves with an excellent thyme flavor. Makes a beautiful border plant.   2. *T. **herba-barona*** or **'Caraway' thyme** — a good spreading thyme that is covered with beautiful lavender-pink flowers in summer. It has a heavy caraway scent and is a good thyme to cook with. I find it to be very hardy in my garden.   3. *T. **herba-barona v.*** or **'Nutmeg' thyme** — has deep pink blooms and a pronounced nutmeg aroma and taste.   4. *T. **pulegioides*** or **'Oregano' thyme** — this plant grows 8 to 10 inches tall and has a strong oregano flavor. It has been a hardy plant in my garden.   5. *T. **'Doone Valley'*** — has green shiny leaves and is lemon-scented. I like this one for cooking.

6. *T.* **'Alba'** — with this name, you know it has white blooms. It is a hardy variety.

7. *T. **pseudolanuginosus*** or **'Silver Wooly Thyme'** — this lovely tiny plant makes a soft cushion of lovely silvery foliage. Be sure to remember where you plant it — it can easily be hoed out in the spring.   8. *T. **serpyllum*** or **'Mother-of-Thyme'** — grows only 2 inches tall. It is not culinary but every garden with a stone path should have Mother-of-Thyme planted between the stones. The most wonderful aroma is released when one walks on this thyme. This variety blooms profusely and the bees really love it. Bees actually love all thymes and bee-pollinated thyme makes delicious honey.

9. *T.* **'Broad-leaf English'** or **English thyme** — similar in taste to common thyme, except the leaves are broader. This is a hardy variety in my garden.   These are only a few of the hundreds of varieties available. If you ever have a chance to visit an all thyme garden, do so. You'll be amazed there are so many colors, leaf forms, and growing habits within the same family.   When we were in southern France a

few years ago, we visited the Roquefort cheese caves in Mount Combalou. It was a wonderful experience. Roquefort is unique as it is the only well-known bleu cheese made from sheep's milk. We were told that the milk's distinctive flavor comes from the sheep grazing in fields of wild thyme. As you drive through the countryside around the caves, the aroma of thyme is overwhelming. Since the stems are woody and tough, the leaves are the part of the plant to use for seasonings. Thyme goes with almost all foods — it is sometimes called the "universal seasoning." It is a great substitute for salt. From a bouquet garni to the making of certain liqueurs, thyme is widely used. It is easy to dry thyme. Bring bunches in from the garden, swish in tepid water to remove any loose dirt, shake off excess water, and let dry until leaves are free of moisture. Tie 8 or 10 stems together to make a bundle. Hang upside down and in about 10 days the leaves will be dry and ready to strip from their stems. Store in an airtight container out of heat and light. Throw the dried stems on the barbecue grill or in the fireplace to give off a wonderful aroma. Besides culinary uses, thyme is a big player in the medicinal world. Ancient Egyptians used thyme in their embalming fluids and I am told it's still used for that purpose today. Thyme is said to aid digestion. It is considered an antiseptic. It is an ingredient in some mouth washes and toothpastes. When thyme is infused in honey, it makes a good cough and cold syrup. Thyme is indeed a most useful, diverse, and universal herb.

How do I use thyme?

- in almost any vegetable dish, especially asparagus, carrots, peas, onions, potatoes, green beans, and tomatoes
- in soup stocks
- in marinades
- in stuffings
- in vegetable sauces
- in meat sauces
- with chicken
- with turkey
- with fish and shellfish
- in breads, muffins, cookies
- to flavor cheeses, such as cream cheese and cottage cheese
- with salad greens
- in fruit salads

- in jellies and jams
- with beef
- with pork
- with lamb
- with veal
- in mushroom dishes
- to season sausages
- in tea
- in vinegars
- in oils
- in egg dishes, especially omelettes and frittatas
- in potpourri making
- in bouquet garnis
- in dried herbal seasoning mixes
- in rice dishes

INDEX

Thyme Recipes

Always Enough Thyme

Appetizer Broccoli-Cheese Tarts (p. 231) *

Roasted Marinated Peppers Salad (p. 234) *

Roast Turkey Breast with Cherry-Thyme Sauce (p. 237) *

Mashed Potatoes

Buttered Frozen Peas

Whole Wheat-Potato Bread (p. 322)

Frozen Lemon Yogurt

Lemon Thyme Cookies (p. 241) *

* Recipe contains thyme

Appetizer Broccoli-Cheese Tarts

18   wonton skins
1   tablespoon butter or margarine, melted
1   egg
1   teaspoon flour
³/₄   cup chopped broccoli
²/₃   cup finely diced cooked ham or cooked chicken
¹/₄   cup roasted red peppers, chopped, or canned pimientos, drained and chopped
1   cup finely shredded cheddar cheese
¹/₄   teaspoon onion powder
¹/₂   teaspoon dried thyme leaves
      Dash of pepper

Spray 18 miniature muffin cups with nonstick cooking spray. Brush one side of each
wonton skin with butter. Carefully press skin, buttered side up, into sprayed cups.
In medium bowl, combine egg and flour. Whisk until blended. Stir in remaining
ingredients and mix well. Spoon mixture into wonton-lined cups. Bake at 350° for
15 to 20 minutes or until mixture is set and skins are a golden brown. Immediately
remove from muffin cups. Serve warm.
Makes 18 terrific tarts.

THE SURPRISE HERE IS THE
TART "PASTRY" — WONTON
SKINS. THIS IS A VERY SPECIAL
APPETIZER THAT IS QUICK
AND EASY.

Minnesota Wild Rice Soup

1	medium onion, coarsely chopped
4	ounces fresh mushrooms, coarsely chopped
1	cup diced smoked ham
3	tablespoons butter
1/4	cup flour
4	cups chicken broth
1 1/2	cups cooked wild rice (a great way to use leftover)
1	cup half-and-half cream
1/4	cup sherry
1	teaspoon dried thyme
	Salt and pepper
	Parsley, finely chopped (optional)

Cook onion, mushrooms and diced ham in butter until onion is tender, but not brown. Add flour and cook and stir for 3 or 4 minutes. Add broth and cook slowly for 15 minutes, stirring frequently. Add wild rice, half-and-half, sherry and thyme. Add salt and pepper to taste and heat through. Add a little chopped parsley to the top of each bowl, if desired. Serves 6 or 8.

Hearty Bean Soup

1	pound soup beans (1 variety or a mixture)
3	quarts chicken broth (see below)
1	bay leaf
1	teaspoon dried thyme
1	smoked ham hock
1	clove garlic, finely chopped
2	13- to 15-ounce cans Italian-style tomatoes
1	large onion, chopped
1	cup celery, diced
1	pound mild Italian sausage, fried and drained
1	frying chicken, cooked (remove skin and bones and dice meat) — save broth
2	tablespoons chopped fresh parsley, or 1 tablespoon dried parsley

Soak beans overnight in a large soup pot. Drain and discard water. Add 3 quarts chicken broth from stewing the chicken, or may need to add enough water to make 3 quarts. Add bay leaf, thyme and ham hock. Cover and simmer for 2 1/2 to 3 hours. Add garlic, tomatoes, onion and celery. Simmer for 1 hour. Remove ham hock and dice meat. Add meat back to the soup pot. Add cooked, crumbled sausage, diced chicken and parsley. Simmer another 15 minutes. Serves 10 or more.

Crab Chowder with Thyme

8	cups bottled clam juice
1	cup dry sherry
$^1/_2$	cup brandy (unflavored)
$^1/_4$	cup minced shallots
1	tablespoon minced garlic
8	leafy stems of fresh parsley
4	bay leaves
4	medium potatoes, peeled and cut into $^1/_2$-inch cubes
2	ounces bacon, diced
2	cups onion, finely chopped
$1^1/_2$	cups celery, finely chopped
1	tablespoon dried thyme
$^1/_2$	cup flour
3	cups heavy cream
$^3/_4$	pound fresh or frozen crabmeat, thawed
	Salt and pepper
	Fresh parsley, chopped

CONSIDERING THE LINE-UP OF INGREDIENTS, YOU JUST KNOW THIS SOUP HAS TO BE SOMETHING SPECIAL. IT IS! A PERFECT LUNCHEON DISH OR THE STAR AT A DINNER PARTY, IT IS SPECIAL INDEED. IT IS BEAUTIFULLY SCENTED AND FLAVORED WITH THYME.

In a large soup pot, heat clam juice, sherry, brandy, shallots, garlic, parsley and bay leaves. Bring to a boil and cook for 15 minutes. Skim, if necessary. Strain through a fine strainer, reserving liquid. In another saucepan, boil cubed potatoes for 5 minutes. Drain. In a large soup pot, cook bacon until crisp. Add onions and celery and sauté in bacon fat for 5 or 6 minutes. Add thyme and sauté for another minute. Stir flour into soup pot and cook and stir constantly over low heat for 4 or 5 minutes, but do not brown the flour. Stir clam broth mixture gradually into the soup pot, still over low heat. Stir constantly while adding broth. When all the broth has been added, heat just to boiling. Quickly reduce heat and simmer for 20 minutes. Stir in cream, potatoes and crabmeat. Heat until hot throughout, but do not boil. Taste and add salt and pepper if necessary. Ladle into soup bowls. Sprinkle a little chopped fresh parsley over each serving. Serves 8 to 10. Absolutely delicious.

Roasted Marinated Peppers Salad

2 large red bell peppers, cut in half and seeded
2 large yellow bell peppers, cut in half and seeded
¼ cup extra virgin olive oil
2 tablespoons red wine vinegar
  Juice of 1 lemon
1 small clove garlic, thinly sliced
6 branches fresh thyme (lemon thyme if you have it)
  Salt and pepper
  Lettuce or spinach leaves
  Black olives
1 navel orange, peeled and cut into slices crosswise
2 or 3 ounces soft mild goat cheese

Arrange pepper halves on a broiler pan and broil until skins turn black, turning a time or two. Or hold pepper half over an open gas flame to blacken. Place peppers in a brown paper bag, close top and let sit for a few minutes to loosen the skins. Make marinade by combining oil, vinegar, lemon juice, garlic, leaves from 3 branches of the thyme, salt and pepper to taste in a large bowl. While peppers are still warm, slip off the skins. Cut pepper halves in half again to make quarters. Place pepper quarters in the marinade and refrigerate 2 to 3 hours. Line 4 salad plates with lettuce or spinach leaves. Divide peppers between the 4 plates, add 3 or 4 olives to each plate, a couple slices of orange and the remaining thyme leaves. Crumble goat cheese over each salad.
Drizzle a little marinade over each salad. Serves 4.

Giardiniera

1   small head cauliflower, broken into large flowerets

3   or 4 medium carrots, left whole or cut into large chunks

1   small head broccoli, broken into large flowerets

    Handful of fresh green beans, stemmed

1   medium yellow zucchini, sliced in half lengthwise

1   medium green zucchini, sliced in half lengthwise

1   medium red onion, sliced or cut into large chunks

    Large pieces of red, orange, yellow, green and purple peppers

    Celery pieces, cut into 2-inch pieces (add some tender celery leaves also)

    Peperoncini

    Black olives

    Green olives (pit in)

    Fresh thyme sprigs

    Dill garlic vinegar or an herb vinegar of your choice, such as thyme vinegar,
       basil vinegar, etc.*

    Optional ingredients: drained capers, salt, pepper, crushed red pepper flakes

    A large clean glass jar which has been sterilized (I use a 2-liter or a half-gallon size)
       Do not use a metal lid.

Bring a large pot of water to a boil. Add the cauliflower pieces and the carrots and boil for 3 minutes. Lift pieces out with a slotted spoon and immediately plunge into ice water to stop the cooking. Now add broccoli pieces and whole green beans and blanch no more than 1 minute. Drain and also place in ice water. Thoroughly drain these vegetables. Clean and prepare all other vegetables. You may wish to cut cauliflower and broccoli into smaller flowerets.

Start packing the jar. Stand carrots, pieces of zucchini and pieces of pepper around inside of jar. Work the cauliflower flowerets, broccoli flowerets, green beans, onion chunks, celery pieces, peperoncini, olives, and thyme sprigs into empty spaces. Continue until jar is full. Add optional ingredients of your choice. Fill jar with an herb vinegar. Refrigerate for at least 2 weeks to develop flavors. Keep refrigerated. Will keep for several weeks.

Sometimes I use ²/₃ herb vinegar and ¹/₃ water — all vinegar can be pretty acidic.

THIS IS A STAPLE IN MOST
ITALIAN KITCHENS. IT JUST
GETS BETTER AND BETTER.
SERVE AS IS OR TOSS WITH SALAD
GREENS FOR A GREAT
ITALIAN SALAD.

Chicken-Thyme Tetrazzini

6	tablespoons butter
12	to 16 ounces fresh mushrooms, cleaned and sliced
3	tablespoons dry white wine
2	tablespoons flour
2	cups hot chicken broth
1	cup hot whipping cream
$1^1/_2$	teaspoons fresh thyme, chopped, or $^1/_2$ teaspoon dried
$^1/_4$	teaspoon ground black pepper
	Salt to taste
4	cups cooked skinless chicken, cut into bite-size pieces
12	ounces egg noodles, cooked and drained

Grease a 13x9x2-inch baking dish and set aside. Melt 3 tablespoons butter in a large skillet over medium heat. Add mushrooms and wine. Cook and stir until mushrooms are soft. Remove from heat and set aside. Melt remaining butter in a medium saucepan over low heat. Add the flour and cook, stirring for 3 minutes. Add hot chicken broth and cream and stir well. Simmer until smooth and thick, about 15 minutes, stirring often. During the last 5 minutes of cooking, add thyme, pepper and salt if needed. Mix the cooked chicken, cooked noodles, mushrooms and sauce in a large bowl. Pour into prepared pan and bake, uncovered, at 375° for about 20 minutes, or until hot through and bubbly. Serves 8.

Cherry-Thyme Sauce for Chicken or Turkey

1 cup unsweetened cherry juice, drained from a can of pie cherries
3/4 cup chicken broth
1/2 cup dried cherries, diced
1/4 cup finely chopped onion
1 teaspoon dried thyme, crushed
1 teaspoon white wine Worcestershire sauce
1 teaspoon sugar
1/4 cup unsweetened cherry juice, drained from a can of pie cherries
4 teaspoons cornstarch

In a small saucepan stir together the 1 cup cherry juice, broth, dried cherries, onion, thyme, white wine Worcestershire sauce, and sugar. Bring to a boil over medium heat. Reduce heat, cover and simmer for 15 minutes. Stir together the 1/4 cup cherry juice and the cornstarch. Add to the first mixture. Cook and stir until thickened and bubbling. Cook 2 more minutes, stirring constantly. Serve warm with chicken or turkey. Makes 2 cups.

BUY TWO 1-POUND CANS OF PIE CHERRIES FOR THIS SAUCE. SAVE THE CHERRIES FOR ANOTHER USE. THIS SAUCE IS BEAUTIFUL AND FULL OF FLAVOR. ANOTHER PLUS — IT CAN BE MADE 2 OR 3 DAYS IN ADVANCE AND HEATED AS NEEDED. THE SAUCE IS ALSO WONDERFUL WITH BAKED HAM.

impressions of
THE ISLAND OF MADEIRA

We recently visited the island of Madeira, about 350 miles west of Morocco, Africa. Most people visit the island from a cruise ship, but it's possible to fly there also. Flowers, flowers everywhere almost any time of the year and the most exquisite hand-made lace I have ever seen. Funchal, the capital city, is a typical bustling seaside town. It is named for the wild fennel that used to grow profusely along the banks. Madeira is a Portuguese island and its largest claim to fame (besides the flowers and lace) is the fabulous dessert wine that is made there.

Madeira is a wine fortified with brandy. Years ago, it was placed in barrels and used as ballast in the holds of ships. It was discovered that after the wine had crossed the equator (in other words, a long journey) and returned to the island, it was then very drinkable and delicious. It became a very popular drink in England and parts of America, especially in Savannah, Georgia. The wine grapes are grown above head height, which makes room for cultivation of flowers underneath. Aging improves the quality of Madeira. The older it gets, the better it gets.

Standing Rib Roast of Beef with Madeira Sauce

1   10-pound standing beef rib roast, or a 10-pound whole rib-eye roast
2   teaspoons salt
3   teaspoons fresh thyme, chopped, or 1 teaspoon dried thyme, crumbled
1   teaspoon pepper
    Fresh sprigs of thyme and parsley for garnish
    Madeira Sauce (recipe follows)

Trim excess fat from the roast and discard. Season meat with salt, thyme and pepper. Place roast on a rack in a large shallow pan. Insert a meat thermometer. Bake, uncovered, at 500° for 10 minutes to seal in juices. Reduce temperature to 350° and bake an additional 2 ½ to 3 hours, or until thermometer registers 155°. Transfer roast to platter. Reserve pan drippings. Garnish with herbs and serve immediately with Madeira Sauce. Roast will serve 6 to 8.

Madeira Sauce
When roast is nearly done, start this sauce.

²/₃ cup water
1 ½ tablespoons butter or margarine
1   tablespoon fresh lemon juice
¼   teaspoon salt
½   pound fresh mushrooms, sliced
½   teaspoon fresh thyme, chopped, or about ¼ teaspoon dried
     Pan drippings
¼   cup butter or margarine, melted
½   cup green onions, chopped
1   cup beef broth
½   cup Madeira wine
1   tablespoon tomato paste
¼   teaspoon salt
¼   teaspoon pepper

Combine water, 1 ½ tablespoons butter and lemon juice. Bring to a boil. Reduce heat and add ¼ teaspoon salt, the mushrooms, and the thyme. Cover and simmer 5 minutes until mushrooms are tender. Drain and reserve liquid. Set mushrooms aside. Combine reserved pan drippings (if a lot of fat has accumulated, skim most of it off), melted butter and onion. Sauté until tender. Add water to reserved mushroom liquid to equal 1 cup. Combine with onion mixture, broth, wine, tomato paste, salt and pepper. Heat thoroughly. Stir in mushrooms. Makes 4 cups.

THE FOLLOWING RECIPE IS OUTSTANDING. I KEEP A BOTTLE OF MADEIRA TO MAKE THIS AND OTHER SAUCES. THYME PLAYS AN IMPORTANT ROLE IN THIS RECIPE ALSO.

Pecan Pilaf

4 tablespoons butter or margarine
1 cup chopped pecans
$^1/_2$ cup chopped onion
2 cups long grain rice (not instant)
2 cups chicken broth
2 cups water
$^1/_2$ teaspoon salt
$^1/_4$ teaspoon dried thyme
   Dash of pepper
3 tablespoons chopped fresh parsley

Melt 3 tablespoons butter in a large skillet over medium heat. Add pecans and toast until lightly browned, 2 or 3 minutes, stirring often. Transfer pecans to a small bowl. Cover bowl and set aside. Melt remaining butter in same skillet. Add onion and sauté until tender, about 5 minutes. Add rice and stir until evenly coated, about 2 minutes. In a large saucepan, bring broth, water, salt, thyme, pepper and 2 tablespoons parsley to a boil over medium heat. Add to rice. Cover, reduce heat and simmer until liquid is absorbed, about 20 minutes. Add pecans and remaining parsley. Fluff with a fork and serve. Serves 6 to 8.

IF YOU'RE TIRED OF POTATOES, PASTA AND PLAIN RICE AS A SIDE DISH, TRY THIS DELICIOUS PILAF. IT DRESSES UP THE SIMPLEST OF ENTRÉES.

Sun-Dried Tomato-Thyme Muffins

2 cups flour
1 tablespoon baking powder
1/2 teaspoon salt
1/4 teaspoon black pepper
1 cup milk
1 egg
1/4 cup olive oil
1/2 cup grated Parmesan cheese (if you don't have fresh, buy it at the deli)
1/3 cup sun-dried tomatoes*, finely chopped
2 teaspoons fresh thyme, chopped, or 1 teaspoon dried

Spray muffin cups (2 1/2-inch diameter) with nonstick vegetable shortening spray. In a large bowl, combine the flour, baking powder, salt and pepper. Set aside. In another bowl, whisk together the milk, egg and oil until smooth. Add the cheese, tomatoes and thyme. Stir. Combine dry ingredients with wet ingredients and stir just until blended. Spoon into muffin cups, filling no more than 2/3 full. Bake at 375° about 20 minutes, or until a tester comes out clean. Cool 2 or 3 minutes, then remove muffins from pan. Makes 12 muffins.

*If tomatoes are packed in oil, remove from oil and rinse under running water. Pat dry with paper towels, then chop.

Cranberry-Thyme Spread

4 cups fresh or frozen cranberries
2 cups water
2 1/2 cups firmly packed light brown sugar
1 tablespoon grated lemon rind
3/4 teaspoon ground thyme
1/2 teaspoon salt

Bring cranberries and water to a boil. Reduce heat, cover and boil gently 5 minutes. Cool and purée in blender or food processor. Press through a strainer, return to pan. Add sugar, lemon rind, thyme and salt. Cook, stirring often, until very thick, about 45 minutes. Pour into sterilized jars, seal and let cool, then refrigerate. Makes about 3 cups.

Lemon Thyme Cookies

2½ cups flour
1   teaspoon cream of tartar
½   teaspoon salt
1   cup butter, softened
1½ cups sugar
2   eggs
1   tablespoon dried lemon thyme leaves

Sift together the dry ingredients. Cream the butter and sugar. Add eggs, one at a time, and mix well after each addition. Stir in the lemon thyme. Form into a ball, place in a zip-type plastic bag and refrigerate several hours or overnight. Preheat oven to 350°. Roll into 1-inch balls and place on a lightly greased baking sheet. Flatten slightly. Bake in a 350° oven for 10 minutes. Watch closely. Makes 4 dozen cookies.

Apple-Thyme Jelly

5   pounds tart apples
5   cups water
1   cup fresh thyme sprigs
1   box Sure Jell pectin
9   cups sugar

Remove blossom and stem ends from apples. Do not peel or core apples. Cut apples into small chunks. Place apples in large kettle. Add 5 cups water and the fresh thyme. Cover and simmer for 10 minutes, stirring occasionally. Uncover pot and crush apples and thyme with a potato masher. Return to heat and simmer 5 minutes longer. Strain apple-thyme mixture through several layers of damp cheesecloth. Add water, if necessary, to make 7 cups of juice. Pour juice into a large kettle. Add 1 box Sure Jell and cook and stir to a full rolling boil. Immediately add the 9 cups sugar. Bring again to a full rolling boil and boil hard for 1 minute, stirring constantly. Remove from heat. Skim foam. Ladle into hot sterilized jelly jars, leaving about ¾ inch headspace. Place a rinsed and dried sprig of thyme in each glass. Seal with hot paraffin, then with hot lids.

WHEN IT'S YOUR TURN TO
TAKE COOKIES TO THE LADIES'
LUNCHEON OR AFTERNOON
BRIDGE PARTY, TAKE A PLATE OF
THESE LEMON THYME-FLAVORED
COOKIES. THEY ARE
PRACTICALLY INDISPENSABLE FOR
THE TEA TABLE.

I TOOK THIS RECIPE FROM MY
BOOK, *IT'S ABOUT THYME!*
BECAUSE IT REALLY BELONGS IN
A THYME CHAPTER. IT IS SUCH A
GOOD JELLY WITH MORNING
TOAST OR BISCUITS.

Other Culinary Herbs

Following are 15 more culinary herbs and seeds important to the cook. There are still others, but these 15 plus the 12 discussed in the herb chapters are truly the herbs most of us cook with. By no means is this a complete book on herbs — I'm not really sure there is such a thing. There are so many herbs from Asia, South America, and other areas of the world that most of us are not familiar with or do not have access to. However, I'm sure that given time, we'll be educated about these herbs also. This whole subject is an ongoing learning experience!

Cilantro and Coriander
CORIANDRUM SATIVUM

This great dual herb has many uses. The green leaves are called cilantro (some call them Chinese parsley), and the dried seeds are called coriander. This ancient plant dates to pre-Biblical times. Today, it seems everybody uses cilantro. Many Mexican,

Mediterranean, and Chinese dishes call for cilantro. Probably the best-known dish in the United States flavored with cilantro is salsa. This annual plant looks a lot like other plants that produce umbel-shaped seedheads. The leaves are dark green, oval, and have sharp-toothed edges. It is best to cook with fresh, young leaves as more mature leaves are very pungent and bitter. Flowers in the umbels are white to pinkish white.

Cilantro, like parsley, chervil, or other plants with taproots, is best planted from seed. For a long harvest season, plant cilantro seeds every 2 or 3 weeks — they germinate and grow quickly. Sow the seeds in fairly rich, moist soil in full sun. Let some plants go to seed so you can harvest coriander in late summer. Don't let the seedheads get too dry, or they'll drop all their seeds. Dry the seedheads in a paper bag. Fresh cilantro leaves and dried coriander seeds are totally different in flavor and usage. Fresh cilantro leaves are pungent and sometimes referred to as "soapy" tasting. A more accurate description of the taste is sagelike, with a slight orange or lemon flavor. The leaves are used in salsa, in guacamole, in salads, to flavor butters, in some soups, in some vegetable dishes, and especially in wok cookery. I never dry cilantro leaves — the fresh are best. Dried coriander seeds have an orange- and lemonlike flavor and are widely used in bread making, in other pastries, with fruits, in meats and sausage dishes, and especially in curry powder mixtures. Coriander is a very important seasoning in Scandinavian breads and cookie recipes.

Garlic

ALLIUM SATIVUM

A whole chapter has been devoted to chives (*A. schoenoprasum*), and no book on culinary herbs would be complete without at least a short discussion on one of its relatives, garlic (*Allium sativum*). Garlic is an herb we take for granted. It enhances so many foods that it is one of the "routine" additions. Like chives, garlic is a member of the well-known lily family of alliums. It has been used by cooks for centuries. Medicinally, garlic is a veritable cure-all. It is touted as a remedy for colds, coughs, lowers high blood pressure, and treats numerous other ailments. Garlic is a perennial bulb composed of several bulblets called cloves. The flat, slender leaves grow about 18 inches tall. In midsummer, round flower heads with tiny white flowers appear on the stem tops. I buy garlic bulbs at the nursery, or even at the grocery store, break them into cloves, and plant each clove about 1 inch deep and 4 inches apart in rich, moist soil and in full sun. When the leaves start to ripen (turn yellow), I pull my new garlic bulbs, hang them by the stems for 2 or 3 weeks in a warm, dry place, then store them for use. In hot climates, garlic is best if planted in the fall and harvested in the spring. Two or three interesting garlics are worthy of mention. **Rocombole**, or **Bavarian garlic** (*A. scorodoprasum*) produces tiny bulbils at the tops of the stems. Rocombole is a beautiful and unusual plant in the garden. **Elephant garlic** (*A. ampeloprasum*) is a bit controversial. Some say it isn't garlic at all. Others say it is a plant that produces giant bulbs that have a milder garlic flavor than *Allium sativum* bulbs. **Society garlic** (*Tulbaghia violacea*) is not garlic at all, but it tastes like garlic and is therefore used as garlic. It has dark green, flat, thin leaves

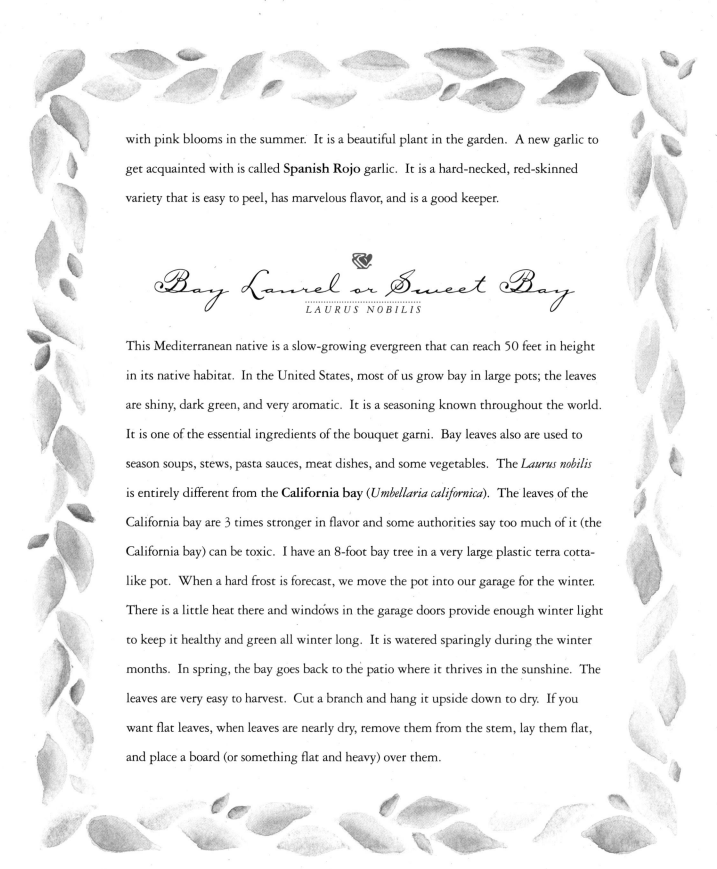

with pink blooms in the summer. It is a beautiful plant in the garden. A new garlic to get acquainted with is called **Spanish Rojo** garlic. It is a hard-necked, red-skinned variety that is easy to peel, has marvelous flavor, and is a good keeper.

Bay Laurel or Sweet Bay
LAURUS NOBILIS

This Mediterranean native is a slow-growing evergreen that can reach 50 feet in height in its native habitat. In the United States, most of us grow bay in large pots; the leaves are shiny, dark green, and very aromatic. It is a seasoning known throughout the world. It is one of the essential ingredients of the bouquet garni. Bay leaves also are used to season soups, stews, pasta sauces, meat dishes, and some vegetables. The *Laurus nobilis* is entirely different from the **California bay** (*Umbellaria californica*). The leaves of the California bay are 3 times stronger in flavor and some authorities say too much of it (the California bay) can be toxic. I have an 8-foot bay tree in a very large plastic terra cotta-like pot. When a hard frost is forecast, we move the pot into our garage for the winter. There is a little heat there and windows in the garage doors provide enough winter light to keep it healthy and green all winter long. It is watered sparingly during the winter months. In spring, the bay goes back to the patio where it thrives in the sunshine. The leaves are very easy to harvest. Cut a branch and hang it upside down to dry. If you want flat leaves, when leaves are nearly dry, remove them from the stem, lay them flat, and place a board (or something flat and heavy) over them.

Summer and Winter Savory

SATUREJA HORTENSIS AND SATUREJA MONTANA

These 2 savories are similar yet quite different from each other. They are both native to the Mediterranean area. **Summer savory** (*Satureja hortensis*) is an annual with gray-green, small, slender leaves. In summer, very tiny pinkish white flowers appear on 12- to 18-inch-tall stems. The leaves are best for cooking before the plant blooms. Summer savory has a delicate peppery flavor that adds marvelous taste to meats, sauces, stuffings, soups, and vegetables, especially green beans. Plants can be started from seed, but I like to set out a few small plants from the nursery. Grow summer savory in moist, light, well-drained soil in full sun. I set my plants fairly close together. They are naturally spindly, so placing them close together helps them support each other. Only fertilizing at planting time is necessary. You can tie bunches of stems together, hang upside down, and let leaves dry in a warm, dry place. Carefully strip off the leaves and store them in airtight containers away from heat and light.

Winter savory (*Satureja montana*) is a hardy perennial that keeps its green leaves most of the winter. It grows 10 to 15 inches tall and also has narrow, gray-green leaves. It is a stronger and heartier plant than the summer savory and it is also much stronger in flavor. I grow some for its beauty as a border or edging plant, but I prefer not to cook with it. The summer savory is so much more delicate and less bitter. Winter savory is a little like garden sage in that after 3 or 4 years, it stalls in its growth and diminishes in beauty, so it should be replanted at that time.

Chervil

ANTHRISCUS CEREFOLIUM

Often called "French parsley" or "gourmet's parsley," chervil, a member of the parsley family, is a pretty little annual plant but milder in flavor than parsley. Like so many herbs, chervil has a slight anise or licorice flavor, as well as parsley flavor. Chervil is native to Europe and parts of Asia. It grows 1 to 1¹/₂ feet tall and makes a nice mound of dark green leaves that are deeply serrated. Umbels of small white flowers appear in midsummer. Sow seeds in early spring in good soil. Chervil likes some shade and moist but well-drained soil. It also likes lower temperatures, so treat chervil as you would spinach — plant it in early spring or early fall for multiple harvests. The leaves are best for cooking just before the plant blooms, so for a longer leaf producing period, keep flower heads pinched back as they appear. Chervil is a favorite of the French cook and is one of the four ingredients in the mixture called *fines herbes*. It also is the herb used to flavor Béarnaise sauce. Fresh chervil must be added to cooking just before it's served as the delicate flavor is quickly lost in heat. Freezing is the best method I have found to preserve fresh chervil. Freeze leaves on a cookie sheet for an hour, place frozen leaves in a zip-top plastic bag, and store in the freezer. Use in soups and sauces as needed. After the leaves have been frozen, they are not suitable for adding to green salads. I add chervil to butters (such as *fines herbes* butter), soups, salads, sauces, and it's especially good with fish dishes.

Salad Burnet

POTERIUM SANGUISORBA

This lovely 1- to 2-feet-tall perennial tastes and smells like cucumber, so it is an important culinary herb to use when cucumber flavoring is desired. The dark green leaves are deeply lobed and roundish-oval in shape. It is another native Mediterranean herb that has been adopted throughout the world. It grows best in full sun and well-drained soil. Since burnet has a long taproot, it can be somewhat difficult to divide. But it does grow easily and quickly from seed. This is a beautiful perennial plant for your garden. It self-seeds very easily, so you may need to keep the seedheads cut off to prevent further spreading. I find that burnet leaves are only good when used fresh. Drying the leaves destroys the flavor. I add the tasty leaves to green salads, make a wonderful vinegar with the leaves, and also use them in flavoring butters and cheese spreads. Salad burnet is a great container plant. I also have seen it in a hanging basket — it had been trimmed to a beautiful mound.

Fennel

FOENICULUM VULGARE

This tender perennial (Midwest gardeners treat it as an annual) is an ancient pre-Biblical plant. It is related to parsley, but looks a lot like dill. It also has hollow stems like dill. Like so many other herbs we have learned about, fennel also is native to the Mediterranean area. Its scientific name is from *foenum*, a Latin word for hay. Therefore, fennel smells somewhat like hay, but it has a wonderful sweet licorice aroma (and flavor) as well. Fennel grows easily from seed in good to rich well-drained soil. It likes full sun. Generally speaking, there are 3 types of fennel for the gardener to choose from. *Foeniculum vulgare*, or common fennel, grows 3 to 5 feet tall and is grown for its leaves and seeds. Flat large umbels of yellow flowers appear in late summer. See the chapter on dill for drying procedures. Do not grow fennel and dill close to each other as they will cross-pollinate. *Finocchio*, or Florence fennel, grows only about 2 feet tall and is grown for its stems and bulblike base, as well as its leaves. Florence fennel has a marvelous sweet taste and I much prefer it over the tall and rangy common fennel. It does require somewhat cool weather, so plant either early spring or late summer for the best bulb formation. When the finocchio bulb is the size of an egg, mound soil around most of the bulb. In about 2 weeks from that time, the bulb is ready to harvest. *F. v. rubrum*, or bronze fennel, is a pretty 2- or 3-feet-tall plant that has bronze-colored leaves. It is used in cooking, but I consider it more of an ornamental plant and a beautiful one at that. Fennel is a favorite herb of Italian cooks. It is used in salads, in pasta dishes, to flavor olive oil, butters, soups, and marinades. If you don't use fennel leaves for anything else, use them with fish — a delicious combination. Fennel seeds are good additions to breads, cakes, cookies, and meats, especially sausages.

Lovage
LEVISTICUM OFFICINALE

Lovage and celery are very much alike, tastewise. Lovage, however, grows much larger than celery. It is a hardy perennial native to the Mediterranean. It grows 3 to 6 feet tall with dark green serrated leaves. The stems are hollow and one of my favorite ways to use lovage is to cut the stems the length of drinking straws and use them to sip favorite tomato drinks. I also use fresh leaves in soups, stews, salads, and in any dish where a celery flavor is desired. I especially love to add a few chopped fresh lovage leaves to my summer potato salad. Lovage likes a moist, well-drained soil. It also likes full sun but will tolerate some shade. It can be started from seed, but I prefer to set out a plant from the nursery in early spring. The plants need to be fertilized in the spring. This plant produces umbels of tiny yellow flowers in midsummer. It usually takes 2 years for lovage to mature. Lovage seeds can be dried and used as a seasoning, but I prefer using the fresh leaves. The leaves can be dried on the stem hanging upside down. Strip dried leaves and store in airtight containers out of heat and light.

Lemon Balm
MELISSA OFFICIANALIS

Lemon balm is so easy to grow it can and often does become a nuisance. This shouldn't come as a surprise since it is a member of the mint family. I often am asked if lemon balm can be substituted for lemon verbena in a recipe. It can if you don't mind adding mint flavor and if you use 2 or 3 times more of it than lemon verbena. For pure lemon taste, lemon verbena is untouchable. Lemon balm is a hardy perennial that grows wherever mint grows. The stems are square, the 1- to 3-inch leaves are light green, serrated, and crinkled, not smooth. The plant will grow 1 to 2 feet tall and 1 to 1½ feet wide and, as stated earlier, it is a good spreader. It likes full sun or a little shade. This is one plant that will thrive even in thin, poor soil. The soil should be moist to get plants established. After that, lemon balm tolerates drought very well. Plants can be started from seed, but I like a nursery plant for an easy and quick start. The leaves can be picked anytime and picking actually helps the plant produce new side growth. Lemon balm leaves can be dried, but they lose a lot of flavor in the process. The fresh leaves are by far the best. Honeybees love a bed of lemon balm. The Greek word *melissa* means bee. Lemon balm is wonderful in hot or cold drinks, with poultry or veal, in jellies, in fruit salads, or wherever lemon or mint would enhance the flavor of a dish. Lemon-based furniture polish often has lemon balm oil added. This is a nice herb to have and to know because it is so easy to grow and to use.

Lemongrass
CYMBOPOGON CITRATUS

The best way to describe the taste of lemongrass is hot and lemony. It has become a very popular herb to use in Oriental cooking. Unfortunately (for me), lemongrass is a perennial tropical plant, so the plant(s) I set out each spring never reaches its full

growth of 6 feet. I have seen it in a southern garden where it was a spectacular clump.
This aromatic grass is native to southeast Asia. Plant lemongrass in full sun in sandy,
well-drained soil. It needs water and fertilizer to thrive. I fertilize the plant every
$1^1/_2$ to 2 months in my garden. The plant is almost always propagated by root division.
Lemongrass is cultivated commercially for its strong lemon-scented oil, which is used in
candy making. Brew a few pieces of the leaf for a delicious lemony tea and of course,
chopped fresh lemongrass is marvelous in Oriental and wok cookery. Anywhere you
want a spicy, lemony flavor, add a little chopped lemongrass. I have preserved
lemongrass by freezing pieces on a cookie sheet, scraping the pieces into a zip-top bag,
and storing the bag in the freezer for winter use.

Angelica
ANGELICA ARCHANGELICA

This biennial relative of parsley produces foliage the first year and magnificent umbels
of yellow-green flowers the second year. It is said angelica got its name because it
blooms on the feast day of the Archangel Michael. Yet another story says that angelica
was the herb of the angels sent as a gift to protect man from the plague. Angelica likes
rather cool, moist conditions and partial shade. It is a handsome 6-feet-tall plant and
2 to 3 feet wide. The stems are strong and hollow. Leaves are very large, dark green,
and serrated. All parts of angelica can be eaten. I remember my Mother buying
candied angelica stem for her fruitcakes. I seldom see it for sale today. All parts of

angelica are useful in cooking. The leaves are somewhat bitter tasting, but also have a slight taste of celery. The juniper-flavored seeds can be (and often are) substituted for real juniper berries in the making of gin.

Sweet Cicely
MYRRHIS ODORATA

I love this plant. Some people call it giant chervil. I don't cook with it much, but I love the way it looks in the garden. Sweet cicely is a member of the parsley family, so it sends up umbels of seedheads in the summer. These heads are first covered with white flowers, then beautiful shiny chocolate-brown seeds appear in early fall. Sweet cicely, a perennial, grows 2 to 3 feet tall and has delicate, dark green, lacy foliage that is almost fernlike. Seeds can be planted in rich, moist soil, or seedlings can be transplanted in spring. The seeds need to go through a cold period before they are planted. Another beauty of this plant is that it is an herb that loves the shade. All parts of sweet cicely are licorice flavored so the fresh leaves are fine to use in sauces, soups, salads, teas, and especially in fish cookery. I find that the leaves do not dry well, so fresh is best. The oil of sweet cicely is used in the making of the liqueur, Chartreuse. To dry the seedheads, place them in paper bags and hang to dry. The dry seeds will fall to the bottom of the bag. Store them in airtight containers. The seeds are splendid in cakes, cookies, and other pastries. Some cooks add them to an apple pie for a unique taste.

Cumin

CUMINUM CYMINUM

I never made good chili until I learned to add cumin powder to it — what a difference this one herb made! Cumin is a member of the carrot family and is related to caraway. It has a hot, spicy flavor. It is a spindly and not-very-attractive annual plant native to Egypt. Like anise, cumin requires a long, hot summer to fully ripen the seeds. The plants grow less than 1 foot tall, and have small, dark green leaves that look a little like fennel or dill leaves. Cumin does best planted in light, well-drained soil. Cumin produces small umbels of pinkish white flowers. Just before the seeds start to ripen, hang the umbel stems upside down in a brown paper bag. Tie the stems and bag top together, poke a few air holes in the sides of the bag, and let dry — this may take 2 or 3 weeks. Dried seeds fall to the bottom of the bag. Store these in airtight containers out of heat and light. (This is a good method for drying any of the aromatic herb seeds mentioned in this section.) Besides adding to chili, cumin seeds are a major ingredient in curry powders, in tomato sauces, in cheeses and cheese dishes, in marinades, in meat dishes, and many other dishes that need a hot and spicy flavor boost. We tried some curry dishes in Katmandu, Nepal, that were highly flavored with cumin — too hot for my taste, but if you're eating yak meat, maybe the taste of cumin is a blessing in disguise!

Caraway
CARUM CARVI

Caraway is another biennial plant with carrotlike leaves the first year, then leaves and umbels of white or pinkish white flowers the second year. Therefore, seeds are harvested the second year. After the crescent-shaped seeds ripen, the plant will die. In its second year, caraway grows about 2 feet tall. It is somewhat licorice flavored and is an important seed for the baker. Rye bread is good, but caraway-rye bread is wonderful! Caraway grows throughout the world, but commercial growing is done in small areas of Germany, Holland, and England. It is easiest to grow caraway from seed as the plant has a taproot that makes it difficult to transplant. Caraway likes well-drained soil and full sun. In midsummer, place the seedheads in a brown paper bag, close bag, and place in a warm, dry place for a couple of weeks. If you leave the seedheads on the plant too long, the seeds will scatter and you'll have little or no harvest. Store the dried seeds in an airtight container away from heat and light. To get full flavor, it is best to slightly crush the seeds before adding to breads, soups, vegetables, cheese and cheese dishes, and liqueurs. Fresh leaves can be added to green salads and they, too, taste of licorice. I understand that the large white carrotlike root also tastes of licorice. Caraway is indeed an important culinary herb.

Anise

PIMPINELLA ANISUM

Sweet and licorice are the words that come to mind when anise is mentioned. This important seed is widely used to flavor breads, cakes, cookies, candies, salads, sausages, and of course the anise-flavored liqueur, Anisette. Anise is a hardy annual native to the Middle East. The plants like full sun and rather dry soil conditions. Anise grows about $1\frac{1}{2}$ to 2 feet tall. Leaves at the base of the plant are rather large and broad, but leaves along the flower stalks are small and lacy. This relative of the parsley family produces umbels of creamy yellow flowers in early summer. It takes a good 3 months for the seeds to ripen. It's fun to have a few anise plants in the garden, but don't expect a big harvest! Unless you have lots of garden space, and plant lots of anise, you'll probably have to rely on your grocer or herb shop for a quantity of the seeds. If you do have some seedheads to dry, follow the general directions found in the cumin or caraway section.

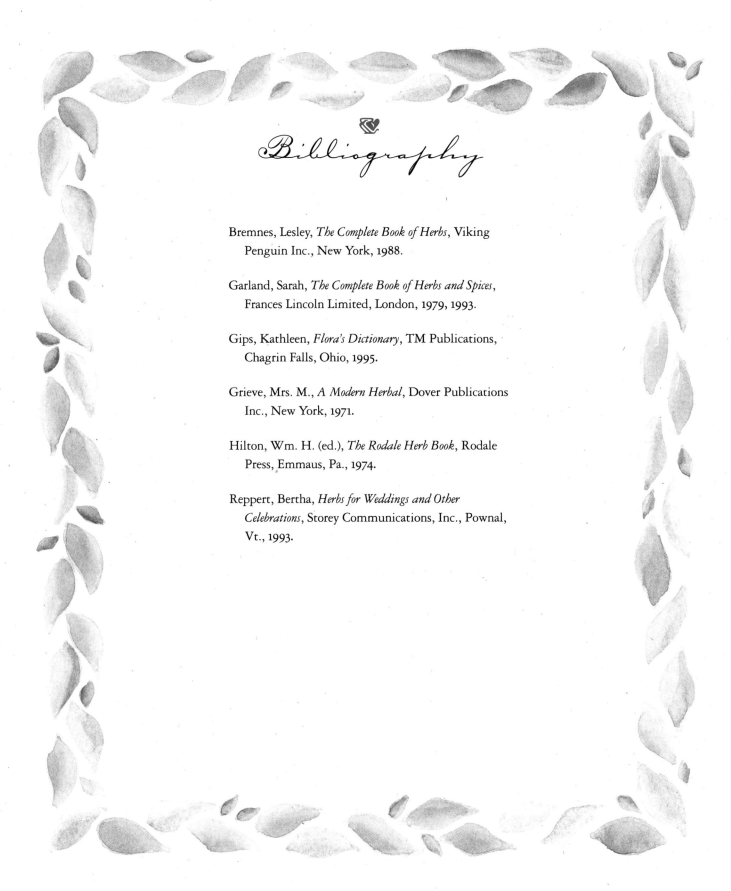

Bibliography

Bremnes, Lesley, *The Complete Book of Herbs*, Viking
 Penguin Inc., New York, 1988.

Garland, Sarah, *The Complete Book of Herbs and Spices*,
 Frances Lincoln Limited, London, 1979, 1993.

Gips, Kathleen, *Flora's Dictionary*, TM Publications,
 Chagrin Falls, Ohio, 1995.

Grieve, Mrs. M., *A Modern Herbal*, Dover Publications
 Inc., New York, 1971.

Hilton, Wm. H. (ed.), *The Rodale Herb Book*, Rodale
 Press, Emmaus, Pa., 1974.

Reppert, Bertha, *Herbs for Weddings and Other
 Celebrations*, Storey Communications, Inc., Pownal,
 Vt., 1993.

THESE ARE A FEW OF

My Favorite Things

I could not call this book complete without giving you the following recipes. The vinegars, oils, seasonings, and other recipes are so basic and so important to me that I can't imagine my kitchen shelves, refrigerator shelves, or pantry shelves without some of or most of them there at any given time. A few of these recipes can be found in one or more of my other books, but if I didn't include them here, the chapter would not be complete. Here indeed are a few of my favorite things and I hope some of them will become yours also!

My Favorite Things
Recipes

Here is a collection of favorites from my kitchen. They are all tried and true and add tremendous appeal to meals and menus. I often make double and give some for gifts. There is no particular order to this section — they're all just wonderful things!

MAKE THIS WITH FRESH HERBS
JUST ONCE AND YOU'LL NEVER
BE SATISFIED WITH DRIED HERBS
IN YOUR BOURSIN AGAIN.
BOURSIN (BORE-SAN) IS A
FRENCH WORD FOR HERBED
CREAM CHEESE. MEASURE THE
HERBS AFTER THEY'RE CHOPPED.

8 ounces cream cheese, at room temperature
1 tablespoon fresh lemon juice
1 or 2 cloves garlic, finely minced
1/2 teaspoon Worcestershire sauce
1/2 teaspoon dry mustard
1 tablespoon fresh parsley, finely chopped
1 tablespoon fresh chives, finely chopped
1 teaspoon fresh basil, finely chopped
1 teaspoon fresh Greek or Italian oregano, finely chopped
1 teaspoon fresh sage leaves, finely chopped
1 teaspoon fresh thyme leaves, finely chopped
1 teaspoon fresh rosemary, finely chopped
1 teaspoon fresh sweet marjoram, finely chopped

Fluff the cream cheese with an electric mixer. Add lemon juice, garlic, Worcestershire sauce and dry mustard and mix well. With a wooden spoon, stir in the chopped fresh herbs — do not use the mixer here. Place in a small bowl, cover and refrigerate. When ready to serve, bring to room temperature. Makes 1 cup, but recipe can easily be doubled.

Herbed Roasted Pepper Strips

Cut **red and yellow peppers** in half (from stem down). Remove ribs and seeds and roast pepper halves, skin side up, under broiler until pepper skins are blackened. Place blackened peppers in a brown grocery bag. Close bag and let peppers steam in bag for about 10 minutes. Remove the skins and cut peppers into strips. Pack strips loosely into a clean glass jar. Add to the jar 3 or 4 small sprigs of **fresh rosemary**, 2 or 3 sprigs of **fresh sweet marjoram or oregano**, a small top sprig of **fresh basil**, 2 **bay leaves** and 2 cloves chopped **garlic**. You may preserve these 1 of 3 ways. 1. Fill jar with a good quality olive oil; 2. Fill jar with a favorite herbed vinegar; or 3. Combine olive oil and vinegar, about half and half, and pour over the strips. Cover jar and refrigerate for 2 weeks to fully develop the flavors. The herbed strips are now ready to add to green salads or chop into pasta dishes, for example. Remember, if oil and garlic are used together, the product must always be kept refrigerated. If olive oil is used, it will congeal when refrigerated. Just bring the jar to room temperature long enough to liquefy, take out the strips you need, then place jar back in the refrigerator. These are one of the best "special" things I make.

Peach Melba Conserve

5   medium ripe peaches (about 1 1/2 pounds)
2   cups fresh red raspberries
1   cup light raisins
2   tablespoons fresh lemon juice
1   2-ounce package powdered fruit pectin (I like Sure Jell)
7   cups sugar
1/2   cup coarsely chopped walnuts

PEACH MELBA DESSERT IS ONE OF MY FAVORITES, SO WHEN I FOUND THIS RECIPE I KNEW I WOULD LOVE IT. I DO.

Drop peaches into boiling water for 30 seconds. Drop into cold water, then peel. Remove pits and chop peaches. Combine peaches, raspberries, raisins, lemon juice and pectin in a large, heavy kettle. Bring quickly to a boil, stirring often. Add sugar and bring again to a rolling boil that can't be stirred down. Boil rapidly for 1 minute, stirring constantly. Remove from heat. Skim off foam. Add walnuts and stir and skim for 6 or 7 minutes to cool and prevent fruit from floating. Ladle into seven or eight 8-ounce jars. Seal immediately. Either process for 5 minutes in a hot water bath, or cool jars and freeze. Delicious.

Hall Sisters' Chili Sauce

24 medium tomatoes, cut up

3 green peppers, seeded and chopped

8 small to medium onions, chopped

2 cups sugar

1 cup cider vinegar

1 teaspoon ground nutmeg

1 teaspoon ground cinnamon

1 teaspoon celery seeds

$^1/_2$ teaspoon ground cloves

3 tablespoons salt

THIS RECIPE IS FROM A COUSIN, ANNA JEAN HUNTER. IT IS SIMPLY THE BEST CHILI SAUCE I HAVE EVER EATEN. ONE OF THE HALL SISTERS WAS ANNA JEAN'S MOTHER, WHO HAPPENED TO BE ONE OF MY MOTHER'S BEST FRIENDS!

Combine tomatoes, green peppers and onions in a large, heavy kettle (Anna Jean uses her heavy pressure canner kettle and the mixture never sticks or burns) and cook until tender. Now add the remainder of ingredients and cook down to desired thickness, stirring often. As Anna Jean says, "It is wonderful on ham and beans, on meats, fried potatoes, hot dogs, to name a few. I freeze this now in pint containers. In the old days, it was canned." Makes 5 to 6 pints of delicious thick sauce.

Cranberry-Apricot Sauce for Poultry and Ham

1 pound fresh cranberries

2 cups sugar

2 cups water

$^3/_4$ cup apricot preserves

$^1/_4$ cup brandy (unflavored or apricot)

VERY EASY AND QUICK. GOES TOGETHER IN MINUTES. THIS SAUCE IS FABULOUS WITH THE HOLIDAY TURKEY OR HAM.

Cook cranberries with sugar and water until they pop — about 15 minutes. Remove from heat and stir in apricot preserves and brandy. Cool, cover and refrigerate. Makes 3 to $3^1/_2$ cups sauce.

Crisp Refrigerator Pickles

1   pint white distilled vinegar
1   large clove garlic, coarsely chopped
1   tablespoon whole cloves
1   tablespoon whole allspice
1   bay leaf
1   stick cinnamon
1   tablespoon celery seeds
1   tablespoon mustard seeds
1   tablespoon whole black peppercorns
1   2-inch piece gingerroot*, coarsely chopped, or 1 teaspoon ground ginger
1½ cups sugar
5   large cucumbers, unpeeled

In a large saucepan, combine all ingredients except the cucumbers. Boil mixture for 15 minutes. Cool, then strain. Slice cucumbers thin and place in a large crock or gallon jar (use no metal). Add cooled vinegar and spice mixture, stir gently and cover tightly. Refrigerate at least 3 days before using and stir pickles once a day. They are now ready to serve. These pickles, if refrigerated, will keep at least 2 weeks.

The gingerroot is best to use here. Use ground ginger only if gingerroot is unavailable.

I LOVE "CANNED THINGS" THAT DON'T HAVE TO BE CANNED! WE THINK OF PICKLES AS "CANNED," BUT THIS RECIPE HAS ALL THE GOOD FLAVOR OF PROCESSED PICKLES WITHOUT ALL THE WORK OF PROCESSING. THESE PICKLES WILL KEEP WELL IN THE REFRIGERATOR FOR SEVERAL WEEKS. WHAT COULD BE HANDIER? EACH RECIPE MAKES 2 QUARTS.

Apple-Ginger Relish

1   cup apples, measured after peeling, coring and chopping
1   cup crushed pineapple, drained
¼   cup walnuts, chopped
2   tablespoons candied ginger, minced
    Dash of salt

Combine all ingredients. Cover and let flavors blend for 2 hours or more before serving. Makes about 2 cups.

THIS IS A WONDERFUL FRESH APPLE RELISH TO SERVE WITH FALL AND WINTER MEALS. SERVE AS A RELISH WITH PORK OR POULTRY DISHES. IT'S VERY GOOD.

Best Barbecue Sauce

2 medium onions, finely chopped
2 tablespoons olive oil
2 cloves garlic, finely chopped
1¹/₂ teaspoons fresh gingerroot, finely chopped
1 14-ounce can plum tomatoes, coarsely chopped
1 cup prepared chili sauce
¹/₃ cup soy sauce
¹/₄ cup ketchup
¹/₄ cup dark brown sugar
¹/₄ cup dry sherry
5 tablespoons honey
1 tablespoon chili powder
¹/₈ teaspoon cayenne pepper
¹/₈ teaspoon dried oregano, crumbled

Sauté onion in oil in a medium-size saucepan for 1 to 2 minutes. Add garlic and gingerroot and sauté 3 more minutes. Stir in remaining ingredients. Bring to a boil. Lower heat and simmer for 30 minutes, stirring often. Cool sauce, then refrigerate in a closed container for up to 2 weeks. This makes 3 cups of sauce, or enough for 5 to 6 pounds of meat. Recipe can be doubled.

Creamy Horseradish Sauce

1 tablespoon confectioner's sugar
1 tablespoon fresh lemon juice
1 tablespoon Worcestershire sauce
2 tablespoons prepared horseradish
1 8-ounce package cream cheese, at room temperature
¹/₂ cup heavy cream, whipped

Blend sugar, lemon juice, Worcestershire sauce and horseradish into the softened cheese. Fold in whipped cream. Refrigerate until serving time. Perfectly wonderful with hot or cold beef, pork or ham. Makes 1¹/₂ cups.

Chili-Cheese-Pimiento Sandwich Filling

1 pound colby or longhorn cheese, shredded
1 4-ounce can green chilies, drained and chopped
1 2-ounce can pimiento, chopped
1 cup pecans, chopped
$^1/_2$ cup ripe olives, chopped
3 tablespoons mayonnaise (you may need to use a little more)

Combine all ingredients in a bowl. Cover and refrigerate. Use as a wonderful sandwich filler, either open-faced or covered. At room temperature, it's great to spread on crackers. Keep any leftover spread refrigerated. Will keep in refrigerator for 2 weeks. Makes $2^1/_2$ to 3 cups.

Bluebarb Jam

3 cups red rhubarb, finely chopped
3 cups fresh blueberries, crushed (I use a potato masher)
7 cups sugar
1 bottle liquid fruit pectin (I like Certo)

I'VE BEEN MAKING THIS SPECIAL JAM FOR YEARS. BLUEBERRIES AND RHUBARB ARE THE PERFECT SWEET-TART COMBINATION HERE. THIS IS TRULY ONE OF THE BEST JAMS I MAKE.

Combine fruits. Add sugar and mix well. Place over high heat in a large, heavy saucepan. Bring to a full boil and boil hard for 1 minute, stirring constantly. Remove from heat. Add pectin. Stir and skim for 6 or 7 minutes. Freeze or can in hot, sterile jars. Makes 8 or 9 half-pints.

Tomato Juice Cocktail

6   quarts tomato juice
1   teaspoon celery salt
3   teaspoons prepared horseradish
3   teaspoons fresh lemon juice
1   teaspoon Worcestershire sauce
1   teaspoon onion salt
   Salt and pepper to taste

Combine all ingredients and heat thoroughly, but do not boil. Stir to mix well. Can in hot, sterile jars in a hot water bath (follow jar manufacturer's directions for canning tomato juice), or refrigerate if using soon. Makes 6 quarts.

Fresh Herbed Tomato Juice

2   gallons ripe tomatoes, peeled and quartered
1   cup fresh basil, cleaned and chopped
1   cup fresh parsley, cleaned and chopped
1   cup onion, chopped
1/2   cup celery, chopped
   Sugar and salt to taste

Place all ingredients, except sugar and salt, in a large kettle and cook over medium heat until tomatoes are soft. Place small quantities at a time in a blender or food processor and blend until smooth. When all is blended, add a little sugar and salt, taste, and adjust seasonings. Makes 8 quarts.

If I make lots of this juice, I will can it in hot, sterile jars in a hot water bath (follow jar manufacturer's directions for canning tomato juice). If I'm going to use it soon, I'll cool the juice then refrigerate it and use within a week or two. Wonderful as a tomato juice cocktail before luncheon or dinner, or use as a base for a delicious tomato soup — just add butter and flour to thicken.

Spiced Tea Mix

2 4-inch sticks cinnamon, coarsely crushed

3 teaspoons whole cloves, coarsely crushed

3 cups orange pekoe tea

1/3 cup shredded, dried orange peel*

1 to 2 tablespoons candied gingerroot, finely chopped

Shred fresh orange peel, then let dry for a day or two. Then combine with remaining ingredients.

Combine cinnamon sticks and whole cloves on a cutting board. Roll over them with a rolling pin to crush and break up. Then combine all ingredients in a 1½-quart casserole. Cover casserole and bake at 300° for 15 to 20 minutes. Cool thoroughly, then spoon tea into a jar with a tight-fitting lid. Store in a cool place for at least a week to develop flavors. Use 1 to 2 teaspoons mix for each cup of boiling water. Makes 3 cups of dry mix.

THIS IS A WONDERFUL MIX TO HAVE FOR THE HOLIDAYS AND THE REMAINDER OF THE WINTER SEASON. MAKE FOR GIFTS — EVERYONE LOVES IT. ALMOST AS GOOD AS CONSTANT COMMENT!

---

helpful hints
THREE EASY HERB IDEAS

1. *To freeze chives, cut into small pieces, lay on a cookie sheet and freeze. When chives are frozen (in 20 to 30 minutes), scrape into a zip-top plastic bag and freeze immediately. All pieces are separated from each other. This is the best method of preserving fresh chives I have found.*

2. *Tie little bunches of rosemary, thyme or lavender together and use as a basting brush for barbecuing. Adds excellent herb flavor to the sauce you're basting with.*

3. *Freeze a supply of mint leaves in ice cube trays — bruise the leaves before adding. Fill tray 1/3 full of water. Lay leaf on water — 1 per cube — and freeze. Then fill up tray with water and quickly freeze. This way the leaf will be beautifully frozen in the middle of the cube!*

a collection of
DRIED SEASONINGS

These are all simple and quick to prepare, but what a difference they make when added to ordinary foods. There are seasonings here to enhance meats, vegetables, seafood, soups and stews. The seasoned salt, as well as the no-salt mixes, are special too.

THIS CLASSIC BLEND OF HERBS IS COMMON IN THE PROVENCE — THE SOUTH OF FRANCE. IT IS A COMBINATION OF DRIED AROMATIC HERBS. COOKS AND CHEFS OF THE PROVENCE SEASON CHEESE, MEAT, POULTRY, FISH AND VEGETABLE DISHES WITH THIS FLAVORFUL MIXTURE.

Herbes de Provence

Combine equal parts of **thyme, lavender, rosemary, savory, marjoram, basil,** and **fennel or anise seeds**. Thyme and lavender are always used. Store mixture in an airtight container away from heat and light. The Provence is a fabulous place to visit!

Goat Cheese à la Provence

Place a block or log of fresh mild **goat cheese** in a flat-bottom refrigerator jar. Combine $1/2$ cup **extra virgin olive oil** and 1 tablespoon **Herbes de Provence**. Pour over the cheese and marinate in the refrigerator for several days before serving. Serve with crusty **French bread**. This is a very typical dish to serve in the Provence.

Bouquet Garni

1   bay leaf
1   teaspoon dried French tarragon
1   teaspoon dried parsley
1   teaspoon dried rosemary
1   teaspoon dried thyme
6   or 8 whole black peppercorns

Place all ingredients in the middle of a coffee filter. Gather up and tie into a bundle. I like to have an assembly line of these herbs and make several at a time. Store them in a tightly covered glass jar.

Shrimp Boil Garni

This garni flavors 2 to 3 pounds of shrimps or crab.

1   teaspoon whole allspice
1   teaspoon dried thyme
1   teaspoon celery seeds
1   teaspoon whole black peppercorns
$1/2$ teaspoon cayenne pepper
$1/2$ teaspoon whole cloves
5   bay leaves, broken
3   dried hot chili peppers
   Salt, to taste

Combine ingredients in the middle of a coffee filter. Tie into a bundle. Bring 4 quarts of water to a boil. Add the garni and salt to taste. Boil 8 to 10 minutes, then add shrimps or crab and cook according to recipe directions.

A GARNI IS A VERY BASIC AND ANCIENT METHOD OF ADDING FLAVORS TO SOUPS, STEWS AND HEARTY DISHES. I USED TO TIE UP THE SEASONINGS IN LITTLE SQUARES OF CHEESECLOTH, BUT THEN I DISCOVERED COFFEE FILTERS! PLACE THE GARNI SEASONINGS IN THE MIDDLE OF A COFFEE FILTER, GATHER UP AND TIE WITH WHITE STRING. DROP THIS LITTLE BUNDLE INTO THE POT AND ALL THE FLAVOR GOES INTO THE BROTH OR STOCK. THIS FILTERED GARNI MAKES FOR A MUCH CLEARER BROTH.

Herb and Garlic Seasonings

Combine the following and blend well:

- 1 tablespoon dried basil, crumbled
- 1 tablespoon dried sweet marjoram, crumbled
- 2 teaspoons dried thyme, crumbled
- 1 teaspoon dried rosemary, crumbled
- $^3/_4$ teaspoon dried oregano, crumbled
- 2 teaspoons garlic powder

Store, covered, in an airtight container out of heat and light. Blend well before using. Use to season pork or beef. Sprinkle on the meat and rub seasonings into the surface. Add salt and pepper, if desired. Makes about $^1/_4$ cup. Use about 1 teaspoon of seasoning per 1 pound of meat.

I FIND THIS INDISPENSABLE IN MY KITCHEN. IT IS A WONDERFULLY SUBTLE BLEND OF FLAVORS THAT I USE TO SEASON MEATS AND VEGETABLES. THE FOOD PROCESSOR MAKES FAST WORK OF THIS JOB.

Gourmet Seasoned Salt

- 1 cup salt
- 2 teaspoons dry mustard
- $1^1/_2$ teaspoons dried oregano
- 1 teaspoon dried sweet marjoram
- 1 teaspoon dried thyme
- 1 teaspoon garlic powder
- 1 teaspoon curry powder
- $^1/_2$ teaspoon onion powder
- $^1/_2$ teaspoon celery seeds
- $^1/_4$ teaspoon dried dillweed

Combine all ingredients in a blender or food processor. Store in an airtight container. Makes about $1^1/_4$ cups.

Herb-Buttered Croutons

3 cups bread cubes cut from stale bread
1/4 cup melted butter
1/2 teaspoon onion powder
1/4 teaspoon garlic powder
1 teaspoon dried oregano, crumbled
1 teaspoon dried thyme, crumbled
1/2 teaspoon rubbed sage
1/4 teaspoon dried rosemary, crumbled

Use a 13x9-inch baking pan. Place bread cubes in pan and place in a 325° oven for 10 minutes. Melt butter and stir in all the seasonings. Remove pan from the oven and pour melted butter mixture over the bread cubes. Toss to coat well. Return to oven and bake until bread cubes are crisp, 20 minutes or so. Stir a time or two. Do not overbrown. Store in an airtight container, or freeze. Makes 3 cups.

SPRINKLE A FEW OF THESE HERBED CROUTONS ON YOUR GREEN SALADS, ON SOUPS, OR TO TOP A FAVORITE CASSEROLE.

Homemade Italian Bread Crumbs

1 teaspoon salt (or omit for salt-free crumbs)
1/4 cup grated Parmesan cheese
1/4 cup dried parsley flakes
1/4 cup dried onion flakes
1 1/2 teaspoons dried oregano
1 tablespoon dried basil
1 tablespoon garlic powder
1 tablespoon dried celery flakes
1 tablespoon paprika
3 cups dry bread crumbs

Combine all ingredients, except the bread crumbs, in a blender or food processor. Process on/off a few times to blend the ingredients. Add to the bread crumbs and toss to coat thoroughly.

TOAST STALE BREAD, PLACE IN A FOOD PROCESSOR AND MAKE YOUR OWN CRUMBS FOR THIS RECIPE, OR IF YOU'RE IN A HURRY, BUY A CAN OF CRUMBS FROM THE GROCERY. THESE FLAVORED CRUMBS ARE WONDERFUL ON CHICKEN OR FISH TO FRY OR BAKE, ON PORK CHOPS, IN ITALIAN DISHES AND TO TOP A CASSEROLE. THESE CRUMBS KEEP FRESHEST IF STORED IN THE REFRIGERATOR. MAKES ABOUT 4 CUPS.

USE TO SEASON MEATS, SOUPS, STEWS AND VEGETABLES. A PERFECT SEASONING FOR SOMEONE WHO SHOULD CUT BACK ON SALT INTAKE.

No-Salt Seasonings with Garlic

1/2 teaspoon cayenne pepper

1 tablespoon garlic powder

1 tablespoon dried basil, crumbled

1 tablespoon dried sweet marjoram, crumbled

1 tablespoon dried thyme, crumbled

1 tablespoon dried parsley, crumbled

1 tablespoon dried summer or winter savory (optional)

1 tablespoon dried mace

1 tablespoon onion powder

1 tablespoon black pepper

1 tablespoon dried sage, crumbled

Combine all ingredients. Store in an airtight container out of heat and light. Makes 1/3 to 1/2 cup.

SHARE SOME WITH A FRIEND ON A SALT-RESTRICTED DIET. ESPECIALLY GOOD ON BAKED CHICKEN, ROAST BEEF, IN SOUPS AND STEWS. USE ABOUT 1 TEASPOON TO SEASON 1 POUND OF MEAT. SPRINKLE INTO SOUPS AND TASTE UNTIL THE SOUP IS JUST RIGHT. DON'T OVERDO ON THESE DRY SEASONINGS — THEY'RE POTENT AND CAN DEFINITELY KILL A DISH WITH TOO MUCH OF A GOOD THING!

No-Salt Herb Seasonings

1/4 cup dried thyme, crumbled

1/4 cup dried parsley, crumbled

1/4 cup dried French tarragon, crumbled

1 tablespoon dried rosemary, crumbled

1 tablespoon dried sage, crumbled

3 tablespoons freeze-dried chives

1 tablespoon celery seeds

Combine all ingredients, mix well and store in a tightly covered container. Makes about 1 cup of seasonings.

Chicken and Turkey Seasonings

Rind of 2 lemons, thinly shredded
$^1\!/_2$ cup dried parsley
1 tablespoon salt
1 tablespoon dried thyme
1 tablespoon dried sweet marjoram
1 teaspoon freshly ground pepper

Spread rind between sheets of paper towels and let dry for 2 or 3 days. Then combine with remainder of ingredients. Store in an airtight container out of heat and light. Sprinkle on chicken, turkey or pork. Makes a little more than $^1\!/_2$ cup.

DRY THE LEMON RIND 2 OR 3 DAYS BEFORE BLENDING WITH OTHER INGREDIENTS. THIS IS MARVELOUS ON A ROASTING CHICKEN OR ON A TURKEY. IF DESIRED, MIX THE SEASONINGS WITH MELTED BUTTER TO BASTE THE BIRD TOWARD THE END OF ROASTING TIME.

Sausage Seasonings

2 teaspoons ground sage
1 to 2 teaspoons salt (to your taste)
$^1\!/_2$ teaspoon ground allspice
$^1\!/_2$ teaspoon dried thyme, crumbled
$^1\!/_4$ teaspoon mace
1 teaspoon freshly ground black pepper
1 teaspoon sweet paprika
3 tablespoons white wine
2 pounds fresh ground pork

Thoroughly mix all seasonings into the pork. Form the sausage into patties. Start patties in a cold skillet and fry until no pink remains. Makes 8 to 10 patties.

I USUALLY DON'T LIKE SEASONED SAUSAGE FROM THE GROCERY. I BUY FRESH GROUND PORK AND USE THESE SEASONINGS TO SEASON MY OWN. WHAT A DIFFERENCE!

ollowing are 3 great herbed and spiced mustards. I can't possibly choose a favorite — they are each that good. The Dill Mustard is perfect with pork or roast beef. The Herbed Dijon Mustard is special on a roast beef sandwich or a ham sandwich. The Spiced German Mustard is a medium-hot spicy mustard that is so good on a pork, beef or ham sandwich.

Spiced German Mustard

1/3	cup mustard seeds
1/2	cup water
1/4	cup dry mustard
1	cup cider vinegar
1	small onion, chopped
2	tablespoons brown sugar
2	cloves garlic, finely minced
1	teaspoon salt
1/2	teaspoon ground cinnamon
1/4	teaspoon ground allspice
1/4	teaspoon dill seeds
1/4	teaspoon dried French tarragon
1/8	teaspoon ground turmeric
2	tablespoons honey

Soak mustard seeds in water for 3 or 4 hours to soften. Combine remaining ingredients, except the honey, in a saucepan. Bring to a boil. Reduce heat and simmer, uncovered, for 20 minutes. This will reduce the volume by about one-half. Pour hot mixture through a wire strainer into the mustard seed and water mixture. Transfer to a blender or food processor and purée until smooth. Place mixture in top of a double boiler and place over simmering water. Cook and stir 5 to 10 minutes. Stir in the honey. Remove from heat. Cover and cool, then refrigerate for a week to develop flavors. Will keep in refrigerator, covered, for at least a month. Makes about 1 cup, but recipe can be doubled.

Dill Mustard

- ⅓ cup dry mustard (I like Coleman's)
- ½ cup prepared mild yellow mustard
- 6 tablespoons sugar
- 6 tablespoons corn oil (or substitute honey another time)
- 1 tablespoon dried dillweed
- 2 tablespoons hot water

Whisk the mustards, sugar and oil together and blend thoroughly. Add the dillweed and hot water. Combine well. Store in the refrigerator. Makes about 1 cup. Stir a tablespoon of this marvelous mustard into the mayonnaise for your next potato salad. I like 1 tablespoon mustard for each cup mayonnaise.

THIS FLAVORFUL MUSTARD IS ESPECIALLY GOOD ON ROAST BEEF OR HAM SANDWICHES. ADD A TABLESPOON OR TWO TO YOUR NEXT POTATO SALAD.

Herbed Dijon Mustard

- ½ teaspoon dried tarragon, crumbled
- ½ teaspoon dried sweet marjoram, crumbled
- ½ teaspoon dried thyme, crumbled
- ⅛ teaspoon dried oregano, crumbled
- ½ teaspoon snipped fresh chives (or freeze-dried)
- 1 teaspoon fresh parsley, finely chopped
- 1 teaspoon fresh lemon juice
  Dash of salt and pepper
- 1 cup smooth (not grainy) Dijon mustard

Add all ingredients to the mustard and blend thoroughly. Keep mustard refrigerated between use. Better than what's passed back and forth between the Rolls Royces! Makes 1 cup.

*Marinades are special mixtures to add flavor and tenderness to meats, poultry and seafood. Marinades are usually made up of 3 major elements: an **acid** (such as vinegar, fruit juices, soy sauce) to break down muscle fiber; an **oil** (such as olive oil, other vegetable oils, flavored oils) to coat and seal the meat; and **aromatics** (such as herbs, spices, hot peppers, onions and garlic) to add flavor. Marinades are definitely basic to much fine cooking — you'll be glad you learned how to use them.*

HERE IS A GOOD HERBY, BUT NOT OVERWHELMING, MARINADE FOR CHICKEN. GRILL OR BROIL THE CHICKEN OUTSIDE OR INSIDE. AN OUTSIDE BARBECUING HINT: BAKE MARINADE CHICKEN (OR BEEF OR PORK) IN A 350° OVEN TO PARTIALLY COOK THE MEAT BEFORE TAKING IT TO THE GRILL. FINISH GRILLING AND BASTING OUTDOORS. YOU WON'T BURN UP THE OUTSIDE TRYING TO COOK THE INSIDE!

Lemon Marinade for Chicken

$1/4$	cup fresh lemon juice
$1/4$	cup soy sauce
$1/2$	cup vegetable oil
2	cloves garlic, finely minced
1	teaspoon dried thyme
1	teaspoon dried basil
1	teaspoon dried rosemary

Combine all ingredients and marinate chicken pieces in a zip-top bag for 4 to 6 hours in the refrigerator. This is enough marinade for 1 frying chicken.

A BASIC MARINADE RECIPE YOU'LL REACH FOR OFTEN. GIVES EXCEPTIONAL FLAVOR TO A PORK TENDERLOIN ROAST.

Marinade for Pork

$1/2$	cup soy sauce
$1/4$	cup vegetable oil
2	tablespoons dark molasses
1	tablespoon ground ginger
2	teaspoons dry mustard
6	cloves garlic, peeled and minced

Combine all ingredients. Pour over a 4- to 5-pound pork roast and marinate 8 hours or overnight. Bake at 325° for about 2 hours, or until a meat thermometer registers 160°.

Pork Marinade with Chili Sauce

³/₄ cup soy sauce
¹/₄ cup fresh lemon juice
1 tablespoon chili sauce
1 tablespoon brown sugar
1 clove garlic, minced
1 teaspoon fresh lemon thyme (if available), or ¹/₃ teaspoon dried thyme leaves

Combine sauce ingredients. Place 4 to 6 pork chops or chicken breast quarters in a zip-top plastic bag. Pour marinade over. Refrigerate pork overnight, or 6 hours or more. If marinating chicken breasts, you won't need to marinate as long — 4 to 6 hours is enough. Grill meat outside over hot coals, or broil inside until done. Garnish with fresh thyme sprigs or parsley. Makes 1 cup.

Teriyaki Sauce

3 green onions, chopped, including green tops
¹/₃ cup soy sauce
2 tablespoons peeled fresh gingerroot, grated
2 tablespoons light brown sugar
4 pork chops each about ³/₄-inch thick

Combine sauce ingredients. Place chops in a zip-top plastic bag. Pour marinade over chops. Marinate at room temperature for about 1 hour. Remove chops from marinade and grill or broil until chops are done (no pink color remains). Serves 4. Use this same marinade on beef steaks, but marinate for several hours before cooking.

THE CHILI SAUCE MAKES THIS MARINADE SPECIAL. I HAVE USED THIS SAME MARINADE ON BONELESS, SKINLESS CHICKEN BREASTS AND LOVE WHAT IT DOES FOR THE CHICKEN.

FOR SOME OF THE BEST PORK CHOPS YOU'LL EVER TASTE, MARINATE THEM IN THIS DELICIOUS SAUCE.

Marinade for Fish and Seafood

$^1/_2$ cup olive oil
    Juice of $^1/_2$ fresh lemon
1   tablespoon fresh lemon thyme leaves, chopped, or lemon verbena leaves, chopped,
        or French tarragon leaves, chopped (or 1 teaspoon dried herb)
2   fresh green onions, finely chopped, including the green tops

Combine all ingredients and add to seafood or fish. Marinate for 30 minutes to 1 hour,
but no more. Broil, grill or bake according to recipe being used. Makes about $^3/_4$ cup.

Hearty Beef Marinade

$^1/_2$ cup olive oil or vegetable oil
$^1/_2$ cup red wine vinegar
2   tablespoons fresh oregano, sweet marjoram or thyme, chopped (or 2 teaspoons
        dried herb)
2   small cloves garlic, peeled and minced
1   bay leaf, crumbled
6   whole black peppercorns
$^1/_4$ to $^1/_2$ teaspoon hot pepper flakes

Combine all ingredients. Pour marinade over red meats and marinate several hours or
overnight. Enough marinade for about $1^1/_2$ to 2 pounds of meat.

my favorite
FLAVORED BUTTERS

A flavored butter is another trick up your culinary sleeve to liven up otherwise dull foods. Herbed butters can be used many ways: season vegetables; spread on bread to bake or broil; add to cheese and cream sauces; use as a sandwich spread; dab on fish, meats or poultry to bake, broil or grill. Any of the following butters packs a lot of flavor.

Fresh Herb Butter

1 tablespoon fresh green basil, chopped
1 tablespoon fresh sweet marjoram, chopped
1 tablespoon fresh chives, chopped
1 teaspoon fresh rosemary, chopped
2 sticks unsalted butter, at room temperature
1 teaspoon fresh lemon juice

Whenever I flavor butters with fresh herbs, I chop the herbs with scissors into small pieces. I don't like to chop them in the food processor because each herb loses its identity and also the butter will be green if the herbs are chopped to a mush. So, for the above recipe, combine the chopped herbs with the softened butter and lemon juice — I use a wooden spoon — for a delicious butter to use on vegetables, on bread and in sauces. Makes 1 cup.

I MAKE THIS BUTTER THROUGHOUT THE SUMMER. NOTHING BEATS FRESH HERBS AND THAT IS ESPECIALLY TRUE IN THIS BUTTER RECIPE. LATE IN THE SUMMER, MAKE THIS BUTTER IN QUANTITY. DIVIDE INTO APPROXIMATELY $1/2$-CUP MEASUREMENTS, WRAP WELL AND FREEZE FOR WINTER USE.

Ginger–Honey Butter

2 sticks butter, at room temperature
1/4 cup honey
1/4 teaspoon ground cardamom
2 tablespoons candied gingerroot, finely minced
1 tablespoon grated orange rind

Combine in a small bowl. Cover and refrigerate or wrap well and freeze. Makes 1 1/4 cups.

THIS BUTTER IS SUPERB ON HOT BISCUITS OR SCONES AND OF COURSE ON TOAST.

Garlic-Parmesan Butter

6 tablespoons unsalted butter, at room temperature
3 tablespoons olive oil
1/2 cup freshly grated Parmesan cheese
2 teaspoons minced garlic
1/4 teaspoon freshly ground black pepper
1 large loaf Italian bread, split lengthwise

Blend the five ingredients together in a small bowl. Butter insides of bread halves. Broil, butter side up, on a baking sheet until bubbly and golden. Makes about 2/3 cup.

Fines Herbes Butter

1 cup butter, at room temperature
2 tablespoons dried parsley flakes
2 tablespoons chopped fresh chives (or freeze-dried)
1 teaspoon dried French tarragon
1 teaspoon dried chervil
1/2 teaspoon salt
Dash of pepper

Blend well in a small bowl. Makes 1 cup of great herb butter. Spread on slices of French bread and toast under the broiler. Dab on steaks to be grilled or broiled. Dab on chicken to be baked, broiled or barbecued.

Lemon-Rosemary Butter

2 sticks butter, at room temperature
1 teaspoon fresh lemon juice
1 tablespoon fresh rosemary, or 1 teaspoon dried, crushed
1 teaspoon fresh lemon thyme or lemon verbena leaves, finely chopped

Combine in a small bowl. Cover and refrigerate or wrap well and freeze. Makes 1 cup.

A STAPLE IN THE FRENCH KITCHEN. THE FOUR HERBS USED HERE ARE USED IN MANY WAYS IN FRENCH COOKERY.

SEASON COOKED VEGETABLES WITH THIS BUTTER OR ADD TO GRAVIES AND SAUCES TO DRESS CHICKEN, TURKEY OR MEATS.

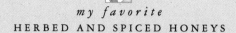

my favorite
HERBED AND SPICED HONEYS

I love honey just as it is, but when I add spices, herbs or flowers, honey takes on a whole new and wonderful taste. These honeys can be used to sweeten teas, to spread on breads, biscuits or scones, to sweeten fruits and other desserts and as a base for salad dressings.

General Method for Flavoring Honeys

The following herbs, spices, seeds and flowers make exceptionally good flavored honeys.

anise seeds	*thyme, dried leaves*
cardamom seeds, crushed	*sweet marjoram, dried*
cinnamon bark, broken	*lemon verbena leaves, fresh or dried*
coriander seeds	*scented geranium leaves, fresh or dried*
fennel seeds	*the mints, fresh or dried*
whole cloves	*lavender flowers*
whole allspice, crushed	*rose petals*
rosemary, dried leaves	*viola flowers*

Bruise fresh leaves (crush dried leaves) and seeds and place them in the bottom of a saucepan. Pour honey over the mixture. Stir and heat only until honey is lukewarm, 2 or 3 minutes. Do not boil. Pour honey into sterilized jars and seal. Store at room temperature about 1 week to develop flavors. Then rewarm the honey gently to liquefy. Strain out leaves, seeds, spices or flowers and reseal. If you wish, add a cinnamon stick to the Spiced Honey or a flower or two to flower-flavored honey. Just don't leave all the ingredients in or it would be difficult to spread.

*This **general method** (above) is for flavoring honeys with all the following recipes.*

Spiced Honey

2   cups honey
6   cinnamon sticks, 2 to 3 inches long
1   teaspoon whole allspice
1   teaspoon whole cloves

Combine and follow the **general method** (above) for flavoring the honey.

283

Orange Spiced Honey

1   or 2 small navel oranges, sliced ½-inch thick
     Whole cloves
3   whole cinnamon sticks
1½ pints honey
3   half-pint canning jars

Stud the peel of each orange slice with whole cloves — 6 or 8 cloves per slice. Follow the **general method** for flavoring (see page 283), then place 2 slices of orange against the sides of each of 3 jars. Add 1 cinnamon stick per jar and divide honey between jars. Cover and refrigerate* this honey. Use within 2 weeks.

Honey refrigerated longer than 2 weeks will probably turn cloudy and milky looking.

Lavender Honey

2   cups honey
2   tablespoons lavender flowers

Combine and follow the **general method** for flavoring the honey (see page 283).

Scented Geranium Honey

For each jar of honey, place 1 clean **scented geranium leaf** in the bottom, pour warm **honey** over, cover and let stand for 1 week. Either discard leaf, or leave leaf in the jar and use honey within a week or two. Very good on tea biscuits or drizzled on pound cake.

Honey Flavored with Seeds

Use 1 tablespoon of **seeds** (anise, cardamom, coriander or fennel) per 1 cup of **honey**. Crush seeds and follow the **general method** for flavoring honey (see page 283).

Herb-Flavored Honey

Use ¹/₂ to 1 tablespoon **herbs** (depending on your taste) per 1 cup of **honey**. Bruise or crush the leaves and follow the **general method** for flavoring honey (see page 283).

*B*y now, you know that I love to take ordinary, everyday staples and turn them into flavorful products. Oils cannot be overlooked in this discussion. If you follow some basic rules, properly made infused oils are safe to use.

Several years ago, oils infused with garlic were removed from grocery store shelves because of the potential (or in some case, the real) problem of botulism. New methods have been found to commercially bottle these oils, so don't be afraid to buy them now from your grocery store, gourmet food shop or your favorite herb shop.

Following are some rules and suggestions for making your own seasoned or infused oils. Read through the entire list before starting your oils.

1. Use only clean and moisture-free herbs or other plant material.

2. Use sterilized wide-mouth jars for olive oil-based flavored oils. Olive oil congeals when it is cold, and you can spoon out the oil needed from a wide-mouth jar. (I actually refrigerate any olive oil — seasoned or plain — after I open it.) I find it stays fresher much longer if refrigerated.

3. Add oil to the herbs or garlic and immediately place in the refrigerator — it will take about 2 weeks to develop the flavors in the refrigerator. Be sure to completely cover the herbs with oil to cut down on the possibility of mold forming.

4. After the desired flavor is achieved, bring oil to room temperature, strain out all plant material and other seasonings and discard them. Now strain the oil through a very fine sieve into another sterilized wide-mouth jar. Cover jar and keep refrigerated at all times.

5. For a little decoration or color, add a dried hot pepper or a whole bay leaf to the jar. Do not leave soft plant material in the oil more than 2 weeks.

6. I like to use extra virgin or virgin olive oil for cold infused oils. Corn, soybean, safflower, canola, grapeseed and especially peanut oils are best for hot infused oils.

7. Make small quantities of oils at a time as flavored or infused oils tend to deteriorate with age.

8. Bruise fresh herbs, or slightly crush dried herbs and seeds before adding them to the oil. This greatly helps to release their flavors into the oil.

9. Oils can be infused in a number of ways and recipes follow to show those ways. Basically, you can infuse oils the cold method, the hot method and a puréed method.

Herbed Olive Oil
COLD METHOD

6 sprigs fresh rosemary (3 to 4 inches long), or 1 tablespoon dried
3 sprigs fresh thyme, or 1½ teaspoons dried
3 fresh sprigs of oregano, or 1½ teaspoons dried
1 large bay leaf
8 to 10 whole black peppercorns
3 cloves garlic, coarsely chopped
¼ teaspoon hot red pepper flakes (optional)
　Good quality olive oil*

Place herbs and seasonings in a sterilized glass jar. Add olive oil to totally cover the herbs (push them down into the oil with a spoon). Seal jar and refrigerate. Leave in refrigerator for about 2 weeks to develop the flavors. Bring oil to room temperature, discard all seasonings and herbs. Filter oil through cheesecloth or fine sieve into a sterilized wide-mouth jar. Oil is now ready to use. Keep refrigerated all the time except when using. As you know, olive oil congeals when cold, so just spoon out what you need and immediately place it back in the refrigerator. Makes 1½ to 2 cups.

If your seasoned oils are to be used for salad dressings or marinades, use an extra virgin olive oil. However, if they're to be used for sautéing, use a lesser grade oil for 2 reasons. First, it will cost less, and second, it can withstand higher temperature before smoking and burning.

Herbed Olive Oil
HOT METHOD

Combine **2 cups olive oil** (*not* extra virgin) in a heavy saucepan with **4 cloves smashed garlic**. Bruise **4 sprigs fresh sage, 10 sprigs fresh thyme**, and **2 sprigs fresh oregano**. Add to oil and garlic. Cook over low heat for 30 to 40 minutes (just barely have oil bubbling). As garlic browns, remove it and discard. Let oil cool, then strain through a sieve into a wide-mouthed jar. Cover jar and refrigerate. Spoon out the congealed oil as you need it. Brush this oil on both sides of French bread slices (toasted first). Lay slices on a cookie sheet and toast again until hot and crisp. Also wonderful brushed on vegetables to roast. Makes 2 cups.

Mushroom-Infused Oil

12	to 15 dried porcini mushrooms
$^2/_3$	cup hot water
2	cups extra virgin olive oil

Place mushrooms in a bowl. Pour hot water over them and let stand until they're soft, about 15 minutes. Remove mushrooms from water and place on layers of paper towels. Pat them dry with more paper towels. Place mushrooms and oil in a microwave-safe bowl. Microwave on high for $1^1/_2$ to 2 minutes until oil is moderately warm to the touch — do not boil. Let oil cool, then cover and refrigerate for 1 week. Bring oil to room temperature, strain out and discard mushrooms. Place oil in a sterilized wide-mouth jar and spoon out as needed. Keep refrigerated.

Garlic Oil

| 5 | whole cloves garlic, peeled |
| 1 | cup peanut oil |

Place garlic and oil in a heavy saucepan over medium heat. Simmer oil until garlic turns golden brown. Remove from heat and let mixture come to room temperature. Remove and discard garlic. Pour oil into a sterilized bottle (peanut oil will not congeal when cold) and refrigerate. It is very flavorful for about 3 weeks. After 3 weeks, discard and make new oil.

Puréed Olive Oil

The usual ratio for this recipe is 1 part puréed herb to 1 part oil. Process clean, dry, fresh **herb leaves** of your choice in the food processor. Measure the purée and add an equal amount of **oil** slowly. Process to blend well with on/off motions.

This is a potent oil and full of herb flavor. Brush on pizza crusts before adding the sauce, cheeses and toppings. Drizzle on pasta dishes to add flavor. This is wonderful brushed on Italian flat bread (focaccia).

For another great oil, see Lemon Herbs Oil in the Lemon Verbena Chapter, p. 97.

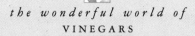

the wonderful world of
VINEGARS

*O*f all the things I make, nothing packs more flavor than the vinegars. Once you learn to make and use them, you'll be a better and more creative cook. First of all, I should say that we aren't actually making vinegars — we're flavoring them. Just like the article on infused oils, there are rules and guidelines to follow to ensure good success.

1. One of the first questions I'm always asked in a lecture is which vinegar to use. I use all of them at one time or another as you'll see by the vinegar recipes in this book. The vinegars are white distilled, cider, white wine, red wine and rice. For color and clarity, I like white distilled vinegar.

2. Use only sterilized bottles and jars for your vinegars.

3. Use no metal in vinegar making. Cork or rubber are best to use for sealing. If non-metallic lids are unavailable, I use 3 or 4 layers of plastic wrap to cover the opening, then secure the wrap with a rubber band.

4. If you choose to heat your vinegar, a nonreactive or noncorrosive pan (such as stainless steel or granite) should be used. The pan must not be affected by the acidity of the vinegar. Heat just to the boiling point.

5. The plant material should be clean and moisture-free. Cut the herbs, swish them in tepid water to clean, then lay them on clean towels or several layers of paper toweling and let dry. Do not add vinegar to wet herbs.

6. Bruise fresh herb leaves before adding to the jar — the flavor will be released into the vinegar more quickly. If seasoning with seeds, crush them slightly (a rolling pin works well) before adding to the jar.

7. An age-old question is whether to heat or not heat the vinegar. You'll find my recipes use both methods and it's really up to you. Heating the vinegar will begin releasing the flavor and color of the flavorings more quickly than not heating it, but I usually prefer pouring the room temperature vinegar over the flavorings — I like the slower and longer release of color and flavor. It's a personal choice.

8. How long to steep vinegars? Flowers will flavor the vinegar in just a few days. Herb vinegar will take 3 to 4 weeks to fully develop flavors. Fruit vinegars will take about 3 weeks to develop. Dried herb vinegars will need 3 to 4 weeks to reach full flavor.

9. I've mentioned this earlier — I do believe straining vinegars through a coffee filter produces the clearest and brightest vinegars. Cheesecloth just doesn't filter out all the little bits like a coffee filter does.

continued on page 290

10. *Store your vinegars out of heat and light. Some of the incredible colors you get from these vinegars will quickly dull and fade if stored in sunny locations. They may look beautiful in a window, but not for long!*

11. *No one ever told me to do this, but I believe my fruit vinegars retain their color and taste longer if they are kept refrigerated.*

12. *Flower vinegars are rather fragile. They will lose their flavor and taste before the fruit- or herb-infused vinegars will. Herb- and seed-infused vinegars should be at optimum flavor, aroma and color for at least a year if properly handled and stored.*

13. *The question about vinegars I am asked most often is, "How do I use them?" Good question — easy answers. Use FLOWER VINEGARS to splash on fresh fruits (splash is the key word here!), or liven up canned or frozen fruits; mix with a little oil to dress a salad (fresh spinach salad dressed with a little nasturtium flower vinegar, a little oil and a handful of fresh nasturtium flowers is memorable). Use BERRY VINEGARS to splash on fruits; to deglaze the fry pan; to add to cream sauces and gravies; to make salad dressings; to make vinaigrettes. Use HERB VINEGARS to make salad dressings; to make marinades; to splash on cold, cooked vegetables; to deglaze the fry pan; to add to sauces and gravies; to make vinaigrettes; to add to mayonnaise-based salads (1 tablespoon of vinegar to 1 cup mayonnaise is about right).*

Besides the vinegars you find in this chapter, look for the following vinegars throughout the book. They are all delicious and add tremendous flavor to otherwise ordinary foods.

Basil Vinegar (p. 26)
Chive Blossom Vinegar (p. 43)
Sage-Caraway Vinegar (p. 201)
Garlic and Parsley Red Wine Vinegar (p. 163)
Dill or Dill-Garlic Vinegar (p. 55)
Herbs and Spices Vinegar (p. 143)
Ginger-Mint Vinegar (p. 117)
Mint Vinegar (p. 110)
French Tarragon Vinegar (p. 81)

My Mixed Herb Vinegar

2   to 3 cups green basil leaves, bruised
1   cup tender thyme sprigs, bruised
1   cup tender sweet marjoram sprigs, bruised
1   cup Greek oregano sprigs, bruised
4   large cloves garlic, peeled and coarsely chopped
10 to 15 whole black peppercorns
1   teaspoon dried hot red pepper flakes
2   bay leaves
1   whole dried cayenne pepper per bottle (optional)
    White distilled or white wine vinegar

Wash herbs. Lay on clean towels and blot with another towel. They must be moisture-
free. Pack herbs into a 1 gallon glass or plastic jar that has been sterilized. Pour cool
(or warm to the boiling point — your choice) white distilled or white wine vinegar over
the herbs. Cover with a nonmetallic lid, set jar in a cool, dark place and let steep for
3 weeks. Taste. If flavored enough, strain out herbs and discard them. Fit a filter into a
small funnel and fill sterilized jars or bottles. Add a whole cayenne pepper, if desired.
Cork, label and enjoy! You can easily cut this recipe in half.

THIS INTENSELY FLAVORED
AND FRAGRANT VINEGAR IS ONE
OF THE BEST I MAKE. IT IS
SUPERB IN SALAD DRESSINGS, ON
MARINATED VEGETABLES AND IN
MEAT MARINADES. THERE ARE
COUNTLESS COMBINATIONS OF
HERBS YOU COULD USE, BUT THE
HERBS AND SEASONINGS I
USUALLY USE ARE IN "MY
MIXED HERB VINEGAR" RECIPE.

Pantry Shelf Herb Vinegar

1   quart white distilled or white wine vinegar
1   large carrot, scraped and cut into quarters
1   rib celery, washed and cut into half lengthwise
1   large bay leaf
2   cloves garlic, peeled and coarsely chopped
1   teaspoon dried basil
1   teaspoon dried parsley flakes
1   teaspoon dried celery flakes

In a half-gallon glass or plastic jar, combine all ingredients. Cover with a nonmetallic lid.
Place in a cool, dark place for 3 to 4 weeks. Shake jar once in awhile. When ready to
bottle, strain through a coffee filter fitted into a funnel. Seal or cork.

AS THE TITLE INDICATES,
YOU DON'T HAVE TO HAVE
FRESH HERBS TO MAKE THIS
VINEGAR. YOU'LL NEED A HALF-
GALLON-SIZE CONTAINER TO
HOLD THE VINEGAR AND ALL
THE SEASONINGS.

Summer Berries Vinegar

2   cups berries (blueberries, red or black raspberries, blackberries or strawberries)
2   cups vinegar (cider, white distilled, rice or white wine)
1   cup dry white wine
$^{1}/_{3}$ cup sugar

In a noncorrosive saucepan, combine fruit, vinegar, wine and sugar. Stir with a spoon to slightly bruise the fruit, but do not mash fruit. Heat to a boil. Reduce heat and simmer, uncovered, for 3 minutes. Remove from heat and cool. Place vinegar in a sterilized jar. Cover with a nonmetallic covering and refrigerate for 3 weeks to develop flavors. Strain vinegar through cheesecloth first. Discard berries and cheesecloth. Strain again (through a coffee filter fitted into a funnel) into a sterilized bottle. Cork or seal. Makes about 3 cups. I have always felt the fruit vinegars stay freshest if kept refrigerated.

Cranberry Vinegar

2   cups fresh or thawed frozen cranberries
$^{1}/_{2}$ cup honey
$^{1}/_{2}$ cup white wine
1   clove garlic
1   cup red wine vinegar
$^{3}/_{4}$ cup cranberry juice

Combine cranberries, honey, wine and garlic in a saucepan and bring to a boil. Reduce heat and simmer for about 20 minutes, stirring occasionally. Cool for 20 to 30 minutes, then place in the bowl of a food processor. Process to a fine purée. Add red wine vinegar and cranberry juice. Process on/off just to thoroughly combine. Place in a sterilized bottle or jar, cover and refrigerate for 1 week. Strain and discard cranberries. Filter into another sterilized container, cover and refrigerate. Makes about 3 cups.

Nasturtium Flower Vinegar

2   cups nasturtium flowers
10 whole black peppercorns
1   quart white distilled or white wine vinegar

Sterilize a quart jar, place clean blooms and peppercorns into the jar and pour in the vinegar. Cover jar with a nonmetallic lid. Set jar in a cool, dark place (a closet is good) for about 1 week to develop. Strain out flowers and discard. Strain this beautiful vinegar through a coffee filter into a sterilized bottle. Cork or seal. Makes 1 quart.

THE COLOR OF THIS VINEGAR IS DETERMINED BY THE COLOR OF NASTURTIUM BLOOMS YOU PICK. ALL YELLOW BLOOMS MAKE A LOVELY LEMON-YELLOW VINEGAR; ALL ORANGE BLOOMS MAKE A DEEP APRICOT-COLORED VINEGAR; ALL RED BLOOMS MAKE A BRIGHT RED VINEGAR; OR YOU COULD CHOOSE SOME OF ALL THE COLORS OF BLOOMS YOU HAVE AND CREATE A SURPRISE COLOR! THIS VINEGAR MUST BE KEPT OUT OF HEAT AND LIGHT.

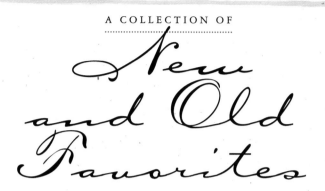

New and Old Favorites

We don't live by herbs alone. And this selection of recipes strongly proves that point. Even though many of the recipes contain herbs, many of them don't. I hope you will use these recipes as much as you use the recipes in the front of the book.

INDEX
Favorite Recipes

Shrimp Dip

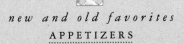

Uncomplicated, rather ordinary, but so good describes this dip. It's one of those basic recipes we all need from time to time.

1½   pounds cooked, peeled and deveined
         shrimps (fresh or frozen)
1   16-ounce container whipped cream cheese
1   cup mayonnaise

1   tablespoon Worcestershire sauce
2   teaspoons hot pepper sauce
2   tablespoons chopped green onion tops
     Crackers of your choice

Thaw shrimps if frozen. Coarsely chop shrimps. In a small bowl, combine all ingredients. Refrigerate several hours or overnight. Serve with crackers. Makes 3 cups of dip.

Marinated Shrimps

If you're looking for a change from shrimps with the red cocktail sauce, do try this recipe.

3   pounds cooked shrimps, peeled and
       deveined
2   large onions, sliced and separated into
       rings
1½ cups salad oil

1   cup white vinegar
2½ teaspoons celery seeds
1   tablespoon capers
4   to 5 bay leaves
4   or 5 dashes Tabasco sauce

Layer warm shrimps and onions in a large bowl. Combine remainder of ingredients and pour over shrimps and onions. Cover tightly and refrigerate at least 24 hours. Drain off marinade, discard onions and serve shrimps with toothpicks. These are delicious. Serves 12 or more.

Herbed Olives

This recipe is in It's About Thyme! *and it has become one of my favorites for the appetizer tray. The recipe can be made with either fresh or dried herbs. The hot pepper flakes add a nice surprise. For 1 quart of herbed olives:*

2   7- or 8-ounce jars whole green olives (pit still in), drained, but save juice

3   or 4 cloves garlic, chopped

1/2   to 1 teaspoon hot pepper flakes

6   3-inch sprigs fresh rosemary, or 1 tablepoon dried

6   3-inch sprigs fresh thyme, or 1 tablespoon dried

6   3-inch sprigs fresh sweet marjoram, or 1 tablespoon dried

10   whole black peppercorns

Cider vinegar, if needed

With a sharp knife, make a small slash in each olive. Place olives in a clean, sterilized jar. Add remainder of ingredients to the jar. Pour olive juice back in the jar. If olives are not covered, add cider vinegar to cover. Put a lid on the jar and refrigerate for at least one week to develop flavors — two weeks is better. These are great.

Fresh Salsa

I love this salsa recipe because there is more to salsa than just cilantro! Try this and you'll see what I mean.

2   cups diced ripe tomatoes

6   green onions, thinly sliced

6   to 8 jalapeño chilies, roasted and chopped, or a 4-ounce can peeled and diced green chilies

1   tablespoon fresh cilantro, finely chopped

1   tablespoon fresh parsley, finely chopped

1   tablespoon fresh basil, finely chopped

1   teaspoon fresh marjoram, finely chopped

1   tablespoon fresh lemon juice

1/4   teaspoon hot pepper sauce, or more for a hotter salsa

1   tablespoon olive oil

Salt and pepper to taste

Combine all ingredients in a serving bowl. Cover and refrigerate until serving time. Serve with tortilla chips. Makes about 2 1/2 cups.

Hot Crabmeat Appetizers

An old and dependable recipe. I keep a can of crabmeat on the shelf to make this quickly for unexpected guests.

1	8-ounce package cream cheese, softened
2	tablespoons chopped onion
1	tablespoon cream or milk
$^1/_2$	teaspoon cream-style horseradish
$^1/_4$	teaspoon salt

Dash pepper

1	6-ounce package frozen crabmeat, or canned crabmeat, well drained
$^1/_3$	cup sliced almonds, toasted

Crackers of your choice

In a mixing bowl, blend cheese, onion, milk, horseradish, salt and pepper. Stir in the crabmeat and toasted almonds. (Toast almonds in a skillet on the stove over medium heat for 2 or 3 minutes, or until light golden brown.) Place crab mixture in an ovenproof bowl or dish. Bake at 375° for 20 to 30 minutes. If mixture has been refrigerated, bake a few minutes longer. Serve with crackers. Makes 2 cups.

Asparagus Roll-Ups

An old favorite for the cocktail party or appetizer tray. Use fresh asparagus if at all possible.

12	thin slices fresh white bread, crusts removed
2	3-ounce packages cream cheese, softened

8	slices bacon, cooked, drained and crumbled
12	fresh asparagus spears, cooked to tender-crisp (don't overcook), or canned spears (but not nearly as good)
$^1/_2$	cup butter, melted

Flatten bread slices with a rolling pin. Beat cream cheese until smooth. Stir in bacon pieces and spread evenly on all the slices. Place an asparagus spear on each bread slice and roll up. Brush outside of bread rolls with melted butter. Place, seam side down, on an ungreased baking sheet and place in freezer until firm, about 1 hour. Remove rolls from freezer. Thaw slightly and cut into thirds. Bake at 400° for 15 minutes, or until golden brown. Serve hot. Makes 36 appetizers. If making rolls ahead of party, store frozen rolls in freezer bags and remove an hour or so before baking. Follow baking instructions above.

Cheese Puffs

A day-old baguette of French bread is transformed into delicious puffy cheese morsels.

1	cup unsalted butter, softened		1	egg, slightly beaten
¹/₂	pound cream cheese, softened		1	day-old baguette French bread, crusts removed
¹/₂	pound sharp cheddar cheese, softened			and bread cut into ¹/₂-inch cubes

Melt butter, cream cheese and cheddar in top of a double boiler set over simmering water. Remove from heat and cool. Mix egg into the mixture. Dip bread cubes into the cheese mixture and place on a waxed, paper-lined cookie sheet. Refrigerate for 4 hours, or may be frozen at this point. If frozen, defrost before proceeding. Transfer cubes to a lightly greased cookie sheet and bake in a 350° oven for 12 to 15 minutes until brown and melted. Serve at once with toothpicks. Serves 12 to 15, or more.

Goat Cheese with Herbed Olive Oil

I think this is about as good as it gets. It is delicious.

1	small bay leaf		¹/₄	teaspoon dried thyme leaves, crumbled
4	cloves garlic, cut into thin slivers		¹/₄	cup extra virgin olive oil
1	tablespoon fresh rosemary leaves		1	¹/₂-pound bag of soft mild goat cheese,
¹/₄	teaspoon coriander seeds, lightly crushed			such as Montrachet, cut into 8 pieces
¹/₄	teaspoon fennel seeds, lightly crushed			Toasted French or Italian bread slices
10	whole black peppercorns			

In a small saucepan, simmer bay leaf, garlic, rosemary, coriander seeds, fennel seeds, peppercorns and thyme in the olive oil for 5 minutes. Arrange goat cheese pieces on a platter. Spoon oil mixture over cheese. Serve with toasted bread slices. Serves 4 to 6.

Anytime Punch

A wonderful basic punch to serve anytime of the year.

1   46-ounce can pineapple juice
1   12-ounce can orange juice concentrate, thawed
1   12-ounce can lemonade concentrate, thawed

1   12-ounce can limeade concentrate, thawed
5   cups cold water
1   quart club soda

Combine juices and water in a punch bowl. Just before serving, add club soda and ice or an ice ring.
Makes 30 servings ($^{1}/_{2}$ cup each).

Spiced Apple Juice

2   quarts apple juice
2   cups water
1   cup orange juice
1   cup brown sugar

2   sticks cinnamon
6   tablespoons fresh lemon juice
$^{1}/_{2}$ teaspoon ground nutmeg

Combine all ingredients in a large pot and heat together. Bring to a simmer and let cook for 5 to
10 minutes. Strain mixture into a large pitcher or container. Cover and refrigerate if serving cold.
If serving hot, after straining mixture, place back in pot and keep warm. Serves 12 or more.

Tangerine Liqueur

There are other great liqueur recipes in It's about Thyme! *and* Christmas Thyme at Oak Hill Farm. *I enjoy making these liqueurs for our own use and especially for gifts.*

6	tangerines	¹/₂	cup water
2¹/₄	cups sugar	1	quart vodka

Remove rinds from tangerines and scrape and discard white part from the inside. Save peeled tangerines for another use. Set rinds on a jelly roll pan. Place in a preheated 250° oven and turn off heat. Leave in oven for 2 hours. Open oven with door just ajar, and leave rinds there overnight. Combine sugar and water in a saucepan. Heat, stirring constantly, until sugar dissolves. Let cool, then stir in 2 cups vodka. Stir again to dissolve any sugar, add remaining vodka and stir again. Place dried tangerine rinds in a half-gallon glass or plastic container that has a screw top. Pour in sugar-vodka mixture. Shake to mix. Cap tightly and let stand in a dark place for about 4 weeks. Strain through a coffee filter into a sterilized bottle. Seal or cork. Makes about 1 quart.

Spiced Iced Tea

8	cups water
4	regular size tea bags
¹/₂	cup sugar
1	5-inch piece fresh gingerroot, peeled
	and coarsely chopped

2	cinnamon sticks, crushed
2	lemons, halved

Bring water to a boil in a large pot. Remove from heat. Add tea bags, sugar, gingerroot and cinnamon sticks. Squeeze juice from lemon halves into the water. Drop lemon rinds into the pot. Cover. After 5 minutes, remove tea bags. Let remainder of ingredients steep for 25 minutes, covered. Strain through a sieve into a 2-quart pitcher. Refrigerate. Serve over ice. Serves 8.

Fresh Cranberry Tea

Serve this beautiful tea either hot or cold. It's wonderful on a Christmas tea table.

1	pound fresh cranberries	1	12-ounce can frozen orange juice concentrate, thawed
2	quarts water		
6	cinnamon sticks	1	quart brewed tea
4	whole cloves	1	6-ounce can frozen lemonade concentrate, thawed
	Grated zest of 1 orange		Sugar to taste

Combine cranberries, water, cinnamon sticks, cloves and orange zest. Bring to a boil and cook until the cranberries pop open. Strain into a large pitcher or container. Add orange juice, tea and lemonade. Stir. Add sugar, a little at a time to desired sweetness, but don't overdo on the sugar — this tea should be somewhat tart. Stir until sugar is dissolved. Serves 15 to 20.

Ginger-Honey Tea

I find this a soothing tea for an upset stomach.

1	cup boiling water	2	teaspoons grated fresh gingerroot*
1	teaspoon tea leaves	2	teaspoons honey

Pour water over tea, ginger and honey. Let steep for 3 or 4 minutes. Strain into a cup or mug. Makes 1 serving, but you can multiply recipe.

* Rub gingerroot over the fine holes of a grater, putting a plate under grater to catch ginger and its juice.

Coffee-Chocolate After Dinner Drink

In a blender, combine $^1/_3$ cup **coffee liqueur**, 1 cup **chocolate ice cream**, $^1/_3$ cup **vodka**, $^1/_2$ cup **milk** and 8 crushed **ice cubes**. Blend until frothy. Pour into balloon wineglasses. Serves 4.

Fruit Punch

1	6-ounce can frozen orange juice concentrate	4	cups cold water
1	6-ounce can frozen lemonade concentrate		Ice ring
2	6-ounce cans frozen limeade concentrate	2	quarts ginger ale, chilled
1	1-pound, 4-ounce can pineapple juice	1	pint club soda, chilled
1	pint cranberry juice cocktail		Mint for garnish, if available

Empty frozen concentrates, pineapple juice and cranberry juice cocktail into a large container. Add water and let stand until juices are thawed. Stir well. Place mixture into a punch bowl. Add an ice ring, then gently pour ginger ale and soda water down the inside of the bowl. Garnish with fresh mint sprigs, if available. Yields 25 to 30 punch cup servings.

Spiced Cocoa

$^1/_4$	cup cocoa	$^1/_2$	teaspoon whole cloves
$^1/_4$	cup sugar	$^1/_2$	cup water
1	cinnamon stick	3	cups milk

Combine cocoa, sugar, cinnamon stick, whole cloves and the $^1/_2$ cup water. Bring to a boil. Reduce heat and simmer 2 minutes. Add 3 cups milk. Heat, but do not boil. Makes 3 cups.

Bellini Cocktail

This is a favorite drink in Italy in the summertime when fresh peaches are available. It is extraordinarily good.

For 1 Bellini:

2 ounces peach purée (fresh or frozen peaches)	2 ice cubes
1 teaspoon fresh lemon juice	4 ounces chilled champagne
1 tablespoon grenadine syrup	

Purée peach in a blender. Measure purée, lemon juice, grenadine and 2 ice cubes in blender and blend until ice is roughly crushed. Pour into a fluted champagne glass and slowly pour champagne into the glass.

Chambord Champagne Cocktail

For 1 cocktail:

1 tablespoon Chambord liqueur	4 ounces champagne, chilled
1/2 teaspoon gin	

Combine Chambord and gin in a fluted glass. Gently pour in champagne. This raspberry-flavored champagne is marvelous.

Cauliflower-Cheese Soup

3½	cups cauliflowerets, divided		¾	cup milk
2	cups potatoes, peeled and diced		¼	teaspoon dried dillweed
1	cup chopped carrots		¼	teaspoon dry mustard
2	cloves garlic			Pepper
1	cup chopped onion		2	tablespoons butter
1½	teaspoons salt		¾	cup buttermilk
4	cups chicken broth			Grated cheddar cheese (optional)
1½	cups grated cheddar cheese			

Combine 2 cups cauliflowerets, potatoes, carrots, garlic, onion, salt and chicken broth in a large soup pot. Bring to a boil. Reduce heat, cover and simmer for 10 to 15 minutes. Remove from heat. Let cool a few minutes. Purée mixture in a blender or food processor until smooth.

Place puréed mixture into a large kettle. Whisk in cheese, milk, dillweed, dry mustard and pepper to taste. Heat soup slowly over low heat. Cut remaining 1½ cups cauliflowerets into tiny bits. Sauté in butter in medium skillet over medium heat until tender. Add to soup mixture. Whisk in buttermilk. Heat through. Serve with extra grated sharp cheddar cheese to sprinkle on top, if desired. Serves 8.

My Chili

As I said earlier, I never really made good chili until I discovered what cumin did for it.

2	pounds ground beef	1	4-ounce can diced green chilies
1	tablespoon cooking oil	1½	teaspoons ground cumin powder
1	medium to large onion, chopped	3	tablespoons chili powder (or more)
1	29-ounce can tomato sauce	2	teaspoons salt
1	29-ounce can hot chili beans	½	teaspoon pepper
1	29-ounce can tomatoes, chopped, with juice	4	cups water

Brown beef in hot oil in a large soup pot. Add onion and sauté with beef until onion is tender and beef is well browned. Drain thoroughly. Place meat and onion back in the soup pot. Add all other ingredients and stir thoroughly. Let come to a boil. Reduce heat and simmer for 30 minutes or more. Stir often. This makes a big pot of chili — will serve 10 or 12.

Broccoli-Cheddar Soup

⅓	cup butter	4	cups extra sharp cheddar cheese, shredded
3	cups chopped onions	1	cup half-and-half cream
2	cups chopped celery	½	teaspoon grated nutmeg
4	10-ounce packages frozen chopped broccoli, thawed and drained	¼	teaspoon salt
7	cups chicken broth		Pepper

Melt butter in a soup pot. Add onions and celery and cook over medium heat, stirring constantly, until tender. Add broccoli and broth. Bring to a boil. Reduce heat, cover and simmer 8 minutes. Cool slightly. Purée 2½ cups of mixture at a time in blender or food processor. Put back into the pot. Add cheese, cream and seasonings. Cook over low heat, stirring constantly with a wooden spoon, until cheese melts and soup is hot. Do not let boil. Serves 8.

Morris-Butler House
AND MULLIGATAWNY SOUP

Not long ago, I gave an herb program for the Morris-Butler House in Indianapolis. It is located at 1204 North Park Avenue, Indianapolis, Indiana 46202. It's a wonderful house/museum to visit. The women who volunteer their services there had a luncheon for the guests that day and Mulligatawny Soup was on the menu. Here is what was written about the soup in their Hoosier Receipts cook booklet that day. Thanks to June Hamblin and Elizabeth Doss for their editing skills. "Mulligatawny is a Tamil word for soup from the language and people of southern Indian and Sri Lanka. The two words, 'Millabee' meaning pepper and 'tanni' meaning water, give you 'pepper water,' thus combined words for this soup. The soup came from the Indian chefs cooking for the British troops. The first time the word appears in England is in 1784. In 1798, it appears in diaries and Hanna Glass's Cookbook. In 1863, it is placed in American cookbooks in a class of curries, pepper pots and country captains (recipes for chicken with vegetables)."

Mulligatawny Soup

3 pounds chicken	2 teaspoons salt
4 strips bacon	¹/₄ teaspoon pepper
1 cup onions, thinly sliced	¹/₂ teaspoon dried thyme leaves
1 cup carrots, thinly sliced	3 tablespoons fresh parsley, finely chopped
1 cup celery, thinly sliced	1 bay leaf
3 cups peeled tart apples, thinly sliced	1 quart tomatoes, chopped
2 tablespoons flour	2 tablespoons fresh lemon juice
1 teaspoon curry powder	

Cook chicken in water. Cool and remove meat from bones. Save broth. Fry bacon in a soup pot and reserve fat. Remove bacon from pot and crumble. To bacon fat, add onions, carrots, celery and apples. Cook, stirring, for about 5 minutes. Remove from heat. Combine flour, curry powder, salt and pepper. Stir into vegetables. Add chicken, thyme, parsley, bay leaf, tomatoes and 1 quart of chicken broth. Bring mixture to a boil. Reduce heat and simmer until vegetables are tender, about 1 hour. Add more chicken broth if needed. Remove bay leaf. Add lemon juice and bacon pieces. Serves 12.

Tomato-Cheese Soup

Here is a great way to add flavor and richness to canned tomato soup. This is so quick and so good, you'll find yourself making it often.

3 cups grated Cheddar cheese

2 10 3/4-ounce cans condensed cream of tomato soup

2 1/2 cups light cream (half-and-half)

Divide the grated cheese among 6 or 7 mugs or bowls. Place the canned soup and the cream in a 2-quart saucepan over medium heat and cook, stirring constantly with a whisk. Be careful not to scorch bottom of soup. Heat and whisk just until soup comes to a simmer. Don't let it boil, however. Ladle hot soup into the bowls over the cheese. Serve immediately. Serves 6 or 7.

Cuban Black Bean Soup

1 pound black beans

8 cups chicken broth, plus 2 to 4 additional cups

1 sweet green pepper, diced

3 ham hocks

2 chopped onions

1/2 pound salt pork (leave in one piece)

3 cloves garlic, chopped

2 teaspoons paprika

3 teaspoons ground cumin

1/4 cup chili powder

2 bay leaves

2 tablespoons red wine vinegar

Sort beans. Place in a large pot, cover with water, cover pot and let soak overnight. The next day, drain beans. Place beans and all other ingredients in the pot. Simmer about 2 hours. Add more chicken broth as soup cooks down, 2 to 4 more cups. Remove ham hocks, dice meat (discard bone and fat) and add back to the pot. Remove salt pork and discard. Remove bay leaves. Add 2 tablespoons red wine vinegar. Stir and heat thoroughly. Serves 10 or more.

Brenda Dumont's Spinach Salad with Chutney Dressing

Thanks to Brenda for sending this fabulous spinach salad recipe. This is what Brenda said in her letter to me: "A few years ago, my husband and I went on a rafting trip down the Colorado River. We spent 3 nights on the river and at the end of the trip, 2 nights in Las Vegas. While lunching at the Mirage Hotel, I came upon this delicious spinach salad. When I asked for the recipe, they handed me a xeroxed copy. (I guess I wasn't the first to ask!) I hope you enjoy the salad as much as we do!"

Spinach Salad

1	cup chopped pecans	2	Red Delicious apples, chopped
1	1-pound bag fresh spinach, cleaned, stemmed and dried	¹/₂	cup raisins
		¹/₂	cup chopped green onions

Combine above ingredients in a large bowl. Set aside.

Chutney Dressing

¹/₂	cup vegetable oil	¹/₂	teaspoon salt
¹/₄	cup mango-ginger chutney*	2	tablespoons fresh lemon juice
1	teaspoon curry powder	2	tablespoons rice wine vinegar (not sweetened)
1	teaspoon dry mustard		

Combine all ingredients in a blender or food processor. Add dressing to the spinach bowl. Toss to mix well and serve. Serves 12 or more.

* *"The mango-ginger chutney is found in the ketchup aisle of most groceries. Packaged under 'Major Grey.' Don't buy the kind in the paper bag. Buy the one that lists ginger as an ingredient," Brenda says.*

Sensational Seafood Salad
with Louis Dressing

Anything I say about this salad wouldn't be adequate. You'll just have to try it for yourself.

1 cup cooked lobster meat, diced	2 teaspoons fresh lemon juice
1 cup cooked crabmeat, chopped	¹/₂ teaspoon fresh chopped dillweed
1 cup cooked shrimps, chopped	¹/₂ teaspoon salt
1 cup mayonnaise	Fresh lettuce leaves
¹/₄ cup sour cream	Hard-boiled egg wedges
¹/₄ cup chili sauce	Ripe tomato wedges
¹/₄ cup green onions, finely chopped	

Prepare seafood and place in a bowl. Combine mayonnaise, sour cream, chili sauce, green onions, lemon juice, dillweed and salt to make a dressing. Line 4 salad plates with lettuce leaves. Add dressing to seafood mixture and toss. Mix well. Divide seafood among the 4 plates. Garnish each plate with hard-boiled egg wedges and tomato wedges. Serves 4.

Creamy Coleslaw

1 medium head green cabbage, cored and shredded (about 10 cups)	³/₄ cup sugar
2 medium carrots, peeled and grated	¹/₄ cup Dijon-style mustard
1 small green pepper, cored, seeded and finely diced	¹/₄ cup cider vinegar
2 tablespoons grated onion	2 tablespoons celery seeds
1 cup mayonnaise	1 teaspoon salt
	¹/₈ teaspoon pepper

Prepare vegetables and place in a large bowl. In a medium bowl combine mayonnaise and all other ingredients. Add dressing to the vegetables and toss well. Cover and refrigerate 4 hours before serving to let flavors develop. Serves 8.

No-Egg Caesar Salad

This recipe is for all of us who try to avoid salad dressings, pie fillings, and other recipes that contain uncooked eggs.

1   large clove garlic, minced and mashed to a paste with a bit of salt
2   tablespoons fresh lemon juice
1   tablespoon Worcestershire sauce
1   teaspoon Dijon mustard
3   tablespoons sour cream

$^1/_4$ teaspoon freshly grated black pepper
$^1/_2$ cup olive oil
$^1/_3$ cup Parmesan cheese, freshly grated
8   cups clean and dry romaine leaves, cut into bite-size pieces

In a large bowl, combine the garlic paste, lemon juice, Worcestershire sauce, mustard, sour cream and pepper. Add the oil slowly whisking vigorously to emulsify dressing. Stir in the Parmesan. Add romaine leaves and toss well. Serves 4.

The Best Chicken Salad

There are wonderful ingredients and seasonings in this classy chicken salad. The luncheon guests will rave over this.

2   cups cooked white meat of chicken, cubed
$^1/_4$ cup sliced water chestnuts
$^1/_2$ pound green seedless grapes, halved
$^1/_2$ cup chopped celery
$^1/_2$ cup toasted slivered almonds
1   8-ounce can pineapple chunks, drained

$^3/_4$ cup best quality mayonnaise
1   teaspoon curry powder
2   teaspoons soy sauce
2   teaspoons fresh lemon juice
    Bibb or Boston lettuce leaves

In a large bowl, combine the chicken, water chestnuts, grapes, celery, almonds and pineapple chunks. In a small bowl, combine the mayonnaise, curry powder, soy sauce and lemon juice. Add dressing to the chicken bowl and gently mix all together. Line 4 plates with Bibb or Boston lettuce leaves. Mound salad on leaves. Serves 4.

Vegetable Salad with Bleu Cheese Vinaigrette

This salad is gorgeous and incredibly delicious!

6   asparagus spears, cut into 1-inch pieces

1/4   pound yellow wax beans, cut into 1-inch pieces

1/4   pound green beans, cut into 1-inch pieces

1/4   pound sugar snap peas, cut open along one side

6   baby beets, boiled, peeled and halved

1   red bell pepper, cleaned and cut into julienne strips

1   yellow bell pepper, cleaned and cut into julienne strips

1   green bell pepper, cleaned and cut into julienne strips

Bleu Cheese Vinaigrette (recipe follows)

2   large carrots, peeled and shredded

1   green zucchini squash, unpeeled, cut into julienne strips

1   yellow zucchini squash, unpeeled, cut into julienne strips

8   black pitted olives, sliced

Blanch asparagus, beans and peas separately in the same boiling salted water. Drain and plunge into ice cold water until serving time, then drain well. In a large bowl, combine blanched vegetables with beets and peppers. Add 3/4 of the bleu cheese vinaigrette and toss well. Arrange carrots and zucchini in a mound on a large serving platter. Pile salad on top. Drizzle with remainder of dressing. Garnish with olives. Serves 6.

Bleu Cheese Vinaigrette

1/4   cup olive oil

2   tablespoons white wine vinegar

1   tablespoon fresh lemon juice

1/2   cup crumbled bleu cheese

Salt and pepper to taste

Combine all ingredients and mix well.

Broccoli Salad Supreme

I have to admit I was skeptical when a friend gave this recipe to me — raisins and broccoli together?! But I tried it, and it is really good. It's now one of my favorite salads.

About 1¹/₂ pounds fresh broccoli	¹/₂ cup raisins
6 slices bacon, browned, drained and cut into bite-size pieces	¹/₂ cup Miracle Whip salad dressing
1 cup unsalted sunflower seeds	2 tablespoons cider vinegar
4 tablespoons minced red onion	1 tablespoon sugar
	4 tablespoons milk

Cut broccoli flowerets into bite-size pieces. Steam broccoli for 2 minutes only. Immediately plunge flowerets into ice water to stop the cooking. Drain thoroughly and place in a salad bowl. Add bacon pieces, sunflower seeds, onion and raisins. In a small bowl, stir together Miracle Whip, vinegar, sugar and milk. Pour over salad ingredients and mix well. Chill at least 1 hour before serving. Serves 6.

Pear and Bleu Cheese Salad

Pears and bleu cheese have an affinity for each other. I love them in this salad. Use ripe pears for this recipe, but not so ripe they are mushy and soft.

2 heads Boston lettuce, washed and torn into bite-size pieces (about 6 cups)	4 tablespoons extra-virgin olive oil
2 large Bartlett pears, peeled, cored, seeded and sliced into thin wedges	¹/₂ teaspoon salt
2 green onions, minced	¹/₂ teaspoon freshly ground pepper
2 tablespoons sherry vinegar	4 tablepoons bleu cheese, crumbled
	4 tablespoons walnut pieces

Divide lettuce among 4 salad plates. Arrange pear wedges on lettuce. In a small bowl, stir together the green onion, vinegar, oil, salt and pepper. Dress each salad with the vinaigrette. Sprinkle 1 tablespoon bleu cheese and 1 tablespoon walnut pieces over each salad and serve. Serves 4.

Orange-Avocado Salad

Another gorgeous salad. Oranges, avocado and red onion team beautifully in this sweet and tangy salad.

The Salad

1 medium head iceberg lettuce, torn into bite-size pieces	1 medium avocado, peeled and sliced
2 cups red leaf lettuce, torn into bite-size pieces	1/4 cup orange juice
	1 small red onion, thinly sliced
	1 11-ounce can mandarin oranges, drained

Prepare greens and place in a large salad bowl. Dip the avocado slices in orange juice, then place them on top of greens. Discard remaining orange juice. Add onion and oranges to salad.

The Dressing

1/2 cup orange juice	1 tablespoon sugar
1/4 cup vegetable oil	1 teaspoon grated orange rind
2 tablespoons red wine vinegar	1/4 teaspoon salt

Combine dressing ingredients in a jar with a tight-fitting lid. Shake well. Dress salad and serve extra dressing on the side. Serves 6 to 8.

Raspberry-Walnut Salad

4 cups Boston lettuce, torn into
    bite-size pieces
4 cups red leaf lettuce, torn into
    bite-size pieces
³/₄ cup walnuts, chopped and toasted

1 cup fresh raspberries
1 avocado, peeled and cubed
1 kiwi fruit, peeled and sliced
    Raspberry Salad Dressing (recipe follows)

Combine lettuces, walnuts, raspberries, avocado and kiwi in a large bowl. Toss gently. Dress with Raspberry Salad Dressing. Refrigerate any dressing not used. Serves 8.

Raspberry Salad Dressing

¹/₃ cup seedless raspberry jam
¹/₃ cup Summer Berries Vinegar (made with
    raspberries) (p. 292)

1 cup vegetable oil
1 tablespoon poppy seeds

Combine jam and vinegar in food processor. Blend 15 or 20 seconds. With processor on high, gradually add oil in a slow, steady stream through the feed tube. Add poppy seeds. Blend briefly. Makes 1¹/₂ cups.

Old-Fashioned Coleslaw

¹/₃ cup water
¹/₃ cup sugar
¹/₃ cup white or cider vinegar
¹/₄ cup vegetable oil
¹/₂ teaspoon celery seeds

¹/₂ teaspoon mustard seeds
1 head green cabbage, about 2 pounds, cored and
    finely shredded
1 small onion, minced
    Salt and pepper

Place water and sugar in a small saucepan. Heat just until sugar dissolves. Remove from heat. Add vinegar, oil, celery seeds and mustard seeds. Mix well. Combine cabbage, onion, salt and pepper to taste in a large bowl. Add vinegar mixture and toss to mix well. Serves 6 or 8.

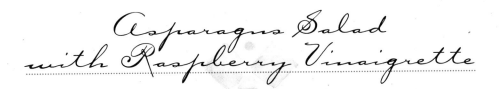

Asparagus Salad
with Raspberry Vinaigrette

24   spears fresh asparagus
     Fresh spinach leaves, cleaned and
       ribs removed

     Freshly ground black pepper
     Raspberry Vinaigrette (recipe follows)
$1/2$ cup fresh red raspberries

Steam the asparagus until just tender. Immediately plunge into ice water to stop the cooking. Drain and reserve the spears. Steam spinach only a few seconds to slightly wilt it. Divide spinach among 4 plates. Place 6 asparagus spears on top of spinach. Sprinkle each salad with freshly ground black pepper. Drizzle about 3 tablespoons of Raspberry Vinaigrette atop each salad. Scatter a few raspberries over each plate. Serves 4.

Raspberry Vinaigrette

1   cup frozen raspberries with juice
$1/3$ cup Summer Berries Vinegar (made with
      raspberries) (p. 292)

$1/2$ cup whipping cream

In a food processor, purée raspberries and strain to remove seeds. Add vinegar and mix well. Whip the cream only to soft peaks. Whisk the cream into the berry pulp and vinegar mixture.

Orange Balsamic Vinaigrette

This simple dressing is perfect for heavier, more bitter greens (than Bibb or Boston, for example). Add some fresh edible flowers, such as nasturtiums, pansies or fuschias, to the salad. Beautiful and peppery tasting.

2 or 3 tablespoons frozen orange juice concentrate	$^1/_2$ cup extra virgin olive oil
$^1/_4$ cup balsamic vinegar	Salt and pepper

Combine all ingredients in a small bowl and whisk thoroughly. Refrigerate a few hours before using. Makes about 1 cup.

Orange Vinaigrette

Serve over citrus salads, drizzle over chicken salad, and of course great on green salads.

1 tablespoon Dijon mustard	1 teaspoon cumin powder
2 teaspoons garlic, finely chopped	1 cup good quality olive oil
1. tablespoon grated orange rind	4 shakes Tabasco sauce
$^1/_4$ cup white wine vinegar	$^1/_4$ cup Grand Marnier liqueur

Combine all ingredients and whisk together thoroughly. Makes about $1^1/_2$ cups.

Benihana Salad Dressing

I found this wonderful dressing recipe in a Florida newspaper. I was ecstatic since I have always loved it on my salad at the restaurant with the same name.

1/4 cup onion, chopped	1 tablespoon soy sauce
1/4 cup peanut oil	1 1/2 teaspoons tomato paste
2 tablespoons rice wine vinegar	1 1/2 teaspoons sugar
2 tablespoons water	1 teaspoon fresh lemon juice
1 tablespoon chopped fresh gingerroot	Dash of salt and pepper
1 tablespoon chopped celery	

Combine ingredients in a blender or food processor. Process until almost smooth. Unused portions may be stored in a covered container in the refrigerator. Makes about 2/3 cup.

Bleu Cheese–Sour Cream Dressing

This is terrific to have made up and in the refrigerator. Will keep for a week or more. Great on green salads or use as an appetizer dip.

1 cup sour cream	1 cup mayonnaise
6 to 8 ounces bleu cheese, crumbled	1/2 teaspoon salt
3 cloves garlic, minced	2 teaspoons vinegar

Mix together thoroughly. Spoon into a quart jar and refrigerate. Best if made and chilled for 24 hours before serving. Makes about 2 1/2 cups.

Herbed Mayonnaise

1½ cups store-bought or homemade mayonnaise
2 tablespoons chopped fresh parsley
2 tablespoons chopped fresh tarragon

2 tablespoons chopped fresh fennel
½ clove garlic, crushed
½ cup sour cream

Combine and mix well. Cover and refrigerate. Use on fish, in salads or as a sandwich spread. Makes about 1²/₃ cups.

Curry Mayonnaise

1½ cups mayonnaise
2 teaspoons curry powder
1 tablespoon onion, finely chopped
½ teaspoon dry mustard

½ teaspoon salt
Dash of black pepper
4 to 6 drops Tabasco sauce

Mix all ingredients together thoroughly. Cover and chill 2 or 3 hours before adding to salad greens. Especially good as a chicken salad dressing. Makes 1½ cups.

Herbed Mayonnaise for Fish

Make a day or two before using to blend flavors. Delicious as a sauce on most any fish.

1 cup mayonnaise
1 teaspoon capers, drained
2 teaspoons fresh basil, chopped

2 teaspoons fresh dillweed, chopped
2 green onions, finely chopped

Combine all ingredients in a small bowl. Makes about 1 cup.

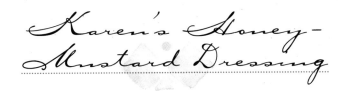

Karen's Honey-Mustard Dressing

Wonderful on salad greens, fresh spinach salad or with chicken or seafood salads.

$^3/_4$ cup mayonnaise

$^1/_3$ cup vegetable oil

$^1/_4$ cup honey

$^1/_4$ cup fresh lemon juice

1 tablespoon minced parsley

1 tablespoon prepared mustard

1 teaspoon pepper

$^1/_2$ teaspoon onion flakes

Whisk all ingredients together in a small bowl until smooth and creamy. Cover and refrigerate until ready to use. Makes about $1^1/_2$ cups.

Lemon-Yogurt Vinaigrette

Try this on fresh spinach salad or salad greens.

4 tablespoons fresh lemon juice

1 tablespoon red wine vinegar

2 small cloves garlic, minced

2 teaspoons Dijon mustard

$^3/_4$ cup nonfat yogurt

$^1/_2$ teaspoon salt

    Pinch of freshly ground black pepper

In a small bowl, mix lemon juice, vinegar, garlic and mustard. Whisk in yogurt. Add salt and pepper. Make this 2 or 3 hours ahead and store in the refrigerator. Makes about 1 cup.

Caraway-Rye Bread

These plump rounds of caraway-studded rye breads are a perfect accompaniment to a German or Scandinavian meal.

2 cups rye flour	$^1/_2$ cup lukewarm water
$^3/_4$ cup dark molasses	$6^1/_2$ cups sifted white flour
$^1/_3$ cup shortening, such as Crisco	1 egg white, slightly beaten
2 teaspoons salt	1 tablespoon water
2 cups boiling water	Caraway seeds
1 package active dry yeast	

Combine rye flour, molasses, shortening and salt in a large bowl. Stir in 2 cups boiling water. Cool to lukewarm. Sprinkle yeast on $^1/_2$ cup lukewarm water and stir to dissolve. Add yeast and 1 cup white flour to rye flour mixture. Beat with electric mixer at medium speed until smooth, 2 minutes, scraping bowl occasionally. Gradually add remaining flour to make a soft dough that leaves the sides of the bowl. Turn dough onto floured surface and knead until smooth and satiny, 8 to 10 minutes. Place in a greased bowl, grease top and cover dough. Let rise in a warm place until doubled, 1 to $1^1/_2$ hours. Divide dough into thirds. Shape into round loaves and place on greased baking sheets. Let rise until doubled. Combine egg white and water and brush on loaves. Sprinkle with caraway seeds. Bake in a 350° oven 40 minutes or until loaves sound hollow when tapped. Remove loaves from baking sheets. Cool thoroughly on racks. Makes 3 loaves.

Oatmeal Yeast Bread

Old-fashioned bread at its best. This bread is unbeatable in flavor. Makes 3 large loaves.

1	package active dry yeast	1/4	cup butter
1/4	cup lukewarm water	1/2	cup light brown sugar
4	cups skim milk, very hot	1	tablespoon salt
2	cups rolled oats (not instant)	8	cups sifted flour

Dissolve yeast in warm water. Set aside. Add hot skim milk to oats and butter in a large bowl. Let stand for 30 minutes. Add brown sugar, salt, dissolved yeast and 4 cups of the flour. Stir with a heavy spoon to mix well. Continue adding flour until a soft dough forms (may not need all 8 cups). Turn out onto a floured board and knead 8 to 10 minutes (or knead in your heavy-duty mixer with the dough hook attached). Place dough in a large greased bowl. Cover and let rise 1½ to 2 hours, or until doubled. Turn out dough, punch down, and divide into 3 loaves. Grease three 9x5x3-inch loaf pans and fill. Let dough rise again until doubled, 45 minutes to 1 hour. Brush loaves with a little melted butter and bake at 400° for 45 minutes or until done.

Whole Wheat–Potato Bread

This recipe has been in my files for many years. The bread is excellent either fresh or toasted.

1½	cups water	1½	cups mashed potato flakes
1¼	cups milk	2½	teaspoons salt
1/4	cup butter or margarine	2	packages active dry yeast
1/4	cup honey	2	eggs
3½	cups unbleached flour	2½	to 3 cups whole wheat flour

continued on the facing page

Whole Wheat-Potato Bread — continued from the facing page

In a large saucepan, heat first 4 ingredients until very warm (120°). In a large bowl, combine warm liquid, 2 cups unbleached flour, potato flakes, salt, yeast and eggs. Beat 4 minutes at medium speed with electric mixer. By hand, stir in remaining flours. On a floured surface, knead dough until smooth and elastic, about 5 minutes. Place in a greased bowl. Grease top of dough and cover. Let rise until doubled, about 45 minutes to 1 hour. Grease two 9x5-inch loaf pans. Punch down dough and divide into 2 halves. Place dough in pans. Cover and let rise in a warm place until doubled, 30 to 45 minutes. Bake at 375° for 35 to 40 minutes to a deep golden brown. If loaves become too brown, loosely cover with foil the last 10 minutes of baking. Immediately remove from pans. Brush tops with melted butter. Cool. Makes 2 loaves.

Seven Grain Yeast Bread

Two or three years ago, I gave a program for a Michigan unit of The Herb Society of America in Frankenmuth, Michigan. Frankenmuth is an absolutely delightful German town famous for good food, hospitality and a huge year-round Christmas shop. Dick and I stayed at The Pines B&B (517/652-9019), where we enjoyed a good night's sleep and a wonderful breakfast the next morning. Seven Grain Yeast Bread is one of the breads Donna Hodge often serves. It is especially good — delicious toasted.

1½	cups boiling water	2	eggs, beaten
1	cup seven grains cereal	1	cup whole wheat flour
2	packages active dry yeast	½	cup honey
½	cup warm water	2	teaspoons salt
6	tablespoons salad oil	4	to 4½ cups white flour

Pour boiling water over the cereal in a large bowl. Dissolve yeast in warm water. When mixture is lukewarm, add yeast, the oil, the eggs, 1 cup whole wheat flour, the honey and the salt. Beat well. Gradually add 4 to 4½ cups white flour to make a dough. Knead dough on a floured board until smooth, 5 minutes or so. Place in a greased bowl, grease top of dough, and let double in size, about 1 hour. Punch down and divide in half. Grease two 9x5-inch loaf pans. Place dough in pans, cover and let rise until almost double. Bake at 375° for 40 to 45 minutes, or until hollow when tapped. Remove from pans and cool. Makes 2 loaves.

*898
very good!*

Buttermilk Batter Bread

This batter bread is foolproof. A good yeast bread recipe for the beginning baker (a new bride perhaps!).

1½ cups cottage cheese (creamed, not dry)	3 packages active dry yeast
1 cup buttermilk	¾ cup lukewarm water
⅓ cup sugar	3 eggs
¼ cup vegetable oil	7½ cups sifted flour
4 teaspoons salt	Melted butter or margarine
¾ teaspoon baking soda	

Mix cottage cheese and buttermilk in a saucepan. Heat until lukewarm (no hotter). Place in a large bowl. Add sugar, oil, salt and baking soda. In a small bowl, add yeast to lukewarm water and stir to dissolve. Add yeast, eggs and 2 cups flour to the buttermilk mixture. Beat with electric mixer at medium speed until smooth, about 2 minutes, scraping bowl occasionally. Gradually stir in remaining flour. Dough will be sticky. Cover and let rise in a warm place until doubled, about 1 hour. Turn dough onto floured surface and knead until smooth and satiny, about 8 to 10 minutes. Divide dough into thirds. Shape each into a loaf. Grease three 9x5-inch loaf pans, place dough in pans, cover and let rise until doubled, about 45 minutes. Bake at 400° for about 30 minutes, or until loaves sound hollow when tapped. Remove from pans and cool. While loaves are hot, brush tops with melted butter. Makes 3 loaves.

Honey-Granola Bread

5 to 5½ cups flour	1 cup plain yogurt
1 cup granola cereal	½ cup honey
2 teaspoons salt	¼ cup vegetable oil
2 packages active dry yeast	2 eggs
1½ cups water	2 cups whole wheat flour

continued on the facing page

Honey-Granola Bread — continued from the facing page

Grease two 9x5-inch loaf pans. In a large bowl, combine 3 cups flour, granola, salt and yeast. Blend well. In a medium saucepan, heat water, yogurt, honey and oil until very warm (120° to 130°). Add warm liquid and eggs to the flour mixture. With mixer, blend at low speed until moistened. Beat 3 minutes at medium speed. By hand, stir in the whole wheat flour and 1 more cup of regular flour to form a stiff dough. On a floured surface, knead in 1 to 1½ cups flour until dough is smooth and elastic, about 10 minutes. Place dough in a greased bowl. Cover loosely with plastic wrap and a clean towel. Let rise in a warm place until doubled, about 1 hour. Punch down dough. Divide in half and shape into 2 loaves. Place in greased pans. Cover and let rise again in a warm place until doubled in size, about 40 minutes. Heat oven to 350°. Uncover and bake 30 to 40 minutes, or until loaves sound hollow when tapped. Remove from pans and cool thoroughly. For a soft crust, brush loaves with melted butter. Makes 2 loaves.

Walnut Bread

I love this nutty walnut bread. It's good with any meal, anytime of the year.

2	packages active dry yeast	2	teaspoons salt
¼	cup warm water (105° to 115°)	2	cups unbleached flour, divided
1½	cups milk	2	cups whole wheat flour
2	tablespoons olive oil	1	cup rye flour
2	tablespoons honey	1	cup walnuts, coarsely chopped

Combine yeast and warm water in a small bowl. Let stand 5 minutes. Combine yeast mixture, milk, olive oil, honey and salt in a large bowl. Beat at medium speed with an electric mixer until well blended. Combine 1½ cups unbleached flour, the whole wheat flour, the rye flour and the walnuts. Gradually add flour mixture to the yeast mixture, beating after each addition of flour. Turn dough out onto a floured surface. Knead in remaining ½ cup unbleached flour and knead until smooth and elastic, about 5 minutes. Place in a well-greased bowl, turning to grease the top. Cover and let rise in a warm place about 1 hour or until doubled in bulk. Punch down dough and divide in half. Shape each half into a round 6-inch ball. Place on a lightly greased cookie sheet. Cover and let rise for about 45 minutes, or until doubled in bulk. Using a sharp knife or razor blade, gently make a ¼-inch-deep cut in the shape of an X in the top of each loaf. Bake at 375° for 20 to 25 minutes, or until loaves sound hollow when tapped. Remove to racks to cool. Makes 2 loaves.

Wonderful Sour Cream Rolls

Sour cream ensures that these rolls will be tender with a fine grain.

2	packages active dry yeast	$^1/_2$	cup shortening (I like Crisco)
$^3/_4$	cup warm water (110°)	2	tablespoons sugar
$^3/_4$	cup buttermilk	2	teaspoons baking powder
$^3/_4$	cup sour cream	2	teaspoons salt
$5^1/_2$	cups flour		

Dissolve yeast in warm water in a large mixing bowl. Add buttermilk, sour cream, $2^1/_2$ cups flour, shortening, sugar, baking powder and salt. Blend $^1/_2$ minute on low speed, scraping bowl often. Beat 2 minutes at medium speed. Stir in remaining flour. Turn dough onto a floured board and knead until smooth, about 5 minutes. Shape rolls as desired. Let rise 1 hour. Bake at 375° for 20 to 25 minutes, or until golden brown. Watch closely. Makes about 3 dozen delicious rolls.

Out-of-This-World Rolls

2	packages active dry yeast	$^1/_2$	cup sugar
$1^1/_4$	cups warm water, divided	2	teaspoons salt
3	eggs, well beaten	$4^1/_2$	cups flour, divided
$^1/_2$	cup shortening (such as Crisco)		

continued on the facing page

Out-of-This-World Rolls — continued from the facing page

Soften yeast in ¼ cup warm water. Combine eggs, shortening, sugar, softened yeast, remaining warm water, salt and 2½ cups flour. Beat until smooth. Add enough remaining flour to make a soft dough. Turn dough out onto a floured board and knead for 3 or 4 minutes. Place in a greased bowl, grease top of dough and cover. Let rise until doubled. Punch down dough and place in the refrigerator overnight. Three hours before baking, remove dough from refrigerator; divide dough in half. Roll each half into a ½-inch-thick rectangle. Spread one half with butter. Roll up jellyroll-style and cut into 1-inch slices. Place in greased muffin tins, cover and let rise 2 or 3 hours, or until doubled. Bake at 400° for 12 to 15 minutes. If desired, make orange rolls out of the other half. Roll out other half of dough. Combine ⅓ cup melted **butter**, ½ cup **sugar** and grated **zest of 1 orange**. Spread this mixture on the rolled-out dough. Continue preparation as for dinner rolls above. Drizzle on a little **confectioner's sugar** icing when orange rolls come out of the oven. These really are out of this world. Each half of the dough makes about 1½ dozen rolls.

Pumpkin Rolls

Don't just save these delicate melt-in-your-mouth pumpkin rolls for Thanksgiving — they're splendid anytime.

¼	cup warm water	½	cup sugar
1¼	tablespoons dry yeast	1	cup canned pumpkin
1	teaspoon sugar	2½	tablespoons canola oil
1	cup hot milk	5	cups flour
1	teaspoon salt		

Place water in a small bowl. Add yeast and sugar to water. Stir to dissolve and set aside. Mixture should be foamy after a few minutes. In a large mixer bowl fitted with the dough hook, combine milk, salt, sugar, pumpkin and oil. Add yeast mixture and mix at low speed. Gradually add the flour until dough forms a ball around the hook, leaving the sides of the bowl. Remove dough from bowl. Place in a large greased bowl, greasing all sides of the dough. Cover bowl with plastic wrap. Place bowl with dough on top rack in oven. Place a large pan of hot water on rack under the dough bowl. Close oven door and let dough rise about 1 hour, or until doubled in size. Remove pan of water from the oven. Punch down and roll dough into about 12 balls. Place balls in each of two greased pie pans, cover pans with a clean tea towel and let rise again, about 45 minutes, until doubled. Bake rolls at 350° about 15 minutes, or until golden brown. Makes 2 dozen rolls.

Orange Blossom Buns

The perfect Easter dinner includes a pan of hot cross buns and a pan or two of these Orange Blossom Buns. These have been a favorite for years at our house.

5½ to 6½ cups unsifted flour
¾ cup sugar
1 teaspoon salt
3 packages active dry yeast
½ cup butter or margarine, softened

1 cup very warm water (120° to 130°)
3 eggs
Melted butter or margarine
Orange Sugar (recipe follows)

In a large bowl, thoroughly mix 1¼ cups flour, sugar, salt and undissolved active dry yeast. Add softened butter. Gradually add water to dry ingredients and beat 2 minutes at medium speed of an electric mixer, scraping bowl occasionally. Add eggs and ¼ cup flour. Beat at high speed 2 minutes, scraping bowl occasionally. Stir in enough additional flour to make a soft dough. Turn out onto a lightly floured board. Knead until smooth and elastic, 5 to 8 minutes. Grease three 8-inch cake pans. Divide dough into 3 equal pieces. Divide 1 piece into 8 equal pieces. Form each of the 8 pieces into smooth balls. Dip each ball into melted butter. Arrange 8 balls in one of the prepared pans. Coat with ⅓ of the prepared Orange Sugar. If freezing to bake later, cover pan tightly with plastic wrap, then aluminum foil and place in the freezer. Repeat with remaining pieces of dough and Orange Sugar. Keep frozen up to 4 weeks. If baking now, cover pan and let rise until doubled in bulk, 45 minutes to 1 hour, or longer. Bake at 350° for 25 to 30 minutes. Remove from pans. If rolls were frozen, remove from freezer. Let stand (loosely covered with plastic wrap) at room temperature until fully thawed, 2 or 3 hours. Let rise in a warm place until more than doubled in bulk, up to 2 hours. Bake as above. Makes 24 buns.

Orange Sugar
Combine 1 cup **sugar** and 2 tablespoons **grated orange peel**.

Oatmeal-Applesauce Bread

This bread is loaded with good things. The oatmeal gives the bread a wonderful texture.

1 cup plus 2 tablespoons flour	2 large eggs, slightly beaten
3/4 cup sugar	1 1/4 cups applesauce
1 teaspoon salt	1/2 cup raisins
1 teaspoon baking powder	1/3 cup vegetable oil
1 teaspoon baking soda	1/4 cup milk
1/2 teaspoon ground cinnamon	1/4 cup light brown sugar, packed
1/2 teaspoon ground nutmeg	1/2 teaspoon ground cinnamon
1 cup quick-cooking rolled oats (not instant)	1/2 cup chopped pecans

In a large bowl, sift together the first 7 ingredients. Stir in the oats. In another bowl, combine the eggs, applesauce, raisins, oil and milk. Stir the applesauce mixture into the flour mixture and turn batter into a greased 9x5-inch loaf pan. In a small bowl, stir together the brown sugar, the 1/2 teaspoon cinnamon and the pecans. Sprinkle this mixture on top of the batter. Bake at 350° for about 1 hour, or until a tester comes out clean. Let bread cool in pan for 15 minutes, turn out loaf and cool completely before slicing. Makes 1 loaf.

Date-Black Walnut Bread

This is simply the best quick bread I make.

³/₄ cup black walnuts, finely chopped	³/₄ cup boiling water
1 cup dates, pitted and sliced	2 eggs
1¹/₂ teaspoons baking soda	¹/₂ teaspoon vanilla
¹/₂ teaspoon salt	1 cup sugar
¹/₄ cup shortening (solid margarine or Crisco)	1¹/₂ cups flour, sifted

Combine nuts, dates, baking soda and salt in a bowl. Add shortening and boiling water. Let stand 15 minutes. Stir. Beat eggs slightly and add vanilla. Sift sugar and flour into the egg mixture. Stir until dry ingredients are moistened. This is a very stiff batter. Add to the date mixture and stir until well blended. Grease two small loaf pans. Pour batter into pans. Cover with foil. Bake at 350° for 25 minutes. Remove foil and bake 10 minutes longer, or until a tester comes out clean. Cool 15 minutes in the pans, then remove from pans. You may wrap well and freeze if desired. If not freezing, wrap well and refrigerate a day or two before slicing. Makes 2 small loaves.

Apricot Bread

1¹/₂ cups dried apricots	³/₄ cup sugar
2³/₄ cups flour	1 cup buttermilk
5 teaspoons baking powder	1 egg
¹/₂ teaspoon salt	3 tablespoons butter, melted
¹/₂ teaspoon baking soda	¹/₂ cup chopped pecans

Cook apricots in water according to package directions. Drain and cool. Cut apricots into thin strips and use a little of the measured flour to dredge strips in. Sift dry ingredients together. Add buttermilk and egg. Add butter. Fold in apricots and pecans. Bake at 350° in a greased 9x5x3-inch loaf pan for 1 hour, or until tester comes out clean. Makes 1 loaf.

Orange-Nut Bread

1	orange	1/4	teaspoon salt
	Boiling water	1	teaspoon baking powder
2	tablespoons shortening (solid margarine)	1/2	teaspoon baking soda
1	egg	1	cup sugar
1	teaspoon vanilla	1/2	cup walnuts or pecans, finely chopped
2	cups flour		

Squeeze the orange and save juice. Discard membranes and grind the peel. Measure juice and add boiling water to make 1 cup. Combine shortening, orange juice, peel, egg and vanilla. Add dry ingredients and mix well. Stir in nuts. Bake in two greased 8x4-inch loaf pans at 350° for about 1 hour, or until tester comes out clean. Cool in pans. Remove from pans and wrap well. This bread **must** be refrigerated for at least 1 day before slicing. Keep well wrapped and keep refrigerated between use. Bread also freezes well. Makes 2 loaves.

Sour Cream-Raisin Bread

When any of these quick bread recipes call for sour cream or buttermilk, you know it's going to produce a moist, tender loaf.

2	cups flour	3	eggs, well beaten
4	teaspoons baking powder	1/2	cup milk
1/2	teaspoon salt	1/2	cup sour cream
1/2	cup light brown sugar, packed	1/4	cup butter, melted
1	cup raisins		

Sift together the flour, baking powder and salt in a large bowl. Add brown sugar and raisins. Stir well. Now add the eggs, milk, sour cream and melted butter. Stir well, but don't overmix. Pour batter into a well-greased 8x4-inch loaf pan. Bake at 350° for about 1 hour. Cool 20 or 30 minutes in the pan. Turn out of pan. Wonderful served warm with a little butter.

Buttermilk-Banana Bread

Here is an excellent banana bread seasoned with molasses, allspice and nutmeg. It has become my favorite banana bread recipe.

3	very ripe bananas (need 1½ cups purée)	1	teaspoon baking powder
½	cup butter, softened	1	teaspoon salt
1	cup light brown sugar, packed	½	teaspoon ground allspice
2	eggs	½	teaspoon ground nutmeg
¼	cup molasses	1	cup buttermilk
2½	cups flour	1	cup English or black walnuts, chopped
1½	cups whole wheat flour		(I love the black walnuts)
2	teaspoons baking soda	1	cup raisins

Purée bananas in a blender. In a large bowl, cream butter and sugar until light and fluffy. Beat in eggs and molasses. Combine flours, soda, baking powder, salt and spices. Add dry ingredients in thirds alternately with puréed bananas and buttermilk. Stir in walnuts and raisins. Pour batter into two well-greased 8x4-inch loaf pans. Bake at 350° for about 1 hour, or until a tester comes out clean. Cool in pans a few minutes. Turn loaves out and cool. Makes 2 loaves. Actually the best if cooled, wrapped and refrigerated a day before slicing.

Rhubarb Bread

1⅓	cups light brown sugar, packed	¾	teaspoon salt
⅔	cup vegetable oil	½	teaspoon ground cinnamon
1	egg, beaten	1	teaspoon baking soda
2	teaspoons vanilla	1½	to 2 cups fresh rhubarb, diced
1	cup buttermilk	½	cup walnuts, chopped
2½	cups flour		

Combine brown sugar and oil. Blend in egg, vanilla and buttermilk. In a separate bowl, combine flour, salt, cinnamon and baking soda. Add to buttermilk mixture. Stir in rhubarb and nuts. Divide batter between two well-greased 8x4-inch loaf pans. Bake at 350° for 45 minutes, or until a tester comes out clean. Makes 2 loaves.

Fig and Cider Muffins

The liquid to moisten these muffins is sweet apple cider. Applesauce is also an addition. You know already these will be moist and wonderful.

6	Calimyrna figs, quartered	1	teaspoon ground ginger
1½	cups sweet apple cider	2	tablespoons ground cinnamon
3	cups flour	2	cups applesauce
1	tablespoon baking powder	2	cups golden raisins
1½	teaspoons baking soda	¾	cup chopped pecans, optional
½	teaspoon salt		

In a microwave-safe bowl, cover figs with cider. Microwave on high for about 3 minutes, turning once or twice. Remove from oven and let fruit soak in cider. Combine flour, baking powder, baking soda and salt in a large bowl. Pour fig mixture, ginger, cinnamon and applesauce into the bowl of a food processor. Blend until smooth. Pour fruit mixture into the dry ingredients. Add raisins and nuts and stir just to combine. Lightly grease muffin pans. Fill cups about ¾ full with batter. Bake at 350° for 18 minutes, or until a tester comes out clean. Makes about 18 muffins.

Hawaiian Corn Bread Muffins

Our son, Mike, came home from Kauai, Hawaii, raving about cornbread he had had at Kokee Lodge on the island. We followed him there a year or two later and I was determined to find this lodge. We did, we had their cornbread and they gave me the recipe. It's almost like eating a piece of cake — it's that good and that rich. I often make the batter into muffins, baking just a few at a time and storing leftover batter in the refrigerator. You can, however, pour the batter into a greased 13x9x2-inch pan and bake it at 350° for 35 to 45 minutes.

3	eggs	2¹/₂	teaspoons baking powder
1¹/₄	cups milk	¹/₄	to ¹/₂ cup yellow corn meal (I use ¹/₂ cup)
3	cups Bisquick	¹/₂	pound butter, melted
¹/₂	cup sugar		

In a large bowl, whisk together eggs and milk. In another bowl, combine dry ingredients. Add egg-milk mixture and melted butter to the dry ingredients. Mix well but do not overmix. Grease muffin pans and spoon batter into cups no more than ²/₃ full. Bake at 350° for 20 minutes, or until a tester comes out clean. Makes about 2¹/₂ dozen.

Rhubarb Muffins

We love these moist, tangy muffins with springtime salads and soups. They are crisp and sugary on top.

2	cups flour	1	egg
³/₄	cup sugar	¹/₄	cup cooking oil
³/₄	cup pecans, finely chopped	2	teaspoons orange peel, finely shredded
1¹/₂	teaspoons baking powder	³/₄	cup orange juice
1	teaspoon salt	1¹/₄	cups rhubarb, finely chopped
¹/₂	teaspoon baking soda	¹/₄	cup sugar

continued on the facing page

Rhubarb Muffins — continued from the facing page

Combine flour, ³/₄ cup sugar, pecans, baking powder, salt and baking soda in a large bowl. In another bowl, combine egg, oil, orange peel and orange juice. Stir in the rhubarb. Pour the rhubarb mixture into the flour mixture and stir only until moistened. Batter will be lumpy. Line muffin cups with paper baking cups. Fill cups ²/₃ full. Sprinkle ¼ cup sugar over muffins. Bake at 400° for about 20 minutes, or until a tester comes out clean. Serve warm with softened butter. Makes about 16 muffins.

Christina Campbell's Tavern Sweet Potato Muffins

Moist and fine-textured muffins from the famous Williamsburg Tavern. Serve with a fall or winter meal.

½	cup butter		¼	teaspoon salt
1¼	cups sugar		1	teaspoon ground cinnamon
2	eggs		¼	teaspoon ground nutmeg
1¼	cups canned sweet potatoes, mashed		1	cup milk
1½	cups flour		¼	cup pecans or walnuts, finely chopped
2	teaspoons baking powder		½	cup raisins or chopped dates

Grease muffin pan or pans (will make about 18 muffins). Cream butter and sugar. Add eggs and mix well. Blend in the sweet potatoes. Sift flour with baking powder, salt, cinnamon and nutmeg. Add the dry ingredients alternately with the milk — do not overmix. Fold in nuts and raisins or dates. Fill muffin cups ²/₃ full. Bake at 400° for 25 to 30 minutes, or until a tester comes out clean.

Orange Muffins

These muffins have an orange and sugar glaze. They are exceptionally good with breakfast or with brunch.

1	cup sugar	1	cup buttermilk
1/2	cup margarine		Rind of 1 orange, finely grated
2	eggs	1	cup raisins
2	cups flour	1/2	cup chopped pecans or walnuts
1	teaspoon baking soda		Juice of 1 orange
1/2	teaspoon salt	1/3	cup sugar

Make a batter of the first 7 ingredients. Stir in the grated rind, the raisins and the nuts. Fill greased muffin pans 2/3 full. Bake at 350° for 25 to 30 minutes or until a tester comes out clean. Combine the juice of 1 orange and 1/3 cup sugar. Bring to a boil. Remove from heat. As soon as muffins come out of the oven, glaze them with the hot orange juice mixture. Makes about 1 dozen splendid muffins.

Cranberry-Orange-Nut Muffins

Make these muffins when cranberries are in season. The orange flavor is a nice sweet contrast to the tangy cranberries.

4 1/2	cups flour	2	eggs
1 1/4	teaspoons baking powder	1	cup water
2	teaspoons salt	3/4	cup orange juice concentrate, undiluted
1/2	teaspoon baking soda	1 1/4	cups pecans, coarsely chopped
1 1/2	cups sugar	1	12-ounce bag of fresh cranberries, thinly sliced
1/2	cup margarine, softened		

Combine flour, baking powder, salt, baking soda, and sugar in a large bowl. Blend in margarine. Add eggs, water and orange juice concentrate. With an electric mixer, beat batter at medium speed for about 5 minutes. Stir in pecans and cranberries. Fill lightly greased muffin pans 2/3 full. Bake in a 350° oven for 30 to 35 minutes, or until a tester comes out clean. Remove muffins from pans and cool. Makes about 2 dozen.

Southern California Casserole

A great lasagna-type dish except soft corn tortillas are used instead of lasagna noodles. You'll need a large 6-quart casserole or baking dish for this recipe. This recipe serves 12, but you can cut it in half for a smaller crowd.

4	pounds ground chuck	24	soft corn tortillas
2	large onions, chopped		Cooking oil
2	cloves garlic, minced	4	cups small curd cottage cheese
1/4	cup chili powder	2	eggs
6	cups tomato sauce	1	pound Monterey Jack cheese, thinly sliced
1	teaspoon sugar	2	cups grated cheddar cheese
1	tablespoon salt	1	cup chopped green onions
2	cups black olives, sliced and divided	1	cup sour cream
2	4-ounce jars green chilis, diced		

Brown meat. Remove meat from pan, add onion and garlic and sauté until tender but not brown. Return meat to pan. Sprinkle chili powder over meat and mix well. Add tomato sauce, sugar, salt, half the olives and all the diced green chilis. Simmer over low heat for 15 minutes. While sauce cooks, fry tortillas in a small amount of hot cooking oil, one at a time, on both sides. Do not brown. Drain on paper towels then cut into quarters. Beat cottage cheese and eggs together and set aside. Spread 1/3 of meat and tomato sauce mixture in the bottom of a 6-quart casserole. Cover with 1/2 pound sliced Monterey Jack cheese, half the cottage cheese and egg mixture and half the tortillas. Repeat, finishing with a final layer of meat and tomato sauce mixture. Top with the grated cheddar cheese and bake, uncovered, at 350° for 30 minutes, or until casserole is thoroughly heated and cheese is melted. Serve with chopped green onions, sour cream and the remainder of the olives. Serves 12.

Flemish Stew

Hearty enough to chase away the winter chill. What a great dish to serve to company on a cold winter night. Add Herb Dumplings to the top the last 20 minutes of cooking. Serve with a green salad and French bread.

3	slices bacon, diced	2½	pounds beef stew meat, cut into 1-inch cubes
3	large onions, peeled and sliced	¼	cup flour
2	teaspoons brown sugar	12	ounces beer (dark beer is best)
2	teaspoons red wine vinegar	1	bay leaf
	Salt and pepper to taste	¾	teaspoon dried thyme
1	tablespoon vegetable oil		Herb Dumplings (recipe follows)

Brown bacon in a heavy flameproof 4-quart baking dish. Remove with a slotted spoon. Add onions to bacon drippings. Cook gently, about 20 minutes. Add sugar. Increase heat to medium and cook, stirring often, until onions are a rich golden brown, 7 or 8 minutes. Add vinegar, salt and pepper. Mix well and set aside. Remove onions to a mixing bowl. In same casserole, add the 1 tablespoon of oil. When hot, add meat in small batches in a single layer and brown well on all sides. Return all beef to the pan and sprinkle with flour. Mix well. Add beer, bay leaf and thyme. Heat to a boil. Add onions and bacon. Place casserole in a 350° oven and bake, covered, until meat is fork tender, about 1½ hours. If desired, add Herb Dumplings the last 20 minutes of baking time. Serves 6 to 8.

Herb Dumplings

½	cup butter, melted	1	tablespoon dried mixed herbs (1 teaspoon each of
2	cups flour		chives, parsley and thyme)
2	teaspoons baking powder		Salt and pepper

Combine melted butter with flour and baking powder. Stir in the herbs, salt and pepper, and mix with a little cold water to make a ball. Pinch off pieces and roll into smaller balls. Place on top of hot stew. Cover stew pot and cook for 20 minutes. Do not lift pot lid during this time.

Grandmother's Swiss Steak

I can still remember Grandma Clem pounding flour into a huge piece of round steak with the edge of a heavy plate. The flour just flew! She assured me that was the best way to get flour into the meat, and in her day, I'm sure it was. Her Swiss steak recipe is very simple, but oh so good.

1 cup flour	1 large onion, coarsely chopped
Salt and pepper	2 or 3 carrots, scraped and cut into chunks
1 3-pound piece of round steak, 1¹/₂ to 2 inches thick	¹/₄ cup flour
	Salt and pepper
¹/₄ cup vegetable oil	2 cups hot water

Combine 1 cup flour and enough salt and pepper to season it. Pound flour into both sides of steak with a meat mallet, the edge of a heavy plate, or whatever you use to pound meat with. Heat vegetable oil in a heavy large skillet (Grandma's was black cast iron). Brown meat well on both sides. Remove meat and pour off most of the grease. In remaining grease, sauté the onion and carrot pieces until onion is tender. With a slotted spoon, remove the onions and carrots. Add the ¹/₄ cup flour and salt and pepper to season to the skillet and brown the flour to a rich, deep golden brown. Slowly add 2 cups of hot water, stirring to make a smooth gravy. Place meat and vegetables in gravy. Ladle gravy up over the meat. Cover and simmer for 1 hour or until meat is very tender. Delicious old-fashioned food. Serves 8.

Wonderful Rib Eye Roast

1	clove garlic	¹/₂	teaspoon cracked or coarse pepper
¹/₂	cup prepared yellow mustard	¹/₄	teaspoon ground ginger
2	tablespoons soy sauce	1	4- to 4¹/₂-pound beef rib eye roast
2	tablespoons salad oil	2	tablespoons fresh parsley, finely chopped

Mince garlic. Add it to the mustard, soy sauce, oil, pepper and ginger. Combine well. Place roast on a rack in an open roasting pan. Use a pastry brush and brush half the mustard mixture over the top of the roast. Insert meat thermometer and roast in a 350° oven to 140° for rare, or cook longer for medium. Do not roast to more than medium done. Will take about 20 minutes per pound for rare (140°). A few minutes before roast is done, brush roast with remainder of the mustard mixture. Place back in oven and roast to desired doneness. Remove meat from oven. Press the chopped parsley onto the mustard glaze. Let stand a few minutes before slicing. Serves 10 to 12. (The mustard glaze seals in the juices.)

Roast Leg of Spring Lamb

A mixture of aromatic herb seeds seasons this lamb roast. It has marvelous flavor.

1	butterflied leg of lamb (ask butcher to do this for you)	2	teaspoons coriander seeds
3	cloves garlic, cut in half and crushed with the side of a heavy knife	2	teaspoons cumin seeds
		1	tablespoon olive oil
2	teaspoons fennel seeds	1¹/₂	to 2 teaspoons salt

Rub all sides of the lamb with the crushed garlic. Discard garlic. Place seeds in a plastic bag and use a rolling pin to crush the seeds. In a small bowl, combine the seeds, olive oil and salt. Using your hands, rub the seed mixture all over top of lamb. Carefully roll up lamb enclosing seeds inside as you roll. Tie roll with kitchen twine. Place lamb on a greased rack in a roasting pan. Roast the meat in a 325° oven until a meat thermometer registers 160° (medium). For a 6- to 8-pound roast, this should take 2¹/₂ to 3¹/₂ hours. Serves 10 to 12.

Sausage and Mozzarella Strata

This is one of my favorite breakfast or brunch dishes. Make it up to 24 hours ahead of time and bake just before serving.

1¹/₂	pounds mild Italian sausage		2	cups milk
6	slices white bread (not lite or diet bread)		¹/₂	teaspoon salt
1	cup shredded mozzarella cheese			Dash of pepper
4	eggs		¹/₂	teaspoon dry mustard

Brown Italian sausage in a large heavy skillet. Stir to break up into small pieces. Drain fat. Cut crusts from slices of bread, then cut bread into cubes. In a 13x9x2-inch baking dish, spread half the sausage. Scatter bread cubes over meat, then add the shredded cheese. Sprinkle on remainder of sausage. In a mixing bowl, combine eggs, milk, salt, pepper and mustard. Pour over the sausage mixture. If not baking now, cover and refrigerate for up to 24 hours. To serve, bake, covered, in a 325° oven for 30 minutes. Uncover and bake for 15 to 20 minutes more. Remove from oven and let stand for 10 minutes. Serves 8 to 10.

Grilled Pork Chops with Spices

Toast coriander seeds in a small heavy skillet over medium heat for about 3 minutes. Shake pan often.

4	boneless pork chops, each about 1 inch thick		1	teaspoon coarsely ground black pepper
2	cloves garlic, crushed		1	tablespoon brown sugar
1	tablespoon toasted and crushed coriander seeds		3	tablespoons soy sauce

Place chops in a shallow glass dish. In a small bowl, combine garlic, toasted coriander seeds, pepper, brown sugar and soy sauce. Pour this marinade over the chops, turning to coat evenly. Set aside and marinate for 30 minutes, or cover and refrigerate overnight. Prepare barbecue grill or broiler. Remove chops from marinade. Grill chops 12 to 15 minutes, turning once or twice. Baste with marinade, if desired. Cook until juices run clear when chop is pierced. Serves 4. (Discard any leftover marinade.)

Spicy Pork and Rice

This dish fairly sings with herbs and spices. It is quick and delicious.

1	tablespoon onion, finely chopped	¹/₄	teaspoon dried oregano
1	tablespoon garlic, finely chopped	¹/₄	teaspoon ground coriander
1¹/₂	pounds lean pork, cut into ¹/₂-inch cubes	¹/₄	teaspoon ground cumin
1	tablespoon olive oil	1	teaspoon cider vinegar
1¹/₂	teaspoons chili powder	¹/₄	teaspoon ground red pepper
¹/₄	teaspoon sweet paprika	¹/₄	teaspoon salt
	Dash of ground cloves	¹/₄	cup water
	Dash of ground cinnamon		Steamed rice

In a large heavy skillet, sauté onion, garlic and pork cubes in hot olive oil 2 or 3 minutes, stirring often. Combine all seasonings and add to the skillet. Continue to cook and stir 2 or 3 minutes more, or until pork is cooked through. Stir in water and heat thoroughly. Serve immediately over hot steamed rice. Serves 4.

Herb-Rubbed Roast Pork

You'll find this recipe in my other books, but it's too good not to include here. It has won blue ribbons in pork cooking contests, and you'll win one too when you serve it.

1	tablespoon sugar	¹/₂	teaspoon dry mustard
2	teaspoons ground sage	¹/₈	teaspoon black pepper
2	teaspoons dried sweet marjoram, crushed		5-pound boneless pork loin roast
1	teaspoon salt	1	tablespoon fresh parsley, chopped
¹/₂	teaspoon celery seed		

continued on the facing page

Herb-Rubbed Roast Pork — continued from the facing page

In a small bowl, combine sugar, sage, sweet marjoram, salt, celery seed, dry mustard and pepper. Thoroughly rub the roast with this mixture. Cover and let stand at least 4 hours (or overnight) in the refrigerator. Set meat on a rack in a shallow roasting pan. Insert meat thermometer. Roast, uncovered, in a 325° oven for 2½ to 3 hours, or until thermometer registers 170°. Sprinkle chopped parsley over roast. Loosely cover and let rest for 15 minutes before carving. Serves 8 or more.

Honey-Gingered Pork Tenderloin

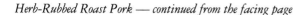

This is another marinated pork tenderloin recipe, but the seasonings are so different and the flavor is also totally different. Thanks to Joan Voas from Biloxi, Mississippi, who sent this recipe. Joan suggests serving with roasted new red potatoes, cooked fresh green beans and a green salad with herb vinaigrette. Sounds good to me!

2	pork tenderloins (¾ pound each)	¼	teaspoon onion powder
¼	cup honey	¼	teaspoon ground red pepper
¼	cup soy sauce	¼	teaspoon ground cinnamon
2	tablespoons brown sugar	¼	teaspoon ground ginger
1	tablespoon onion, finely chopped	¼	teaspoon garlic powder
1	tablespoon ketchup		

Place tenderloins in a 13x9x2-inch baking pan. Combine honey and remainder of ingredients. Pour over the tenderloins. Cover and marinate 8 hours or overnight. Remove from marinade and grill over medium-hot coals 25 to 35 minutes, or until a meat thermometer registers 160°.* Or roast in the oven until thermometer registers 160°. Thinly slice and serve. Will serve 6.

* This is the perfect cut of meat to use an instant-read thermometer with.

Elegant Chicken and Shrimp Casserole

There are a few party dishes in all our files that we consider special. This is one of them from my files. Serve with a crisp green salad and fresh fruit for dessert. Another plus — the entire dish may be made ahead and baked at party time.

2	14-ounce cans plain artichoke hearts, cubed
4	whole chicken breasts, cooked and cut into large chunks
1¹/₂	pounds shrimps, cooked, peeled and deveined
1¹/₂	pounds fresh mushrooms, sliced and sautéed in 1 stick of butter and 2 cloves of minced garlic (reserve liquid)

¹/₂	cup plus 2 tablespoons butter
¹/₂	cup plus 2 tablespoons flour
3	cups half-and-half cream
¹/₂	cup dry white wine
1	tablespoon Worcestershire sauce
¹/₂	cup grated Parmesan cheese

Grease a 13x9x2-inch baking dish or casserole. Layer ingredients in the following order: artichokes on bottom, then chicken chunks, then shrimps, then mushrooms. Now make the sauce. Melt butter in a large heavy saucepan. Add the flour and cook and stir for 2 to 3 minutes. Add the cream and the reserved mushroom liquid and cook until thickened. Add the wine and Worcestershire sauce and mix well. Pour sauce over the layers and sprinkle with the Parmesan cheese. Bake at 400° for about 40 minutes, or until very hot and bubbly. Serves 8 to 10.

Chicken Parmesan

I have used this recipe many times over the years. Sometimes I serve the chicken as is, sometimes I serve it over pasta with additional sauce and cheese. We love it either way. This makes more sauce than needed for the recipe. Refrigerate leftover sauce and use to dress pasta for another meal.

3	29-ounce cans tomato sauce	1/4	cup grated Parmesan cheese
4	cloves garlic, finely chopped	4	chicken breast halves, skinned and boned
1	tablespoon dried red pepper flakes	1	egg, beaten
1	teaspoon dried oregano	3	tablespoons olive oil
1	teaspoon dried basil	1	cup shredded mozzarella cheese
1/2	cup fine bread crumbs		

In a large heavy pan, combine tomato sauce, garlic, red pepper flakes, oregano and basil. Bring to a boil, reduce heat and simmer for 30 minutes, stirring occasionally. While sauce is cooking, combine bread crumbs and Parmesan cheese. Dip chicken in beaten egg and then in bread crumbs and Parmesan cheese mixture to coat. Preheat oil in a heavy skillet, add chicken and cook 3 to 5 minutes on each side, or until golden brown and almost done. After sauce has cooked for 30 minutes, pour some over each piece of chicken. Cook another 5 minutes, or until chicken is done. Sprinkle mozzarella cheese on top and cook until cheese melts. Serves 4.

Marinated Bacon-Wrapped Chicken Breasts

This is a terrific party dish because it must be prepared several hours or even a day ahead of serving. It is delicious.

8	strips bacon	3	cloves garlic, minced
4	chicken breast halves (you may remove skin, but I like to leave the bones in)	2	teaspoons ground ginger
1	cup soy sauce	1/4	teaspoon paprika
1/2	cup sugar	4	or 5 drops hot pepper sauce

Wrap 2 bacon strips around each breast half. Secure with toothpicks if necessary. Place breasts in a shallow glass baking dish. In a small bowl, combine soy sauce, sugar, garlic, ginger, paprika and pepper sauce. Pour over the chicken, turning to coat all sides. Cover with plastic wrap and refrigerate several hours or overnight. Drain and reserve marinade. Bake in a 325° oven for about 1 hour, or until chicken tests done. Baste occasionally with the marinade. Discard any leftover marinade. Serves 4.

Herbed Turkey Breast

Use this wonderful basting sauce for roast chicken also.

1/2	cup butter or margarine	1	teaspoon dried marjoram, crushed
1/4	cup fresh lemon juice	1	teaspoon dried sage, crushed
2	tablespoons onion, finely chopped	1/2	teaspoon salt
2	tablespoons soy sauce	1/4	teaspoon pepper
1	teaspoon Worcestershire sauce	1	bone-in turkey breast, 5 to 7 pounds
1	teaspoon dried thyme, crushed		

continued on the facing page

Herbed Turkey Breast — continued from the facing page

Combine all ingredients, except turkey, in a small saucepan. Bring to a boil over medium heat. Turn off heat. Place turkey breast, skin side up, in a greased 13x9x2-inch baking pan. Baste with the warm butter mixture. Loosely cover turkey with foil. Roast, basting often with the butter mixture. Roast to 170° on a meat thermometer, about 2 to 2½ hours. Do not overcook. Meat is white and succulent. Serves 10.

Pita Pocket Chicken with Yogurt Sauce

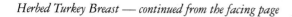

These are great luncheon or supper sandwiches. The sauce is delicious.

4 large pita pockets	1 medium sweet onion (Vidalia, for example), thinly sliced
2 or 3 chicken breast halves	Yogurt Sauce (recipe follows)
1 tomato, thinly sliced	
¼ head lettuce, shredded	

Toast pita pockets and cut each one in half from top to bottom. Cook chicken in boiling salted water until tender. Remove chicken from liquid and slice into thin strips. Evenly divide the chicken between the pita pockets. Tuck in some tomato, some lettuce and some onion. Spoon 1 tablespoon (or perhaps a little more) Yogurt Sauce inside each pocket.

Yogurt Sauce

1 cup nonfat plain yogurt	¼ cup chopped parsley
1 teaspoon fresh lemon juice	¼ teaspoon salt
1 clove garlic, finely minced	¼ teaspoon black pepper
½ teaspoon ground cumin	Dash hot pepper sauce

Combine all ingredients in a small bowl. Mix well. Cover and keep refrigerated until ready to use. Serves 6 or 8.

Chicken and Meatball Lasagna

This dish takes some time to prepare, but it can be made and frozen up to 1 month before baking. It is an excellent one-dish meal. Make the sauce first, then the meatballs, then the cheese filling.

Tomato Sauce

1/3	cup olive oil	2	28-ounce cans Italian or plum tomatoes
1	large whole chicken breast, skinned	2	teaspoons sugar
1	small onion, chopped	1	teaspoon dried basil
1/2	cup dry white wine		Salt and pepper

Heat oil in a large heavy saucepan. Add chicken and sauté until lightly browned. Stir in onion and cook until soft, but do not brown. Add wine and cook and stir for about 15 minutes. Add remainder of ingredients. Simmer, partially covered, for 1 1/2 hours. Remove chicken, cool slightly and cut into cubes. Set aside. Save sauce.

Meatballs

1/2	pound ground beef (I like ground chuck)	1	slice white bread softened in water, squeezed dry
2	tablespoons grated Parmesan cheese	2	teaspoons fresh parsley, finely chopped
1	garlic clove, minced		Salt and pepper
1	egg	1/4	cup olive oil

Mix all ingredients together except the oil. Form into tiny meatballs. Sauté in hot oil, browning on all sides. Remove browned meatballs and add to the tomato sauce. Simmer 30 minutes.

Cheese Filling

1/2	pound ricotta cheese	1/2	cup grated Parmesan cheese
1	egg	2	thin slices chopped ham
1/4	pound diced mozzarella cheese	6	green or regular lasagna noodles, cooked
2	tablespoons fresh parsley, finely chopped		according to package directions

Beat ricotta and egg until smooth. Add remaining ingredients, except noodles. Spread a 13x9x2-inch baking dish with 1/4 of the tomato sauce. Place 2 lasagna noodles in the bottom. Top with half the cubed chicken. Cover with 1/2 the meatballs and 1/4 of the sauce. Spoon 1/2 of the cheese filling over the sauce. Top with 2 more lasagna noodles. Cover noodles with other half of chicken cubes, other half of meatballs and 1/4 of the tomato sauce. Cover with remainder of cheese filling. End with a layer of noodles on top and the last 1/4 of tomato sauce on noodles. Cover with foil. Bake at 350° for 30 minutes or until lasagna is very hot and bubbly. Serves 8 to 10.

Chicken Paprika

This is good anytime of the year, but we particularly love it in the winter. It's hearty and very delicious.

2	tablespoons olive oil		$^1/_2$	teaspoon cumin seeds, crushed
8	choice pieces of frying chicken		$1^1/_2$	to 2 cups chicken broth
1	small onion, finely chopped		2	tablespoons tomato paste
2	cloves garlic, chopped			Salt and pepper to taste
2	carrots, peeled and cut into 1-inch chunks		$^1/_4$	cup sour cream
1	tablespoon paprika (see below)			Buttered noodles

Heat oil in a large heavy skillet. When hot, add chicken pieces and brown well on all sides. Set chicken aside. Remove all but 1 tablespoon fat from the pan. Add onion and garlic to the pan and cook and stir for about 2 minutes. Add carrots, paprika and cumin seeds. Stir to blend well. Add $1^1/_2$ cups chicken broth, tomato paste, salt and pepper. Add chicken to the skillet. Heat to a boil. Reduce heat and cover. Simmer until chicken is tender, about 1 hour. Add remaining $^1/_2$ cup chicken broth if necessary. Just before removing from heat, stir in the sour cream. Serve with buttered noodles. Serves 4.

---

some thoughts on
PAPRIKA

My firsthand experience with paprika was in a little street corner market in Pest (across the Danube River from Buda — link them with a bridge and you have Budapest). There were strings of dried sweet paprikas hanging everywhere in that little shop and literally hundreds of cans of Hungarian sweet paprika lining the shelves. I bought some to bring home. It was the finest paprika I ever tasted and I've been unable to duplicate it since. Goulash soup is served in every café and restaurant in Budapest (probably in all of Hungary) and it is flavored with the sweet paprika. As you no doubt know by now, visiting markets is one of the favorite things I do when we travel — what a great way to learn about a country and its cuisine.

Perfect Pan-Fried Fish

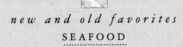

¹/₂	cup cracker meal	1	large egg, slightly beaten
¹/₂	cup flour	8	fish fillets (approximately 6 ounces each)
¹/₄	cup yellow cornmeal	2	tablespoons bacon fat
1	teaspoon salt	2	tablespoons margarine
	Dash of pepper		Tartar Sauce (recipe follows)
1	cup whole milk		

Mix cracker meal, flour, cornmeal, salt and pepper in a pie plate. Place milk in another pie plate and the beaten egg in yet another pie plate. Dip the fish first in milk, then in egg, then in the flour mixture, coating both sides. Heat the bacon fat and margarine in a large heavy skillet. When hot, add fish, skin side down, in a single layer. Fry, turning occasionally, until fish easily flakes with a fork, 8 to 10 minutes. Serve with Tartar Sauce. Serves 8.

Tartar Sauce

1	cup mayonnaise	2	tablespoons fresh lemon juice
¹/₂	cup sour cream	1	tablespoon fresh parsley, chopped
2	tablespoons grated onion	1	teaspoon fresh fennel leaves, chopped
2	tablespoons dill pickles, finely chopped	1	teaspoon fresh dillweed, chopped
1	tablespoon dill pickle juice (may need a little more for proper consistency)		

Combine all ingredients in a small bowl at least 2 or 3 hours ahead of using, if possible, to blend flavors. Cover and refrigerate. You may substitute other favorite herbs in this recipe, but the mayonnaise, sour cream, onion, dill pickles, pickle juice, and the lemon juice are all essential. If you've never tasted tartar sauce with fresh herbs, you're in for a treat. Makes about 1¹/₂ cups.

Roasted Marinated Salmon Steaks

This sweet and sour marinade is perfect on salmon steaks.

1/4 cup soy sauce	1 1/2 tablespoons vegetable oil
1/4 cup fresh lemon juice	1 clove garlic, crushed
3 tablespoons brown sugar, packed	1 4-pound salmon fillet, skin left on

Stir together the soy sauce, lemon juice, brown sugar, oil and garlic. Line a baking pan with heavy-duty foil. Place fillet on the foil, skin side down. Be sure to remove the bones from the fish. Brush the marinade on fish and roast at 350° for about 20 to 30 minutes, or until fish is cooked through and flakes easily. When fish is almost done, turn on the broiler and brown the top of the fillet, but do not allow to burn. Remove from oven, brush on a little marinade and serve to 6 or 8.

Shrimp Creole

I have used this recipe for years. I am always on the lookout for an improvement, but so far this is still the easiest and the best.

1/2 large green pepper, seeded and chopped	1 1/2 teaspoons salt
2 medium onions, chopped	1/2 teaspoon pepper
3/4 cup celery, chopped	1/8 teaspoon cayenne pepper
3 tablespoons butter	1 tablespoon fresh parsley, chopped, or 1 teaspoon dried
1 28-ounce can tomatoes, chopped	4 cups shrimps, cooked and cleaned
1 16-ounce can tomato sauce	Steamed white rice

Lightly sauté green pepper, onions and celery in butter. Add tomatoes, tomato sauce and seasonings. Add shrimp and heat thoroughly, but do not overcook. Serve over steamed white rice. Serves 4 to 6.

Fish with Mediterranean Herbs

This is my favorite way to prepare cod. The flavors of fresh vegetables and herbs stand out in this dish.

1/4	cup flour	1/4	cup pine nuts, toasted
2	pounds cod, cut into 6 pieces	1/2	cup pitted black olives, coarsely chopped
3	tablespoons olive oil		Salt and pepper to taste
1	cup celery, chopped	1	tablespoon fresh thyme, chopped
1	cup onions, chopped	1	tablespoon fresh rosemary, chopped
2 1/2	cups fresh tomatoes, finely chopped	1	tablespoon fresh green basil, chopped
1	clove garlic, finely chopped	1	tablespoon fresh oregano or sweet marjoram, chopped

Lightly flour cod on all sides. Heat olive oil in a heavy skillet. Sauté fillets in hot oil until lightly browned on both sides. Remove cod and cover to keep warm. If necessary, add a little more oil to the skillet and sauté the celery and onions until tender, but do not brown. Add tomatoes, garlic, pine nuts, olives, salt and pepper and herbs. Cook and stir for about 5 minutes. Add fish back to skillet and simmer about 5 minutes more or until fish is done. Serves 6.

Tuna-Cheese Loaf

A great standby for a busy day. This is especially good served with a warm cheese sauce.

1	egg, beaten	2	tablespoons canned pimiento, chopped
3	tablespoons milk	4	6 1/2-ounce cans tuna, drained
1	tablespoon butter, melted	1 1/2	cups grated cheddar cheese
1/2	teaspoon salt	1/2	to 3/4 cup cracker crumbs, finely ground
	Dash of pepper		

Combine all ingredients and pack into a greased 9x5x3-inch loaf pan. Chill for 2 hours or longer. Bake at 375° for 45 minutes. Serves 6.

Scalloped Cauliflower and Peas

I love this cheesy dish. It's wonderful with chicken, beef or pork entrées.

1	head cauliflower, broken into flowerets	$1/4$	teaspoon pepper
$1/2$	cup sliced celery	$2^1/2$	cups milk
$1/4$	cup diced green pepper	2	cups shredded cheddar cheese
4	tablespoons butter	1	10-ounce package frozen peas
$1/4$	cup flour	4	tablespoons butter
$1^1/2$	teaspoons salt	1	cup fresh bread crumbs*

Cook flowerets only until tender-crisp in boiling water. Do not overcook. Drain. In a large skillet, sauté celery and green pepper in butter. Stir in flour, salt and pepper. Add milk and cook until thickened, stirring constantly. Fold in cheese and peas. Carefully combine cauliflower and cheese sauce. Place in a greased 2-quart baking dish or casserole. Melt the 4 tablespoons butter. Toss with 1 cup fresh bread crumbs. Sprinkle crumbs on top and bake at 400° for about 30 minutes. Serves 6 to 8.

* Make your own fresh bread crumbs in the food processor. Process 3 or 4 slices of bread for about 1 cup of fresh bread crumbs.

Portobello Mushrooms

I love these as a warm salad or as a first course. Almost as good as steak, but no cholesterol!

2   tablespoons Mushroom-Infused Oil (p. 288)

2   cloves garlic, finely chopped

1   teaspoon fresh rosemary, chopped

About 6 ounces fresh portobello mushrooms

2   tablespoons Balsamic vinegar

In hot oil, sauté garlic and rosemary a few seconds only — do not brown garlic. Add portobellos and sauté until lightly browned, stirring often. Place mushrooms on a platter. Drizzle Balsamic vinegar over them and serve. Serves 4.

Ratatouille

A lovely Greek vegetable stew. Long, slow cooking creates a very flavorful dish. Exactly right for late summer and early autumn days before frost ruins the herb garden.

3   medium onions, thinly sliced

1   red pepper, cleaned and cut into strips

1   green pepper, cleaned and cut into strips

2   zucchini, cut into chunks

1   large eggplant, cut into chunks

1   cup mixed fresh herbs, chopped (basil, oregano, parsley, sweet marjoram, summer savory — a combination of these is best, but use what you have)

1   28-ounce can tomatoes, chopped

$^{1}/_{2}$ cup olive oil

$^{1}/_{2}$ cup tomato sauce

Salt and pepper

Combine all ingredients in a large mixing bowl. Toss gently. Place in a large roasting pan. Bake at 350° for 1 hour. Reduce temperature to 300° and bake 1$^{1}/_{2}$ hours longer, stirring occasionally, until vegetables are very tender. Serve hot or at room temperature. Serves 8 to 10.

Caramelized Tomatoes

It seems that we roast everything today — roasted vegetables and now roasted tomatoes. You have to admit, it's quick and easy and delicious.

3   pounds plum tomatoes, or other small
    firm tomatoes (not cherry tomatoes)
$^1/_3$ cup sugar
1   teaspoon minced garlic
2   teaspoons fresh basil, chopped
2   teaspoons fresh oregano, chopped

2   teaspoons fresh thyme, chopped
1   teaspoon pepper, freshly grated
$^1/_3$ cup olive oil
2   or 3 green onions, finely chopped
$^1/_2$ to 1 teaspoon salt

Drop tomatoes into boiling water for a few seconds. Remove from water and quickly slip off the skins. In a large bowl, combine tomatoes and all other ingredients. Transfer to a large rectangular baking dish. Roast in a 250° oven for 2 hours. Cool some, but serve warm. Fabulous with grilled or broiled meats. Serves 8.

Fresh Corn Pudding

Remember this recipe when fresh sweet corn is plentiful. Don't substitute canned or frozen corn — it just isn't the same.

4   eggs, separated
2   tablespoons butter or margarine, melted
    and cooled
1   tablespoon granulated sugar
1   tablespoon brown sugar

1   teaspoon salt
$^1/_2$ teaspoon vanilla
2   cups fresh whole kernel corn (4 or 5 ears)
1   cup half-and-half cream
1   cup milk

In a mixing bowl, beat egg yolks until thick and lemon-colored, about 5 minutes. Add butter, sugars, salt and vanilla. Mix well. Add corn. Stir in cream and milk. Beat egg whites until stiff. Fold into the corn mixture. Pour into a greased $1^1/_2$-quart baking dish. Bake, uncovered, at 350° for 35 minutes or until a knife inserted near the center comes out clean. Cover loosely the last 10 minutes of baking to prevent overbrowning. Serves 8.

Cheesy Onion Casserole

Serve this marvelous onion dish with beef, steaks or roast.

2	tablespoons butter or margarine	1	10 ³/₄-ounce can condensed cream of chicken soup
3	large sweet onions (such as Vidalia or Walla Walla), peeled and sliced	²/₃	cup milk
2	cups shredded Swiss cheese, divided	1	teaspoon soy sauce
	Dash of pepper	8	slices French bread, buttered on both sides

Melt butter in a large skillet. Sauté onions in butter until slightly browned — cook over low heat — about 30 minutes. Butter a 2-quart casserole. Place onions in the bottom, cover with ²/₃ of the cheese and sprinkle with pepper. Heat soup, milk and soy sauce in a saucepan, stirring to blend. Pour into casserole dish and stir gently. Top with French bread slices, overlapping to fit inside the dish. Bake at 350° for 15 minutes. Remove from oven and push bread down into the liquid. Top with remaining cheese and bake another 15 minutes, or until golden brown. Serves 8.

Carrots with Orange and Ginger

Here is a really great way to prepare carrots for guests or family.

8	medium carrots	¹/₄	teaspoon ground ginger
1	tablespoon sugar	¹/₄	cup orange juice
1	teaspoon cornstarch	2	tablespoons butter
¹/₄	teaspoon salt		Chopped fresh parsley or mint

Clean carrots. Cut into ¹/₄-inch-thick slices. Cook, covered, in boiling salted water about 7 or 8 minutes, or until just tender. Drain. Combine sugar, cornstarch, salt and ginger in a small saucepan. Add orange juice and cook, stirring constantly, until mixture thickens and bubbles. Boil 1 minute, then add butter. Let butter melt and pour juice mixture over hot carrots. Toss to coat. Garnish with chopped parsley or mint. Serves 4.

Casserole of Wild Rice

A splendid dish to accompany most any entrée.

¹/₂	cup chopped celery	1	cup long grain white rice
3	tablespoons chopped onion	3	tablespoons soy sauce
1	tablespoon butter, melted	¹/₂	teaspoon salt
1	quart chicken broth	1	tablespoon chopped fresh parsley
1	cup wild rice, washed and drained		

In a small skillet, sauté celery and onion in butter about 5 minutes. Stir often. Combine all other ingredients, except parsley, in a lightly greased 2-quart covered casserole. Stir in celery and onion. Bake, covered, at 350° for 30 minutes. Remove cover and bake another 15 to 20 minutes, or until rice is tender (the wild rice will still have a crunch to it, however). Garnish with fresh parsley. Serves 8.

Sweet Potato Soufflé

For years, this has been one of the vegetables on our Thanksgiving table. It's sweet and crunchy.

4	cups cooked and mashed sweet potatoes	¹/₂	cup butter, melted
3	tablespoons sherry wine	¹/₂	cup whipping cream
¹/₄	teaspoon salt	²/₃	cup light brown sugar, packed
¹/₂	cup granulated sugar	¹/₃	cup butter, melted
2	eggs, beaten	1	cup chopped pecans

Combine sweet potatoes, sherry, salt, granulated sugar, eggs and ¹/₂ cup melted butter. Place in a greased 2-quart casserole. In a small heavy saucepan, bring cream just to a boil, add brown sugar and stir to dissolve. Cook over medium heat until mixture reaches the soft ball stage on a candy thermometer, about 10 minutes. Remove from heat. Add butter and pecans and mix well. Pour topping over sweet potatoes and bake at 350° until hot and bubbly, 45 minutes to 1 hour. Serves 8.

Scalloped Asparagus

1/2	cup water	1/4	teaspoon pepper
2	pounds asparagus (tough ends removed), washed and cut into 1-inch pieces	1	2-ounce jar diced pimiento, drained
1 3/4	cups milk (approximately)	4	hard-cooked eggs, sliced
1/3	cup butter or margarine	1/2	cup shredded mild cheddar cheese
1/4	cup flour	1/2	cup fine dry bread crumbs
1/4	teaspoon salt	2	tablespoons butter, melted

Bring 1/2 cup water to boil and cook asparagus for 3 minutes. Drain but reserve liquid. Add enough milk to the cooking liquid to make 2 cups. In a medium saucepan, melt 1/3 cup butter or margarine. Stir in flour, salt and pepper. Stir in milk mixture all at once and cook, stirring constantly, until thick and bubbly. Remove from heat. Stir in pimiento. Grease a 1 1/2-quart baking dish. Place half the asparagus on the bottom; arrange half the eggs over asparagus; spoon half the sauce on top; sprinkle with half the cheese. Repeat layers. Sprinkle with bread crumbs and drizzle crumbs with butter. Bake at 425° for 20 minutes, or until bubbly. Serves 6.

Golden Potato Casserole

6	medium-large potatoes	1	teaspoon salt
1	pint sour cream	1/8	teaspoon pepper
10	ounces sharp cheddar cheese, grated	2	tablespoons butter, melted
1	bunch green onions, cleaned and chopped	1/3	cup dry bread crumbs
3	tablespoons milk		

Wash potatoes and cook in boiling salted water until tender. Cool. Peel potatoes and grate with a coarse grater into a large bowl. Add sour cream, cheese, onions, milk, salt and pepper. Mix thoroughly. Turn into a buttered 13x9x2-inch baking pan. Smooth top. Combine melted butter and bread crumbs. Sprinkle over top of potatoes. Bake at 350° for 45 minutes to 1 hour. Serves 6.

Easy Fudge Cake

If I need a chocolate cake in a hurry, this is the recipe I use.

The Cake

2	cups flour		2	large eggs, beaten
2	cups granulated sugar		1/2	cup milk
1	cup butter		1	teaspoon baking soda
4	tablespoons unsweetened cocoa powder		1	teaspoon vanilla
1	cup water			

For cake, lightly grease a 17x11-inch jelly roll pan. Set aside. Sift flour and granulated sugar into a bowl. In a saucepan, combine butter, cocoa and water over medium heat. Cook until butter melts and mixture boils. Pour butter mixture over flour mixture and stir well. Add eggs, milk, baking soda and vanilla. Blend well. Pour batter into prepared pan and bake at 400° for 20 minutes. Serves 14 to 16.

The Icing

1	cup butter		1	1-pound box confectioner's sugar, sifted
6	tablespoons milk		1	teaspoon vanilla
4	tablespoons unsweetened cocoa powder		1	cup chopped nuts

During the last few minutes of baking, combine butter, milk and cocoa in a saucepan. Heat to a boil. Stir in confectioner's sugar and vanilla and mix well. Gently mix in chopped nuts. As soon as cake comes out of the oven, pour the icing over the hot cake. Spread evenly. Cool cake before cutting.

Raisin-Apple Spice Cake with Penuche Icing

Spicy and moist cake with a fabulous penuche icing. This is one of our favorite cakes.

2½	cups flour		1¼	cups granulated sugar
1½	teaspoons baking soda		2	eggs
1	teaspoon salt		½	cup light molasses
1	teaspoon ground cinnamon		2¼	cups thick applesauce
½	teaspoon ground cloves		½	cup pecans, walnuts or black walnuts, finely chopped
½	teaspoon ground nutmeg			Penuche Icing (recipe follows)
¾	cup butter, at room temperature			Walnut or pecan halves

Sift flour with soda, salt and spices. Cream butter. Add granulated sugar gradually and beat until fluffy. Add eggs, one at a time. Add molasses and beat thoroughly. Stir in applesauce and nuts. Gradually blend in sifted dry ingredients. Pour batter into 3 waxed paper-lined and greased 8-inch round baking pans. Bake at 350° for 20 to 25 minutes. Cool layers, remove from pan and spread with Penuche Icing. Ice both the top and sides. If desired, decorate top or sides with nut halves. Serves 12 or more.

Penuche Icing

⅓	cup butter, at room temperature		1	teaspoon vanilla
⅓	cup light brown sugar, packed		¼	cup chopped nuts
⅓	cup half-and-half cream		1	cup raisins, coarsely chopped
3	to 3½ cups sifted confectioner's sugar			

Combine butter, brown sugar and cream in a heavy saucepan. Bring to a boil over medium heat. Remove from heat and gradually stir in confectioner's sugar until mixture is velvety and very smooth. Stir in vanilla, nuts and raisins.

Coconut Cake

This luscious bundt cake is a hit every time it's served. Frost with Fluffy White Frosting.

1¼ cups butter, at room temperature
2 cups sugar
5 large eggs, separated
1 teaspoon vanilla
2½ cups cake flour

1 cup minus 1 tablespoon milk
1⅔ cups flaked coconut
Fluffy White Frosting (recipe follows)
Extra coconut for top

With electric mixer, beat butter and sugar until very light. Add egg yolks and beat again until light and fluffy. Add vanilla. Gradually beat in cake flour alternately with milk. Add coconut and beat until smooth. Beat egg whites until stiff and fold gently into the batter. Turn batter into a greased and floured 10-inch tube or bundt pan. Bake at 300° for 2 hours, or until a tester comes out clean. Let cake cool in pan for 30 minutes, then turn out onto a serving platter. Cool cake completely. Frost. Sprinkle a little coconut over the top. Serves 14 to 16.

Fluffy White Frosting

I have never had this frosting fail. Just don't overcook it. This frosting (minus the coconut) is wonderful on almost any cake. It never gets grainy.

2 egg whites, unbeaten
1½ cups light corn syrup

Dash of salt
1 teaspoon vanilla

Combine egg whites, corn syrup and salt in top of a double boiler. Beat with rotary mixer until well mixed. (I use my portable electric hand mixer.) Place over boiling water. Start timer for 7 minutes. Cook for 7 minutes, beating constantly on medium-high speed, until whites stand in stiff peaks. Remove from boiling water, add vanilla and beat until thick enough to spread on cooled cake — won't take long — don't overbeat. Spread frosting on top and sides of cake.

Fabulous Chocolate Cake with Vanilla Buttercream

A delicious moist cake with an equally delicious buttercream frosting.

The Cake

4	ounces unsweetened chocolate	¹/₂	cup sour cream
2	cups granulated sugar	¹/₂	cup vegetable oil
1¹/₂	cups sifted flour	2	large eggs, at room temperature
³/₄	teaspoon baking soda	1	teaspoon vanilla
¹/₂	teaspoon salt		Buttercream Frosting (recipe follows)
1	cup brewed coffee, hot and strong		Fresh mint leaves for decoration (optional)

Lightly butter and flour two 8-inch cake pans. Melt chocolate in a small bowl placed over simmering water (or use a double boiler). Sift together the granulated sugar, flour, baking soda and salt into a large mixing bowl. In another bowl, whisk together the hot coffee, sour cream and vegetable oil. Set the mixer on low speed and gradually add the coffee mixture to the dry ingredients. Blend until mixed. Scrape the bowl and blend 10 more seconds. Add the eggs, one at a time, and mix on medium-low speed for 15 seconds after each addition. Scrape bowl and add vanilla. Blend 10 seconds more. Pour into prepared pans and bake at 350° for about 30 minutes, or until the tester comes out clean. Remove from oven and cool. Frost with Buttercream Frosting and garnish with fresh mint leaves, if desired. Serves 12.

Buttercream Frosting

1	stick unsalted butter, at room temperature	³/₄	cup plus 2 tablespoons cold whipping cream
1¹/₄	cups confectioner's sugar	1¹/₂	teaspoons vanilla

Place all ingredients in a food processor and process until light and fluffy, about 5 minutes. Scrape sides of processor several times. Transfer mixture to the mixing bowl of a heavy duty mixer and beat on medium-high speed for about 15 minutes until white and fluffy, stopping occasionally to scrape the bowl.

To frost cake, place a cooled cake layer on a plate and cover with buttercream. Top with second cake layer. Use remaining buttercream to frost top and sides of cake, leaving the cake with a smooth coat of frosting. Decorate the cake with fresh mint leaves or small fresh scented geranium leaves if they're available. This is a very, very good cake.

Fresh Lemon Cake

If you love lemon as I do, then you'll really love this cake. The cake is delicious, the frosting is out-of-this world.

8 egg yolks (save whites for another recipe)	³/₄ cup whole milk
³/₄ cup butter, softened	1 teaspoon grated lemon rind
1¹/₄ cups granulated sugar	1 teaspoon fresh lemon juice
2¹/₂ cups sifted cake flour	1 teaspoon vanilla
1 tablespoon baking powder	Lemon Frosting (recipe follows)
¹/₄ teaspoon salt	Lemon slices for garnish, if desired

With an electric mixer, beat egg yolks at high speed for 4 minutes. Set aside. In another bowl, beat butter until creamy. Gradually add granulated sugar and beat well. Add egg yolks and, again, beat well. Combine flour, baking powder and salt. Add to butter mixture alternately with milk, beginning and ending with flour. Mix well after each addition. Stir in lemon rind, juice and vanilla. Spoon batter into 3 greased and floured 8-inch round cake pans. Bake at 375° for 18 to 20 minutes, or until cake tests done. Cool in pans for 10 minutes, then remove from pans and cool completely. Frost with Lemon Frosting between layers and on top and sides of cake. Decorate with thin lemon slices, if desired. Serves 12 to 15.

Lemon Frosting

1 cup butter, at room temperature	8 cups sifted confectioner's sugar
2 teaspoons grated lemon rind	1 to 2 tablespoons light cream or half-and-half
¹/₃ cup fresh lemon juice	

Beat butter with electric mixer until very creamy. Stir in rind and juice. Gradually add confectioner's sugar and beat at high speed for 4 minutes. Add half-and-half, if necessary, for proper spreading consistency.

Orange Kiss Me Cake

Pillsbury's Bake-Off grand prize winner in 1950 was this cake. It's every bit as good today as it was when it won the prize.

1	thin-skinned juice orange	1	cup milk
1	cup raisins	1/2	cup shortening
1/3	cup walnuts	2	eggs
2	cups flour	1/3	cup sugar
1	cup sugar	1	teaspoon ground cinnamon
1	teaspoon baking soda	1/4	cup walnuts, finely chopped
1	teaspoon salt		

Squeeze the orange and reserve 1/3 cup of juice. In a food processor, grind together the orange peel and pulp, raisins and walnuts. Set aside. Combine flour, sugar, baking soda, salt, milk, shortening and eggs. With an electric mixer, beat at low speed until moistened, then at medium speed for 3 minutes. Stir in orange-raisin mixture. Pour batter into a greased and floured 13x9x2-inch baking pan. Bake in a 350° oven for 35 to 45 minutes, or until a toothpick inserted in the center comes out clean. Drizzle reserved 1/3 cup orange juice over the warm cake while it's still in the pan. To prepare the topping, in a small bowl, stir together sugar and cinnamon. Stir in walnuts. Sprinkle over cake and cool completely. Serves 12 to 15.

Chocolate Whipped Cream Frosting

2	cups whipping cream	6	tablespoons sugar
6	tablespoons unsweetened cocoa powder		

In a 1-quart mixing bowl, combine cream, cocoa and sugar. Stir until well mixed. Cover bowl and refrigerate 8 hours, or overnight. With an electric mixer, beat the cream mixture on low speed until frothy. Increase speed to high and beat until stiff. Makes about 3 1/2 cups.

Cranberry-Orange Pound Cake with Butter Rum Sauce

Makes a splendid large cake that will serve 16 or more. The sauce is served warm over the cake. Alone, this cake is wonderful. With the Butter Rum Sauce, it is extraordinary! Serve this for your next holiday party — your guests will rave.

2³/₄	cups sugar	1	teaspoon baking powder
1¹/₂	cups butter, at room temperature	¹/₂	teaspoon salt
1	teaspoon vanilla	1	8-ounce container sour cream
1	teaspoon grated orange rind	1¹/₂	cups fresh or frozen cranberries, chopped
6	eggs		Butter Rum Sauce (recipe follows)
3	cups flour		

Generously grease and lightly flour a 12-cup tube pan. Set aside. Beat sugar, butter and vanilla in a large mixer bowl until light and fluffy. Add orange rind. Add eggs, one at a time, beating well after each addition. Combine flour, baking powder and salt in a medium bowl. Add flour mixture to egg mixture alternately with the sour cream. Beat well after each addition. Gently stir in cranberries and pour batter into the prepared pan. Bake at 350° for 1 to 1¹/₄ hours, or until a tester comes out clean. Cool in pan for 15 minutes, then turn cake out onto a serving platter. Make Butter Rum Sauce. Serves 16 or more.

Butter Rum Sauce

1	cup sugar	¹/₂	cup butter, melted
1	tablespoon flour	4	or 5 teaspoons light rum
¹/₂	cup half-and-half cream		

Combine sugar and flour in a small saucepan. Stir in half-and-half and butter. Cook over medium heat until thickened and bubbly, stirring constantly. Remove from heat and stir in rum. Serve a slice of cake with a spoonful of warm sauce over each slice.

Apple Streusel Crumb Cake

This cake has a thick layer of apples. Cut into squares to serve. Whorl a dollop of whipped cream on top of each serving. Absolutely delicious.

6	cups flour, divided	2	teaspoons vanilla
1¹/₂	cups sugar, divided	4	cups McIntosh or Rome Beauty apples, peeled, cored and sliced
2	teaspoons baking powder		
3	cups butter, softened and divided	2	teaspoons ground cinnamon
2	large eggs		

Mix 3 cups flour, ¹/₂ cup sugar and the baking powder in a large bowl. Mix well. Add half the softened butter, the eggs and vanilla. Mix just to moisten. Spread in an ungreased 18-inch jelly roll pan and layer the apple slices over the top. For streusel, mix remaining 3 cups flour and 1 cup sugar with cinnamon. Mix well. Mix in remaining softened butter with a pastry blender until crumbs form. Sprinkle topping over the apples. Bake at 350° until golden brown, about 45 minutes. Cool. Serves 16.

Ginger–Pear Loaf

Pears and two kinds of ginger flavor this moist cake.

1	16-ounce can pears in unsweetened juice	1	teaspoon baking soda
¹/₂	cup butter, softened	¹/₂	teaspoon salt
¹/₂	cup granulated sugar	¹/₂	teaspoon ground allspice
¹/₂	cup light brown sugar, packed	¹/₄	cup crystallized ginger, finely minced
2	tablespoons molasses	2	firm but ripe pears, peeled cored and diced
1	large egg, or 2 small eggs		Confectioner's sugar (optional)
2	cups flour		Vanilla ice cream (optional)
2	teaspoons ground ginger		

continued on the facing page

Ginger-Pear Loaf — continued from the facing page

Grease a 9x5-inch loaf pan. Purée canned pears with their juice in a food processor. Set aside. Cream butter and both sugars with an electric mixer until light and fluffy, about 2 minutes. Add molasses and egg and mix well. Beat in the puréed pears (mixture will look curdled). Mix together the flour, ground ginger, baking soda, salt and allspice. Add crystallized ginger and toss to coat well. Add to the batter and stir thoroughly. Fold in the diced fresh pears. Pour into prepared pan and bake at 325° for $1^1/_4$ to $1^1/_2$ hours, or until a tester comes out clean. Cool in pan 10 minutes, then loosen from sides and invert on a rack to cool. Cool completely before slicing. Serve with a dusting of confectioner's sugar, if desired, or a scoop of vanilla ice cream on the side. Serves 8.

Velvet Angel Cake

When is an angel food cake not an angel food cake? Here, in this recipe. It has the qualities of an angel food, but here is a very unconventional method of putting the cake together. At any rate, the texture is like velvet and the taste is superb.

$1^1/_2$ cups cake flour	1 cup sugar
2 teaspoons baking powder	1 teaspoon vanilla
1 cup whipping cream	Frosting and filling of your choice
4 large egg whites	

Grease one 13x9x2-inch baking pan, or two 9-inch cake pans. Sift together flour and baking powder and set aside. Whip cream in a large bowl of an electric mixer on high speed until it holds soft peaks. Pour in the egg whites and continue beating until well combined. Gradually beat in the sugar, mixing thoroughly. Mix in vanilla. Stop the mixer. Add sifted dry ingredients and fold in with a rubber spatula. Pour batter into prepared baking pan or pans. Bake at 350° until cake(s) spring back when touched lightly in the center, about 30 minutes. Cool in pan(s) for 5 minutes, then turn cake(s) out of pan(s) and cool completely. Frost as desired. Some of my suggestions are: 1. Frost with Chocolate Whipped Cream Frosting (p. 364); 2. Cut a wedge from one of the layers and place on a plate. Surround with fresh peach slices, raspberries, blueberries or nectarine slices and add a dollop of whipped cream on the side; 3. Frost layers with a confectioner's sugar frosting; 4. Serve squares or wedges with Raspberry Sauce (p. 401). This wonderful cake serves 12 or more.

Peach Upside Down Cake

I try to give you a really easy recipe or two in every chapter, if possible. By easy, I mean "dressed-up" prepared foods or, in this case, a cake mix that is turned into a delicious upside down cake. This will go together in 10 to 15 minutes.

4   tablespoons butter
1/2   cup light brown sugar, packed
2/3   cup peach schnapps
3   or 4 large peaches, peeled, pitted and
    sliced, or one 1 pound, 13 ounce can
    peach slices, drained

1   18¼-ounce package yellow cake mix
    Whipped cream (optional)

Place the butter and brown sugar in a 13x9x2-inch aluminum cake pan. Place pan over very low heat to melt sugar. Remove from heat. Add schnapps and mix well. Arrange peach slices in pan. Make the cake batter according to package directions and pour over the peaches. Bake at 350° for 35 to 45 minutes, or until a tester comes out clean. Loosen cake from sides of pan and quickly invert onto a large rectangular tray or serving platter. Best served warm with a little whipped cream on the side. Serves 10 or 12.

Black Walnut Cake

If you love black walnuts, you'll love this cake. It's one of the finest cakes I've ever made.

1   cup unsalted butter, softened
2   cups granulated sugar
5   eggs, separated (at room temperature)
1   cup buttermilk
1   teaspoon baking soda
2   cups flour

    Dash of salt
1   teaspoon vanilla
1½   cups black walnuts, plus extra for topping
1   3-ounce can flaked coconut (1 heaping cup)
1/2   teaspoon cream of tartar
    Cream Cheese Frosting (recipe follows)

continued on the facing page

Black Walnut Cake — continued from the facing page

Beat butter until light and fluffy. Gradually add granulated sugar, beating until sugar is dissolved. Add egg yolks, beating well. Combine buttermilk and soda in a small bowl. Stir until soda dissolves. Add flour and salt to butter mixture alternately with buttermilk mixture, beginning and ending with flour. Stir in vanilla, black walnuts and coconut, mixing well. Beat egg whites with cream of tartar until stiff peaks form. Fold whites into the batter. Pour into 3 greased and floured 9-inch round cake pans. Bake at 350° for 30 minutes, or until a tester comes out clean. Cool layers 10 minutes. Remove from pans and let cool completely on racks. Frost with Cream Cheese Frosting. Serves 12.

Cream Cheese Frosting

³/₄	cup butter, softened	6³/₄	to 7 cups confectioner's sugar, sifted
1	8-ounce package cream cheese, softened	1¹/₂	teaspoons vanilla
1	3-ounce package cream cheese, softened		

With an electric mixer, beat butter and cream cheese until very light. Gradually add confectioner's sugar, beating until fluffy. Stir in vanilla. Spread frosting between layers and on top and sides of cake. Sprinkle extra black walnuts on top, if desired.

Wonderful Rhubarb Cake

A great cake for springtime. Be sure to use an 11x7x1¹/₂-inch pan — a 13x9x2-inch pan is too large.

1	stick butter, softened	1	cup buttermilk
1¹/₂	cups light brown sugar, packed	1	teaspoon vanilla
1	egg	2	cups diced fresh rhubarb
2	cups flour	¹/₂	cup granulated sugar
1	teaspoon baking soda	¹/₂	teaspoon ground cinnamon

In a mixing bowl, beat butter and brown sugar until light and fluffy. Add egg and beat well. In another bowl, sift together flour and baking soda. Alternately add buttermilk and flour mixture to the butter mixture, making sure ingredients are well blended. Stir in vanilla and rhubarb. Pour batter into a greased 11x7x1¹/₂-inch baking pan. Stir together the granulated sugar and cinnamon. Sprinkle over the cake. Bake at 350° for 45 to 50 minutes, or until a tester comes out clean. Serves 8.

Buttermilk Fudge Frosting

½	cup butter	1	teaspoon baking soda
1	cup buttermilk	2	tablespoons butter
2	cups sugar	1	teaspoon vanilla

Place the first 4 ingredients in a heavy 3-quart saucepan. Stir over low heat until sugar is completely dissolved. Increase heat and bring mixture to a boil. Put candy thermometer in place. Cook, stirring constantly, until thermometer registers 232°. Remove from heat and place 2 tablespoons butter on top of frosting. Set aside to cool to 110° on the thermometer. Do not disturb during cooling period. Add vanilla, then beat frosting until smooth, satiny and of spreading consistency. Enough to frost two 9-inch layers, or one 13x9-inch cake.

Bakery Creamy Frosting

Many bakers and bakeries use a recipe just like this one. It is incredibly light and fluffy.

2	tablespoons cornstarch	½	cup solid vegetable shortening (such as Crisco)
1	cup sugar, divided		Dash of salt
1½	cups milk	1	teaspoon vanilla
½	cup margarine, softened		

In a small saucepan, stir together cornstarch and 1 teaspoon sugar. Add milk and stir until smooth. Cook over medium heat until thick, about 5 minutes, stirring constantly. Set aside to cool. In an electric mixer bowl, mix together margarine, solid shortening, salt and the remaining sugar. Beat for 10 minutes, or until mixture is very fluffy. Add the cooled cornstarch-milk mixture and vanilla. Continue beating until well mixed and very fluffy, about 3 minutes. Enough frosting for a 9-inch double layer cake.

Easiest Cheesecake

I'm not a big fan of frozen dessert toppings, but this is a very good recipe using one of those toppings. It is embellished with butter brickle pieces (which would improve almost anything). So before we say "no" to those toppings, make and try this dessert. I'll just bet there will be a time when you need a real good dessert real fast. This recipe could be it.

1 3-ounce package cream cheese, at room temperature	1 12-ounce carton frozen dessert topping, thawed (such as Cool Whip)
2 tablespoons sugar	1 prepared 9-inch graham cracker crust
1 cup butter brickle pieces, or chopped Heath bars	1/4 cup butter brickle pieces, crumbled
	2 tablespoons chocolate syrup (from a can)

Beat cheese and sugar until sugar is dissolved. Fold in brickle pieces and dessert topping. Pour into a graham cracker crust. Place in the freezer for 4 hours or longer before serving. To serve, remove from freezer, scatter butter brickle pieces over the pie and drizzle top with about 2 tablespoons chocolate syrup. Serves 6 or 8.

Apple Cheesecake

I consider this cheesecake (and the Raspberry Cheesecake, p. 373) as restaurant quality. You know how the chef can and does "dress up" the ordinary dishes. This is a good cheesecake on its own and becomes even better when apples, nuts and cinnamon are added as a topping. This is a splendid autumn dessert, but of course, it's good anytime.

The Crust

2	cups flour	1	teaspoon vanilla
$^2/_3$	cup sugar	1	cup cold butter, cut into chunks

Place flour and sugar in a food processor bowl and pulse on/off until mixed. Add vanilla and butter and pulse on/off until a dough is formed. Press dough over the bottom and most of the way up the sides of a 10-inch springform pan.

The Filling

4	eggs, at room temperature	32	ounces cream cheese, softened
1	cup sugar	2	teaspoons vanilla

Make sure all ingredients are at room temperature. Beat eggs and sugar to combine well. Add cream cheese and vanilla and beat until smooth. Pour into the prepared crust.

The Topping

$^1/_4$	cup sugar	$^1/_2$	cup chopped walnuts
1	teaspoon ground cinnamon	4	tart apples, peeled and sliced

In a medium bowl, toss together sugar, cinnamon and walnuts. Add apples and toss. Arrange apple slices in overlapping circles on top of filling. Sprinkle with any walnut mixture left in the bowl. Bake in a 450° oven for 15 minutes. Reduce heat to 350° and bake another 45 minutes, or until filling is set. If apples start to brown too much, loosely place a sheet of foil over top of cheesecake. Remove from oven and cool on wire rack. Cover and refrigerate for several hours. Remove sides of pan just before serving. Serves 12 to 15.

Raspberry Cheesecake

Cheesecake and raspberries together. Could anything be better?

The Crust

$1/2$	cup unsalted butter, at room temperature, divided	$1/8$	teaspoon ground cinnamon
$1/4$	cup sugar	$1/4$	teaspoon vanilla
1	medium egg yolk	$1/2$	cup flour
		1	cup chopped pecans

Use an electric mixer and beat half the butter with the $1/4$ cup sugar until light and fluffy. Add egg yolk, cinnamon, vanilla and flour. Mix well. Pat mixture in a $1/4$-inch-thick layer onto an ungreased nonstick cookie sheet. Bake at 350° for 25 minutes, or until golden brown. Remove from oven and cool completely. Crush with a rolling pin (or in the food processor) to make fine cookie crumbs. Melt remaining $1/4$ cup butter. In a small bowl, combine with crumbs and pecans. Grease the bottom and sides of a 9-inch springform pan with butter. Press crumbs into bottom of pan. Set aside.

The Filling

2	pounds cream cheese, at room temperature	$1/2$	cup whipping cream
$1 1/2$	cups sugar plus 2 tablespoons	1	to $1 1/2$ pints fresh red raspberries, divided
4	eggs	1	cup sour cream
1	teaspoon vanilla		

With an electric mixer, beat cream cheese with $1 1/2$ cups sugar until lump-free. Beat in eggs, one at a time. Beat in vanilla and then the whipping cream. Wash and dry $1/2$ pint raspberries. Roll berries in 2 tablespoons of sugar to coat them. Pour $3/4$ of the filling into the crumb-prepared pan. Scatter sugared berries evenly over the top. Pour in remaining filling. Lightly tap pan on countertop so any trapped bubbles can rise to the top. Set pan on a sheet of heavy-duty foil larger than the springform pan. Turn up edges all the way around to hold any drips or butter that might leak out. Place pan with foil under it in a large baking pan. Fill baking pan with $3/4$-inch hot water. Place on low rack in a 300° oven. Bake for 1 hour and 40 minutes, or until cake tests done — should be solid in the middle, not soupy. Remove from oven and cool to room temperature. Cover and refrigerate several hours. To serve, carefully remove pan sides. Spread the sour cream over top of cake and arrange remaining raspberries on top. Serves 12 or more.

Jody's Basic Pie Crust

This recipe, from a friend, is in all my books, but I can't imagine a pie chapter without it. It is the recipe I use nearly every time I bake a pie.

3	cups flour	1	egg
1	teaspoon salt	5	tablespoons cold water
1¼	cups solid vegetable shortening (Crisco)	1	tablespoon vinegar

Combine flour, salt and shortening in a mixer bowl. Mix only until crumbs form. In a small bowl, beat 1 egg slightly. Add the water and the vinegar and mix well. Add egg mixture all at once to the flour mixture. Mix on low speed only until a ball of dough forms. Do **not** overmix. Gather dough into a ball. You may wrap and chill dough, or roll out now. Use a floured rolling pin and plenty of flour on the rolling surface. Makes three 9-inch single pie crusts.

To make dough in your food processor, combine the flour, salt and shortening in the processor bowl. Process on/off a couple of times to mix. Add egg, vinegar and water through the feed tube with the motor running. Process only seconds until a ball of dough forms along one side of the work bowl. Do **not** overprocess.

Chocolate-Peanut Butter Pie

Only someone who doesn't like peanut butter would dislike this pie. Everyone else will love it. It's very rich, so small servings will suffice.

The Crust

1³/₄ cups chocolate wafer cookie crumbs

3 tablespoons sugar

5 tablespoons butter, melted

The Filling

8 ounces cream cheese, softened

1 cup creamy peanut butter

1 cup sugar

1¹/₂ cups cold heavy whipping cream

The Topping

¹/₂ cup heavy whipping cream

6 ounces semisweet chocolate chips

For the crust, blend the cookie crumbs, sugar, and butter in a bowl. Press the mixture onto the bottom and up the sides of a 9-inch pie plate. Bake crust in a 350° oven for 10 minutes. Let crust cool.

For the filling, in a large bowl with an electric mixer, beat the cream cheese with the peanut butter until the mixture is smooth. Beat in the sugar until well combined. In a chilled bowl, beat the cream until it forms soft peaks. Fold ¹/₄ of the whipped cream into the peanut butter mixture, than gradually fold in the remaining cream gently but thoroughly. Place filling in the crust, cover and chill several hours or overnight.

For the topping, in a small heavy saucepan, bring the ¹/₂ cup cream to a boil. Immediately remove the pan from the heat and stir in the chocolate chips. Stir until mixture is smooth. Let topping cool for about 20 minutes, or until nearly cool, then pour it evenly over the pie. Chill pie for at least 30 minutes before cutting. Serves 8.

Rhubarb Pie with Phyllo Crust

This recipe came from a newspaper clipping. It is simply wonderful for a spring treat. Look for phyllo dough in the frozen food section of your grocery. Don't be intimidated by phyllo — it's really very easy to work with if you follow some easy directions.

6 sheets phyllo dough (wrap and return remaining sheets to the freezer for later use)	$^1/_2$ teaspoon grated orange rind
	4 cups fresh rhubarb, cut into $^1/_2$-inch dice
1 cup granulated sugar	1 teaspoon butter
2 tablespoons cornstarch	2 tablespoons vegetable oil
$^1/_3$ cup fresh orange juice	Confectioner's sugar

Remove package of phyllo dough from the freezer several hours before using and place package in the refrigerator to thaw. In a medium saucepan, combine granulated sugar, cornstarch, orange juice and orange rind. Add rhubarb and cook over low heat, stirring, until rhubarb is tender and sauce thickens, about 5 minutes. Remove from heat and let cool. Melt butter and oil together. Lay out 1 sheet of phyllo dough (keep the other 5 sheets under a slightly damp towel to prevent drying out), and dab very lightly with the butter-oil mixture. Lay sheet in a 9-inch pie plate, letting edges hang over sides of pan. Dab a second sheet and lay in pan perpendicular to the first sheet. Repeat with the other 4 sheets of dough. Spread rhubarb filling evenly into the phyllo-lined pie plate. Pick up the overhanging edges of the dough and let them drop over the filling, creating a free-form top crust. Bake at 425° for about 30 minutes, or until the crust is a deep golden brown. Best served slightly warm. Dust the pie top lightly with confectioner's sugar. Serves 6 to 8.

Brown Sugar–Pumpkin Pie

This is the best pumpkin pie recipe I've found.

1½ cups canned pumpkin	3 eggs
1 cup light brown sugar, packed	1 cup half-and-half cream
2 teaspoons pumpkin pie spice*	1 unbaked 9-inch pie crust

Combine all ingredients, except the crust, in a large mixer bowl. Mix thoroughly. Pour filling into the crust. Sprinkle a little pumpkin pie spice over the filling. Bake at 425° for 15 minutes. Reduce heat to 350° and bake another 30 to 40 minutes, or until a knife inserted near the center comes out clean. Cool. If crust browns too much, make a ring of aluminum foil and lay over crust the last 15 minutes of baking time. Serve with whipped cream, if desired. Serves 6.

* *You can make your own spice blend — combine 1 teaspoon **ground cinnamon**, ½ teaspoon **ground nutmeg**, ¼ teaspoon **ground ginger** and ¼ teaspoon **ground cloves**. Enough to season 1 pumpkin pie.*

Peach Cobbler Pie

This is a great crust-on-top pie. Serve with a scoop of vanilla or cinnamon ice cream.

6 cups fresh peaches, peeled and sliced	2 teaspoons ground cinnamon
1½ cups sugar	1½ cups flour
¼ teaspoon salt	¼ teaspoon salt
2 eggs	2 teaspoons sugar
¼ cup flour	¾ cup shortening
4 tablespoons butter	4 tablespoons ice water

Combine peaches, sugar, salt, eggs and flour. Place in a flat, buttered, 3-quart baking dish. Dot with butter and sprinkle with cinnamon. Combine flour, salt and sugar. Cut in shortening with a pastry blender, adding water to make a soft dough. Roll out on a floured board, cut into wide strips and cover fruit, lattice-style. Bake at 400° for 30 to 40 minutes, or until thickened and bubbly. Serves 10 or 12.

Florida Lime Pie

Key limes are getting scarce in Florida. The bottled juice is still available in many markets and groceries, but I seldom see the actual key lime anymore. If you have key limes, by all means use them, but for those of us who don't have them, a regular green (Persian) lime is substituted in this recipe. I really like this recipe mainly because it is so good, but also because the filling is baked — no raw eggs. Raw eggs may harbor harmful bacteria, the danger of which is eliminated only by thorough heating.

3	eggs, separated	¹/₄	teaspoon salt
1	cup milk		Pastry for a 9-inch crust (either a regular crust, a
¹/₂	cup fresh lime juice		graham cracker crust, or a chocolate crumb crust)
1¹/₄	cups sugar		Whipped cream
¹/₄	cup flour		Lime slices (optional for decoration)

Beat egg whites in a large bowl until stiff peaks form. Set aside. In a small bowl, beat egg yolks. Add milk and lime juice, then sugar, flour and salt. Beat until smooth. Fold lime mixture into beaten egg whites. Pour into crust of your choice. Bake at 350° for 30 to 40 minutes, or until golden brown. The surface may crack. Garnish each slice with whipped cream and a twisted slice of lime, if desired. Serves 6 to 8.

Coconut Custard Pie

Here is old-fashioned Southern cooking at its best. This pie is quick, easy and delicious.

2	tablespoons butter, softened	¹/₄	cup half-and-half cream
1¹/₄	cups sugar	1¹/₂	cups coconut
2	eggs	1	unbaked 9-inch pie crust

Cream butter. Gradually add sugar and beat well. Add eggs, one at a time, beating well after each addition. Stir in cream and coconut. Pour filling into the unbaked crust. Bake at 300° for about 1 hour. Cool before serving. Serves 6 or 8.

Heavenly Lemon Pie

The filling here takes on the quality of a chiffon pie — part of the egg whites are incorporated into the filling. This is a delicious lemon pie.

2 cups plus 2 tablespoons sugar	2 tablespoons butter
$^1/_3$ cup cornstarch	2 teaspoons grated lemon rind
$^1/_4$ teaspoon salt	1 baked 9-inch pastry shell
$1^1/_2$ cups cold water	$^1/_4$ teaspoon cream of tartar
$^1/_2$ cup fresh lemon juice	
6 eggs, separated (place 6 yolks in one small bowl, 3 whites in one bowl, and 3 whites in another bowl)	

Combine $1^1/_2$ cups sugar, cornstarch and salt in a large heavy saucepan. Mix well. Gradually stir in water and lemon juice, stirring until mixture is smooth. Whisk in the 6 egg yolks. Add butter. Cook over medium heat, stirring constantly, until thickened and bubbly. Cook 1 minute after mixture comes to a boil. Remove from heat and stir in lemon rind. Cover and set aside. Let cool for 15 minutes. Beat 3 egg whites until stiff. Uncover cooked filling and stir until smooth. With a rubber spatula, incorporate beaten egg whites into the filling. Place filling in the baked shell. Beat the other 3 egg whites with cream of tartar, gradually adding the other $^1/_2$ cup plus 2 tablespoons of sugar. Beat until stiff peaks form. Spread meringue over the filling, sealing to edge of pastry. Bake at 350° for 12 to 15 minutes, or until golden brown. Serves 6 to 8.

Grandmother Clark's
Rocky Mountain Apple Pie

This pie is anxiously anticipated at Clark Christmas celebrations. Dick's Mother made two or three of these pies for every Christmas dinner for as long as I can remember. Now that Grandma has gone, a niece, Margy, has taken over the apple pie baking for our dinners. She has gotten so good at it that this past Christmas we thought that surely Grandma had a hand in the making of these pies — perhaps she did.

1	cup sugar	1	large apple, peeled and diced
1/2	cup flour	1	unbaked 9-inch pie crust
1	cup whipping cream		Ground nutmeg
1/2	cup half-and-half cream		

Thoroughly combine the sugar and flour. (Grandma always said it should feel like silk). Gradually add the cream and half-and-half to make a smooth filling. Add apple to cream mixture. Pour into an unbaked 9-inch crust. Sprinkle ground nutmeg over the top. Bake at 350° for about 1 hour, or until pie is set in the middle. Serves 6.

Blueberry-Peach Pie

Nothing sings the praises of summer like fresh peaches and blueberries. Put them together and your family and guests will sing your praises.

6	cups fresh peaches, sliced	1/2	teaspoon ground cinnamon
1	cup fresh or frozen blueberries	1/4	teaspoon ground nutmeg
1	teaspoon lemon juice	1/4	cup flour
1/2	cup granulated sugar		Pie crust for a double crust 10-inch pie
1/2	cup brown sugar, packed	1	tablespoon butter or margarine, cut into bits

continued on the facing page

Blueberry-Peach Pie — continued from the facing page

In a large bowl, combine peaches, blueberries and lemon juice. Mix well and set aside. In another bowl, stir together sugars, cinnamon, nutmeg and flour. Add to fruit mixture and blend gently, but thoroughly. Spoon fruit into the prepared bottom crust. Dot with butter. Place prepared top crust on top. Trim and flute edges. Slash the top crust for steam to escape. Place pie on a cookie sheet to catch drips. Bake at 425° until crust is golden brown and filling is bubbling through the steam vents, about 45 minutes to 1 hour. This big, juicy pie will serve 8 or more.

Marvelous Cheese Pie with Fresh Raspberries

A rich and satisfying party pie. It is beautiful to serve. Another time use strawberries or blueberries.

1	8-ounce package cream cheese, softened	½	cup water
¾	cup confectioner's sugar	¼	cup granulated sugar
1	teaspoon vanilla	1	tablespoon cornstarch
1	cup whipping cream, whipped	1	tablespoon quick-cooking tapioca
1	baked and cooled 9-inch pie crust	1	teaspoon vanilla
1	cup fresh raspberries	2	cups fresh raspberries

For the filling, beat cream cheese, confectioner's sugar and vanilla in a large mixer bowl until smooth. Fold in the whipped cream. Spoon filling into the baked crust and smooth top.

For the topping, combine 1 cup raspberries, water, granulated sugar, cornstarch and tapioca in a small saucepan. Cook, breaking up the berries with the back of a spoon, until thick, 4 or 5 minutes. Remove from heat and add vanilla. Cover and cool completely. Stir in 2 cups fresh berries. Spread berry mixture over the filling. Refrigerate before serving. Will easily serve 8.

"Be sorry for people whoever they are, who live in a house where there's no cookie jar."
— *Anonymous*

This is a sad fate indeed. When our boys were growing up, I tried to keep the jar stocked. Nothing beats a good homemade cookie and a glass of milk for an after-school treat.

Glazed Apple Cookies

1¹/₃	cups brown sugar, packed	¹/₄	cup apple juice or cider
¹/₂	cup shortening	1¹/₂	cups apples, peeled and chopped
1	egg	1	cup chopped nuts
2	cups flour	1	cup raisins
1	teaspoon baking soda	1¹/₂	cups confectioner's sugar, sifted
1	teaspoon ground cinnamon	2	tablespoons milk
¹/₄	teaspoon salt	1	tablespoon butter or margarine, softened
¹/₄	teaspoon ground cloves	¹/₄	teaspoon vanilla

In a mixing bowl, beat brown sugar and shortening with an electric mixer on medium speed until well combined. Beat in egg. In another bowl, combine flour, baking soda, cinnamon, salt and cloves. On low speed, beat flour mixture into creamed mixture. Beat in apple juice. By hand, stir in apple bits, nuts and raisins. Drop dough by rounded tablespoons onto a greased cookie sheet. Bake at 400° for 7 or 8 minutes. In a small bowl, combine the confectioner's sugar, milk, butter or margarine and vanilla. Stir mixture until smooth. Spread on warm cookies. Makes about 3 dozen cookies.

Linda Atteberry's Oatmeal Cookies

This great cookie recipe is one of many I have received through the mail. Thanks, Linda.

2 cups unbleached all-purpose flour	2 cups light brown sugar, packed
1 teaspoon baking powder	2 large eggs
Pinch of salt	1 teaspoon baking soda
1 heaping teaspoon ground cinnamon	4 tablespoons hot water
¼ teaspoon ground cloves	4 cups quick oats
1 heaping teaspoon ground allspice	1 cup chopped pecans
¼ teaspoon ground ginger	1 cup raisins
1 cup shortening (Crisco)	

Combine the first 7 ingredients in a large mixing bowl. Blend well. In another large bowl, cream shortening, brown sugar and eggs. Blend dry mixture, a cup at a time, into the creamed mixture. In a cup, stir together the baking soda and hot water and add to the creamed mixture. Add the quick oats and pecans and stir in thoroughly. Grind the raisins in a meat grinder or a food processor (this is an important step). Add to the dough and mix well. Roll dough into 1-inch balls and place on a greased cookie sheet. Heat oven to 350° and bake for 13 minutes. Makes about 4 dozen cookies. Cookies are very moist and chewy.

Chocolate-Filled Snowballs

These are wonderful any time of the year, but especially at Christmas time. The mailman would love a box of them!

1	cup butter, softened	1	cup walnuts, finely chopped
¹/₂	cup granulated sugar	1	5³/₄-ounce package Hershey's Kisses
1	teaspoon vanilla		Confectioner's sugar
2	cups sifted flour		

Beat butter, granulated sugar and vanilla until light and fluffy. Add flour and nuts and blend well. Chill for 2 hours. Unwrap the Kisses. Shape about 1 rounded teaspoon of dough around each Kiss, completely covering chocolate. Roll to form a ball. Place on ungreased cookie sheets. Bake at 375° for 15 to 18 minutes, or until set, but not browned. Let cookies cool slightly on pan, then remove to racks to cool. While still warm, roll cookies in confectioner's sugar. Let cool completely. Store in a tightly covered container. Roll in confectioner's sugar again before serving, if desired. Makes about 3 dozen cookies.

Macadamia-White Chocolate Cookies

6	ounces unsalted butter, at room temperature	1¹/₂	cups flour
¹/₂	cup light brown sugar, packed	¹/₂	teaspoon baking powder
¹/₂	cup granulated sugar	¹/₂	teaspoon salt
1	egg	2	tablespoons light corn syrup
1	teaspoon vanilla	1	cup macadamia nuts, cut in half
		12	ounces white chocolate, cut into chunks

In a large bowl, cream butter and sugars. Add egg and vanilla and mix thoroughly. Gradually add flour, baking powder and salt and mix well. Add corn syrup, then nuts, then chocolate and mix well. Drop by tablespoonfuls onto an ungreased cookie sheet, about 4 inches apart. Bake at 375° for 9 to 12 minutes or until golden brown. Cool and store in an airtight container. Makes about 3¹/₂ dozen.

Maple-Rum Bars

Use only pure maple syrup in this recipe. These are delicious.

Crust

$^3/_4$	cup unsalted butter, softened		$^3/_4$	cup rolled oats
$^2/_3$	cup light brown sugar, packed		1	teaspoon baking powder
2	cups flour		$^1/_2$	teaspoon salt

Butter a glass 12x8x2-inch baking dish. Cream butter and brown sugar with electric mixer until light colored. In another bowl, stir together the flour, oats, baking powder and salt. Add to creamed mixture and blend with a wooden spoon. Spread about half the dough into the baking dish. Press into the bottom and a little up the sides. (Cover and refrigerate remainder of dough.) Bake the crust at 375° until light golden brown, 15 minutes. Remove from oven and cool crust.

Filling

1	cup whipping cream		$^1/_4$	cup unsalted butter
$^2/_3$	cup pure maple syrup		2	tablespoons dark rum
$^1/_3$	cup light brown sugar, packed		$^1/_2$	cup pecans, finely chopped

Combine cream, maple syrup, brown sugar and butter in a small saucepan. Heat to a boil, then boil vigorously for 2 minutes. Remove from heat and stir in the rum. Pour filling over the crust and sprinkle with pecans. Crumble the remaining dough over the filling. Reduce oven to 350° and bake until light brown, about 25 minutes. Cool to room temperature, then cover and refrigerate for several hours before slicing. Makes 2$^1/_2$ dozen bars.

Rolled-Up Date Cookies

1	pound dates, finely chopped	3	eggs
$^1/_2$	cup granulated sugar	1	teaspoon vanilla
$^1/_2$	cup water	4	cups flour
1	cup butter, at room temperature	1	teaspoon salt
1	cup granulated sugar	1	teaspoon baking soda
1	cup brown sugar, packed		

Combine dates, $^1/_2$ cup sugar and water in a saucepan. Bring to a boil over medium heat, stirring constantly. Boil 1 minute. Remove from heat and set aside to cool. Cream butter in a large bowl. Add both sugars and eggs and beat until light and fluffy. Add vanilla and mix. Stir in flour, salt and soda. Mix well. Wrap dough and chill. Roll out on a lightly floured board and spread with filling. Roll up like a jelly roll. Chill overnight. Slice $^1/_8$-inch thick and place on lightly greased baking sheets. Bake at 375° for 10 to 12 minutes, or until golden brown. Makes about 6 dozen delicious cookies.

Charlene Glorioso's Peanut Crunchies

Charlene, from Willard, Ohio, sent several recipes. They are all good, but I particularly like this recipe. Charlene says she makes these only at Christmas time. They are too good to limit to just one time of the year!

$1^1/_4$	cups butter or margarine, at room temperature	2	eggs
$^3/_4$	cup granulated sugar	2	cups flour
$1^1/_4$	cups light brown sugar, packed	1	teaspoon baking soda
1	teaspoon vanilla	2	cups quick-cooking rolled oats
		1	cup chopped salted peanuts

continued on the facing page

Charlene Glorioso's Peanut Crunchies — continued from the facing page

Cream butter and sugars until light and fluffy. Add vanilla and eggs and continue to beat. Sift flour and baking soda together and add to creamed mixture. Stir in oats and peanuts. Drop by rounded teaspoons on well-greased baking sheet. Bake at 400° for approximately 10 minutes or until light brown. Makes 2 to 3 dozen.

Old-Fashioned Refrigerator Black Walnut Cookies

My Mother and her Mother made mountains of these cookies. I can remember Dad husking the walnuts — his hands would be stained for days. After the walnuts dried, the tricky part was getting the meats out. Black walnuts must have the toughest hulls of all nuts. The nut meats were worth all the staining and straining, however. I hope you'll like these cookies as much as we do.

1¼	cups butter, at room temperature	1	teaspoon salt
1	cup light brown sugar, packed	3¼	cups sifted flour
⅔	cup granulated sugar	¼	teaspoon baking soda
1	teaspoon vanilla	1½	cups chopped black walnuts
2	eggs		Confectioner's sugar (optional)
1	teaspoon baking powder		

Beat butter until light and fluffy. Add both sugars and mix with a wooden spoon until fluffy. Stir in vanilla. Add eggs, one at a time, beating well. Sift together baking powder, salt, flour and baking soda. Add to butter mixture. Stir in walnuts. Shape dough into rolls 1½ inches wide and about 10 to 11 inches long. (If dough is sticky, chill it for 30 minutes to 1 hour before shaping.) Wrap rolls in plastic wrap and refrigerate for several hours. To bake, slice rolls into ¼-inch-thick slices with a sharp knife. Place on ungreased cookie sheet and bake in a 400° oven for 8 to 10 minutes, or until light brown. Remove from sheets and, while still warm, sprinkle with a little confectioner's sugar, if desired. Makes about 8 dozen cookies.

Special Chocolate Chip Cookies

Special because this is the best chocolate chip cookie recipe I've found yet. I think the addition of sour cream is the secret. Whatever the secret, I hope you enjoy these as much as my family does.

2¹/₂ cups flour	³/₄ cup butter or margarine, softened
³/₄ cup granulated sugar	¹/₄ cup sour cream
³/₄ cup light brown sugar, packed	1 teaspoon vanilla
1 teaspoon baking powder	12 ounces semisweet chocolate chips
2 eggs	1 cup chopped pecans or walnuts (optional)

Combine dry ingredients. Add eggs, one at a time, beating well after each addition. Add butter, sour cream and vanilla. Mix well. Stir in the chocolate chips and nuts. Drop by heaping teaspoons onto a lightly greased cookie sheet. Cookies spread, so leave room between them. Bake at 375° for 10 minutes. Makes about 3¹/₂ to 4 dozen.

Lemon and Cheese Bars

This 3-layered bar cookie is delicious. Sweet and tangy. A wonderful way to end a summer meal.

Crust

1	cup butter, at room temperature	$^1/_2$	cup confectioner's sugar
2	cups flour	$^1/_4$	teaspoon salt

Cut butter into flour, confectioner's sugar and salt until crumbly. Press into a 13x9x2-inch baking pan. Bake at 350° for 15 to 20 minutes, or until light brown. Remove from oven to add the cheese layer.

Cream Cheese Layer

$^1/_4$	cup granulated sugar	1	8-ounce package cream cheese, at room
1	egg		temperature

Cream granulated sugar, egg and cream cheese until smooth. Spread over crust and bake at 350° for 8 to 10 minutes. Remove from oven to add lemon layer.

Lemon Layer

4	eggs	4	tablespoons fresh lemon juice
2	cups granulated sugar	1	teaspoon grated lemon rind
4	tablespoons flour		Confectioner's sugar

Combine eggs, granulated sugar, flour, lemon juice and rind. Mix well. Spoon over cheese layer. Bake at 350° for 20 to 25 minutes. Sprinkle with confectioner's sugar while still warm. Makes $2^1/_2$ to 3 dozen bars.

Chocolate-Covered Raisin Cookies

Why didn't we think of this sooner? I love chocolate-covered raisins and they are a terrific addition to this cookie recipe.

2½	cups flour	½	cup light brown sugar, packed
1	teaspoon baking soda	2	large eggs
½	teaspoon salt	2	teaspoons vanilla
1	cup unsalted butter or margarine, softened	2	cups chocolate-covered raisins
1	cup granulated sugar	2	cups chopped pecans

Grease cookie sheets. Sift flour, baking soda and salt together. Set aside. Beat butter and sugars together in large bowl of electric mixer on high speed. Beat 2 minutes. Add eggs, one at a time, mixing well after each addition. Add vanilla. Stop the mixer and add dry ingredients. Mix on low speed only until combined. Stir in raisins and pecans. Drop dough by heaping teaspoons onto the greased cookie sheet. Bake at 375° until golden brown, 12 to 15 minutes. Cool for 1 minute, then transfer cookies to wire racks to cool. Makes about 4 dozen cookies.

Fabulous Macaroons

These are just that — fabulous!

1	7-ounce package almond paste	1	tablespoon cornstarch
¾	cup sugar		Dash of salt
2	large egg whites, slightly beaten	¼	teaspoon lemon rind, finely grated

Line 2 baking sheets with parchment paper or aluminum foil. If using foil, lightly spray it with nonstick vegetable coating. Place almond paste and sugar in a bowl and blend, using an electric mixer. Add egg whites and blend until smooth but not runny. Beat in cornstarch, salt and lemon rind. Drop by rounded teaspoonfuls onto the sheets. Leave room for macaroons to double in size. Bake at 325° for about 15 minutes, or until golden brown. Allow to cool completely before removing from the paper or foil. Makes about 4 dozen.

Classic Flan

One of the most popular desserts in the world, flan is found on the menu nearly everywhere we travel. This version bakes with the caramel on the bottom, then is turned out, carmel side up to serve. It's easy and delicious.

Caramel

¹/₃	cup sugar	2	tablespoons water

In a small saucepan, heat sugar and water to boiling over medium-high heat, swirling pan to dissolve sugar. Boil 5 to 7 minutes, swirling pan once or twice, or until syrup is medium amber color (note that you do not stir the syrup). Immediately pour into a 4-cup (6 or 7 inches in diameter) soufflé dish. Tilt dish to evenly coat the bottom. Place this dish in a larger pan and set aside.

Custard

1	cup milk	¹/₃	cup sugar
1	cup half-and-half cream	2	large eggs plus 2 egg yolks
1¹/₂	teaspoons vanilla		

Bring milk and half-and-half to just under a boil. Remove from heat and stir in vanilla along with the sugar. Stir until sugar dissolves. In a bowl, beat eggs and egg yolks until mixed. Stir (not beat or whisk) into the sugar and vanilla mixture. Pour custard through a fine sieve into the prepared soufflé dish. Place oven rack in lowest position. Set pan with dish inside it in the oven. Add boiling water to the pan to come halfway up sides of soufflé dish. Bake at 325° for about 1 hour (test after 50 minutes), or until a knife inserted in the center comes out clean. Set pan on a cooling rack for 15 minutes. Remove dish from pan and cool the custard. Cover and refrigerate for at least 3 or 4 hours. Run knife around edge of custard. Invert onto a rimmed platter. Serves 8.

Rhubarb Pinwheels

This marvelous spring recipe comes from my good friend, Annie Blacketer. She is a gifted cook and baker and I know any recipe she gives me will be splendid.

Dough

2 cups flour	1/3 cup shortening (solid margarine or Crisco)
1 tablespoon sugar	1 egg, beaten
4 teaspoons baking powder	1/2 cup milk
1/2 teaspoon salt	

In a mixing bowl, sift together the dry ingredients. Cut in shortening until mixture resembles crumbs. Combine egg and milk. Add to crumb mixture, stirring just until moistened. Turn out onto a floured surface. Roll into a 10x12-inch rectangle.

Filling

2 tablespoons butter or margarine, melted	3 to 4 cups fresh or frozen rhubarb, diced
1 cup sugar	

Brush the rolled-out dough with melted butter, sprinkle with the sugar and top with the rhubarb, spreading rhubarb evenly over the sugar. Carefully roll up dough jelly roll-style, starting with the shorter side. Cut into 1-inch slices. Reshape the slices as needed to form round pinwheels. Place in a greased 13x9x2-inch baking dish.

Syrup

1 1/2 cups water	Few drops of red food coloring, if desired
1 cup sugar	Heavy cream to pour or whip (optional)

For syrup, bring water and sugar to a boil in a small saucepan. Cook and stir until sugar dissolves. Stir in food coloring, if desired. Carefully spoon hot syrup over pinwheels. Bake at 400° for 30 minutes or until golden brown. Serve warm with cream or whipped cream, if desired. Serves 12.

Australian Sticky Date Pudding

This popular dessert is taking Australia by storm. It's gooey and rich and everyone there seems to love it. Meanwhile, more than 10,000 miles away (in the United States), it's starting to make a name for itself. I think you'll agree — it's a great dessert.

1	teaspoon butter	$^1/_2$	teaspoon salt
8	ounces pitted dates, chopped	$^1/_2$	teaspoon vanilla
2	cups water	$1^3/_4$	tablespoons baking powder
1	teaspoon baking soda	$^1/_2$	cup butter
$^1/_2$	cup butter, at room temperature	$^1/_4$	cup heavy cream
5	tablespoons granulated sugar	$^1/_2$	cup brown sugar, packed
2	eggs	$^1/_2$	teaspoon vanilla
$1^1/_4$	cups flour	1	cup heavy cream, whipped (optional)

Butter a 9-inch round or square deep-dish baking pan or dish with the 1 teaspoon butter. Place dates in a saucepan and cover with water. Bring to a boil, reduce heat and simmer for 3 minutes. Add baking soda. Set aside. In a bowl, cream $^1/_2$ cup butter, the 5 tablespoons granulated sugar and the eggs, adding one at a time. Mix well after each egg addition. Gently fold in flour, salt and $^1/_2$ teaspoon vanilla. Slowly stir in baking powder and $^1/_4$ cup of the date cooking liquid until the cake mixture resembles thick pancake batter. (Discard remaining cooking liquid.) Stir in the dates. Pour into prepared pan and bake at 350° for 30 to 40 minutes, or until cooked in the center. Make a sauce by combining $^1/_2$ cup butter, $^1/_4$ cup heavy cream, brown sugar and $^1/_2$ teaspoon vanilla in a medium saucepan.
Bring to a boil. Reduce heat and simmer for 3 minutes. Drizzle some of the sauce over the cake as it is cooling. Serve the remainder of sauce separately. Garnish with whipped cream, if desired. Serves 8 to 10.

Apple Pudding with Rum Sauce

This pudding is like Grandma used to make. My Grandma never served it with rum sauce, however. She served it with scoops of ice cream. It's delicious either way.

Apple Pudding

1/4	cup butter or margarine	3/4	teaspoon ground nutmeg
1	cup sugar	1/4	teaspoon salt
1	egg	4	cups apples, peeled and chopped
1	cup flour	1/2	cup chopped pecans or walnuts
1	teaspoon baking soda		Rum Sauce (recipe follows)

In a large bowl, beat butter with an electric mixer on medium speed for 30 seconds. Add sugar and mix well. Add egg and mix in. In a small bowl, combine dry ingredients. Add to the creamed mixture and beat on low speed until combined. Fold apples and nuts into batter and spread batter in a greased 8x8x2-inch pan. Bake at 350° for about 1 hour, or until golden brown. Serve with Rum Sauce or ice cream to 9.

Rum Sauce

Melt 1/2 cup **butter or margarine**. Add 1 cup **sugar** and 1/2 cup **light cream**. Bring just to a boil over medium heat. Reduce heat and cook for 3 minutes, stirring often. Remove from heat, stir in 2 tablespoons **rum**, 1 teaspoon **ground nutmeg** and 1 teaspoon **vanilla**. Serve over warm Apple Pudding. Makes about 1 1/2 cups sauce.

Cranberry Ice

2	cups fresh cranberries	2	tablespoons cold water
1	cup sugar	1	teaspoon unflavored gelatin
1	cup boiling water	1	cup ginger ale

Cook cranberries and sugar in boiling water for 4 or 5 minutes, or until berries pop. Cool slightly. Meanwhile in a small pan, combine cold water and gelatin. Let stand 5 minutes to soften. Cook and stir over low heat to dissolve gelatin. Place cranberry mixture in blender or food processor. Cover and blend until smooth. Return the puréed mixture to the saucepan. Stir in gelatin mixture and the ginger ale. Pour cranberry mixture into an 8x8x2-inch baking pan. Cool to room temperature, then place in freezer and freeze until mushy. Transfer the partially frozen mixture to a large chilled mixing bowl. Beat with electric mixer until smooth, but not melted. Return to pan and keep frozen until ready to serve. Spoon into 8 serving dishes.

Rhubarb Cobbler

1	cup sugar	1^1/$_2$	teaspoons baking powder
2	tablespoons cornstarch	^{1}/$_2$	teaspoon salt
^{1}/$_2$	teaspoon ground cinnamon	4	tablespoons butter
4	cups red rhubarb, cut into 1-inch pieces	^{1}/$_3$	cup milk
1	tablespoon water	^{1}/$_2$	cup chopped pecans
2	tablespoons butter	1	teaspoon shredded orange peel
1	cup flour		Light cream, milk or ice cream (optional)
^{1}/$_3$	cup sugar		

Combine the 1 cup sugar, cornstarch and cinnamon. Add rhubarb and water. Cook and stir until mixture boils. Cook 1 minute longer. Pour into a lightly greased 8x1^1/$_2$-inch round baking dish. Dot with the 2 tablespoons butter. Place in a 400° oven while preparing biscuits. Sift together flour, ^{1}/$_3$ cup sugar, baking powder and salt. Cut in 4 tablespoons butter. Stir in milk, pecans and orange peel. Drop spoonfuls of batter onto hot rhubarb mixture. Bake at 400° for another 25 minutes. Serve with light cream, milk or ice cream. Serves 6.

Pecan-Praline Bread Pudding

1	tablespoon butter, softened		1	tablespoon vanilla
1/2	cup raisins		1/4	teaspoon salt
1/4	cup bourbon		1/8	teaspoon ground nutmeg
6	cups French bread (cut in 1/2-inch cubes)		2	tablespoons unsalted butter
4	cups half-and-half cream		1/2	cup light brown sugar, packed
6	large eggs		1/3	cup heavy cream
1/2	cup granulated sugar		1/2	cup pecans, coarsely chopped and toasted

Butter a 2½-quart baking dish. In a small bowl, mix raisins and bourbon. In a large bowl, mix bread cubes and half-and-half. Let soak 10 minutes. In medium bowl, whisk eggs, granulated sugar, vanilla, salt and nutmeg to mix well. Stir raisin and egg mixture into bread mixture. Spoon into prepared dish. Bake at 350° for 45 to 50 minutes or until pudding is puffed, top is brown and knife inserted 1 inch from the edge comes out clean. Cool 30 minutes. Make topping. In a saucepan over medium heat, stir butter and brown sugar together until butter melts. Add cream and mix well. Heat to boiling. Cook 2 minutes or until sugar dissolves and mixture thickens. Add pecans. Pour into a bowl. Cool 15 minutes. Drizzle over pudding. Serve warm. Makes 12 servings.

The Best Rice Pudding

Well, here it is — the best one. The vanilla bean is very important here.

1	cup water		1	cup heavy whipping cream
1/2	cup short- or medium-grain white rice		1/2	cup sugar
1/2	vanilla bean (split lengthwise from one whole bean)		2	eggs
1/4	teaspoon salt		1/2	cup raisins (or dried sour cherries, or dried cranberries)
2	cups milk		1/4	teaspoon ground cinnamon

continued on the facing page

The Best Rice Pudding — continued from the facing page

Bring water to a boil in a 2-quart saucepan. Add the rice, vanilla bean and salt. Cook 10 minutes. Add milk and cook over very low heat until rice is tender, about 10 more minutes. Lightly butter a 1½-quart shallow baking dish. In a small bowl, combine the cream, sugar and eggs, then fold into the rice mixture. Remove the vanilla bean and discard. Pour rice mixture into the buttered baking dish. Stir in the raisins, cherries or cranberries. Sprinkle with cinnamon. Place dish into larger baking pan in the oven. Pour boiling water into the larger pan to a depth of 1 inch. Bake at 350° for 30 to 45 minutes, or until pudding is firm and the surface is golden brown. Cool to room temperature. Serve at room temperature, or refrigerate, covered, to serve chilled. Serves 6 or 8.

Lemon Mousse with Raspberry Sauce

6 large eggs	¾ cup chilled whipping cream
6 large egg yolks	1½ cups fresh raspberries or frozen unsweetened
1½ cups sugar	raspberries, thawed
1 cup fresh lemon juice, strained	2 tablespoons sugar (or more to taste)
2 tablespoons minced lemon peel	Fresh mint sprigs for garnish
1¾ sticks cold unsalted butter, cut into	
small pieces	

Whisk eggs and yolks in a heavy nonaluminum saucepan until foamy. Whisk in 1½ cups sugar, then lemon juice. Stir in peel. Stir over low heat until mixture thickens to look and feel like heavy custard, about 10 minutes. Do not boil. Remove from heat and whisk in butter. Transfer mixture to bowl and cool until very thick, stirring occasionally, about 1 hour. Whip cream in a medium bowl to soft peaks. Fold cream into lemon mixture until just combined. Spoon mousse into 8 serving glasses. Cover and refrigerate at least 2 hours, or overnight.

For the sauce, mash berries in a small bowl using a fork. Mix in 2 tablespoons sugar. Taste. Add more sugar if desired. Cover and refrigerate berries 1 hour to release juices. Spoon sauce over each serving. Garnish with mint sprigs. Serves 8.

Brandied Pear Crisp

1½	cups old-fashioned rolled oats	¼	cup brandy
¼	cup flour	¼	pound cold butter, cut into small pieces
1	cup dark brown sugar, packed	2	pounds pears, peeled and sliced
1½	teaspoons ground cinnamon	1	tablespoon fresh lemon juice
½	teaspoon ground ginger	2	tablespoons granulated sugar
¼	teaspoon ground nutmeg	1	quart vanilla ice cream

Blend oats, flour, brown sugar, cinnamon, ginger, nutmeg and 1 tablespoon of the brandy. Work in the butter with your fingers or a pastry blender until mixture looks like coarse meal. Set aside. Place pears in a bowl with the lemon juice and granulated sugar and remainder of the brandy. Toss to coat the pear pieces thoroughly. Butter a 1½- to 2-quart baking dish and place pear mixture in it. Spread the oat mixture evenly over the top of the pears. Bake at 350° for about 45 minutes or until topping is golden brown and crisp. Remove from oven and let set for 15 minutes. Serve with ice cream to 6.

Caribbean Bananas with Rum-Raisin Sauce

½	cup dark raisins	¼	cup dark brown sugar, packed
¼	cup dark rum	¼	teaspoon ground nutmeg
8	ripe, firm bananas	¼	teaspoon ground cinnamon
4	tablespoons unsalted butter		Vanilla ice cream

Place raisins and rum in a small bowl. Let stand for 30 minutes. Peel bananas and slice in half lengthwise. Heat butter in a large skillet until foamy, but don't burn. Add bananas, round side down. Cook each side for 3 minutes (you may need to reduce the heat a little), turning carefully so they don't break. Remove bananas from skillet and arrange 2 halves on each of 8 plates. Add rum and raisins to butter left in the skillet. Stir in brown sugar and spices. Heat until warm and just beginning to bubble. Add a scoop of ice cream to each plate. Divide sauce among the 8 plates, drizzling over both bananas and ice cream. Serve immediately.

Ginger-Baked Pears

I could use lots of words to describe the goodness of this dessert, but I'll let you find out for yourself.

8	large, firm and ripe Bosc or Anjou pears	5	tablespoons fresh gingerroot, peeled and minced
5	tablespoons honey	2	tablespoons fresh lemon juice
5	tablespoons dark brown sugar, firmly packed		Whipped cream

Peel the pears, leave stems on and cut a thin slice from the bottom of each pear so it will stand up. Stand pears in a large baking dish, drizzle them with honey, and sprinkle them with the brown sugar and gingerroot. Sprinkle lemon juice around the pears. Add enough water to reach halfway up the sides of the dish. Bake pears, covered with foil, in a 350° oven for 45 minutes to 1 hour, or until pears are just tender when pierced. Transfer pears to a serving dish, pour the cooking liquid into a saucepan, and boil it until it is reduced and thickened. Pour sauce over pears and serve each pear with a dollop of whipped cream. Serves 8.

Pears Poached in Red Wine

I am very fond of pears for dessert. I especially love this recipe — the finished pear is a beautiful wine red in color.

3	cups dry red wine	2	tablespoons vanilla
1	cup sugar	4	whole cloves
1	cinnamon stick, broken into pieces	4	firm ripe pears, peeled

Combine wine, sugar, cinnamon, vanilla and whole cloves together in a heavy pan. Bring mixture to a boil. Add pears and simmer until tender but not mushy, turning them often. Cook about 15 minutes. Place pears and syrup in a bowl. Cover and refrigerate several hours, or overnight. To serve, cut pears in half lengthwise and remove cores. Starting $1/2$ inch from stem end, make several lengthwise cuts in each pear half. Lay pear half onto a serving plate. Press gently on pear to fan out the slices. Spoon a little syrup over each half. Pass more syrup, if desired. Serve 2 halves to each of 4 people, or serve 1 half to each of 8 people. I think each guest will want 2 halves!

my favorite
APPLES

I have 8 favorite apples. I cook with some, bake with some, make applesauce with some, and, of course, eat some raw. If I lived nearer the east coast, I would add some of their apples (such as Winesap and Northern Spy) to my list, but I don't often see their apples for sale in my markets or groceries.

1. **Rome Beauty** — *my favorite of all apples. It's crisp, tangy and delicious. This apple bakes well, is great in breads, cakes, pies, cobblers and other pastries, and I love it as an eating apple.*

2. **Early Transparent or Early Harvest** — *this apple make the list because of the superb applesauce made from it. It's a yellow-green apple that turns to a transparent yellow when ripe. It ripens in August. Besides applesauce, they make good pies also — even though they don't retain their apple-slice-shape like a true pie apple does, the flavor of an Early Harvest pie is unforgettable.*

3. **Granny Smith** — *this tart green apple is prized for pies, cobblers, breads, cakes and muffins. Some people like to eat these raw, but they are too tart for my taste. This apple has become one of the top-selling apples in the world. I always use this apple when I make Apple Brandy.*

4. **McIntosh and Jonathan** — *I know these are two separate varieties, but they are totally interchangeable in use. They are aromatic and tangy. They make very good applesauce, they are used extensively in baking and they are good to eat raw. Both are readily available and good all-around apples.*

5. **Golden Delicious** — *this is a favorite apple to bake. It is sweet and juicy and holds its shape well when baked. It was Mother's favorite apple for pie baking and it's actually splendid in all categories except applesauce making. Since it holds its shape so well, it won't cook down into smooth applesauce. A good ripe Golden Delicious is unbeatable to eat raw.*

6. **Red Delicious** — *repeat everything I said about Golden Delicious apples and it applies to the Red Delicious also. The main difference is in the raw category. The Red Delicious is a little tangier and a little crisper. This is the apple that comes to mind when you sit down with a bowl of popcorn — a Red Delicious apple just has to go with it.*

7. **Royal Gala** — *a beautiful gold-streaked red apple that is delicious to bake and especially to eat raw. I use this apple also in breads, cakes, pies, apple crisp and cobblers. A very good all-around sweet apple.*

8. **Fuji** — *Everyone puts this apple on a pedestal! It is good, but I'm not so sure I'd elevate it to such heights. It is a splendid apple to eat raw — it is crisp and juicy, but because it is always the highest priced apple (in my markets), I don't bake with it often. I guess I would have to say it is a splendid choice for an eating apple.*

Raspberry Sauce

Of all the dessert sauces I make, this is my favorite one. It is delicious with angel food cake, pound cake, over ice cream, over baked custards and heavenly over lemon mousse.

1   10-ounce package frozen raspberries, thawed and drained

6   tablespoons raspberry jam

1   tablespoon cornstarch

1   tablespoon cold water

2   tablespoons raspberry liqueur (I like Chambord)

Combine raspberries and jam in a heavy saucepan. Bring to a boil. Combine cornstarch and water and add to raspberry mixture. Stir constantly and boil until sauce is clear and thick. Remove from heat. Pour sauce through a fine sieve to strain out seeds. Cool a few minutes. Add liqueur. Stir well. Cool. Cover and refrigerate. Serve chilled. Makes about 1 cup.

Orange-Rum Sauce

This sauce is terrific over coffee ice cream or almost as good over vanilla ice cream.

Juice of 2 oranges

$^1/_2$ cup sugar

$^1/_2$ cup water

1   teaspoon cornstarch

Dash of salt

$^1/_4$ cup rum

1   teaspoon grated orange rind

Combine orange juice, sugar, water, cornstarch and salt. Cook in a double boiler over simmering water until thickened. Add rum and orange rind. Stir well. Cool sauce and serve cold. It has the consistency of heavy cream. Makes about $^3/_4$ cup sauce.

Yogurt Fruit Sauce

1	3-ounce package cream cheese, softened	1/2	teaspoon vanilla
1/3	cup brown sugar, packed	1	cup plain nonfat yogurt

Combine cream cheese, brown sugar and vanilla in a small mixer bowl. Beat with an electric mixer on medium speed until fluffy. Add yogurt. Beat until smooth. Spoon sauce over fresh fruit and top with toasted nuts or coconut, if desired. Makes a little more than a cup.

Devonshire Cream

3/4	cup sour cream	2	tablespoons vanilla
1/4	cup half-and-half cream	1	tablespoon honey
1/4	cup confectioner's sugar		Fresh fruit, cut into pieces

Combine sour cream, half-and-half, confectioner's sugar, vanilla and honey. Mix until very smooth. Pour over servings of fresh fruit. Makes 1 cup sauce. A delicious English dessert sauce.

Cocoa Fudge Sauce

1/2	cup unsalted butter	2/3	cup dark brown sugar, packed
1	cup unsweetened cocoa powder	1/2	cup granulated sugar
1	cup whipping cream		Dash of salt

Melt butter in a heavy saucepan over medium heat. Add cocoa and whisk until smooth. Gradually add cream. Stir in sugars and salt. Simmer until mixture is smooth and sugars dissolve completely, about 3 minutes. Best served warm over ice cream. Makes about 2 cups. It can be prepared and refrigerated for a week ahead.

Brandied Pear Sauce

Simply wonderful over vanilla ice cream. Also serve as a sauce for plain baked pears.

6	tablespoons butter, divided	3	tablespoons water
4	Bosc pears, peeled, cored and sliced	1/4	cup pear-flavored brandy, or plain unflavored
1/2	cup brown sugar, packed		brandy if pear brandy is unavailable

Melt 3 tablespoons butter in a skillet and cook the pear slices until lightly browned, a single layer of slices at a time. Remove slices as they brown. Add sugar and water. Let sugar dissolve, then add brandy. Heat to a boil and boil until syrupy, about 5 minutes. Return pears to skillet, add remaining 3 tablespoons butter and cook 5 minutes longer. Do not overcook or pear slices will fall apart. Serve now, or refrigerate. Carefully rewarm pears and syrup and serve warm. Enough for 8 dishes of ice cream.

Grand Marnier Custard Sauce

Serve this sauce over or under a slice of cake, or whenever a dessert needs a flavor boost, spoon on a little of this grand sauce.

	Ice cubes	1/3	cup whole milk
3	egg yolks	1/4	cup Grand Marnier orange liqueur
1/3	cup sugar		Pinch of salt
1	cup heavy or whipping cream		

Fill a large mixing bowl with ice cubes. Set bowl aside. Beat egg yolks and sugar until well blended. In a heavy saucepan, bring cream and milk to a boil. Remove pan from heat. Gradually whisk 1/2 cup hot cream and milk mixture into egg mixture. Whisk egg mixture into remaining hot cream. Place pan over medium-low heat and whisk constantly until cream begins to thicken. Do **not** boil. Remove pan from heat. Stir in Grand Marnier and salt. Strain sauce into a small bowl and cool it quickly by placing bowl into the bowl of ice cubes. Makes about 1 1/2 cups sauce.